Gay Voluntary Associations
in New York

GAY VOLUNTARY ASSOCIATIONS IN NEW YORK

Public Sharing and Private Lives

Moshe Shokeid

PENN

UNIVERSITY OF PENNSYLVANIA PRESS

PHILADELPHIA

Published by
University of Pennsylvania Press
Philadelphia, Pennsylvania 19104-4112
www.upenn.edu/pennpress

Printed in the United States of America on acid-free paper
1 3 5 7 9 10 8 6 4 2

A Cataloging-in-Publication Record is available from the Library of Congress

ISBN 978-0-8122-4657-5

CONTENTS

Introduction

In the early 1980s my family and I lived in Queens, New York, where I studied the Israeli immigrant community, nicknamed Yordim (Hebrew for "those who go down"; singular, Yored). I found that the Israelis there were reluctant to admit that their relocation to the United States was more than temporary. As a result, they organized nostalgic get-togethers, what I defined as "one-night-stand ethnicity," but did not form the voluntary associations—often leading to enduring social institutions—that other earlier and present-day, Jewish and non-Jewish "permanent" immigrants had (Shokeid 1988). It was during that time that I was invited to attend a service at the gay and lesbian synagogue, Congregation Beth Simchat Torah (CBST) in the West Village of Manhattan. I was fascinated by that social experience, and a few years later (1989) I returned to New York and started research at CBST. The period of my observation there coincided with a time of challenge for the synagogue. It was faced with the question of whether, as a lay-led, all-volunteer organization, it could still continue to meet the needs of its now sizeable congregation, many of whom were ill with AIDS. Or would it have to hire a full-time paid rabbi and paid staff, thus transforming its founding social bricks and the ethos of a voluntary organization (Shokeid 2003 [1995], 2001)?

In the mid-1990s, while still maintaining contact with CBST, I broadened my field of interest to the Lesbian and Gay Community Services Center in the West Village (the Center). Starting in 1995, during sabbaticals and research fellowships, I observed a number of the voluntary groups holding meetings there. Located in a massive New York landmark school building (on Thirteenth Street), the Center hosts a wide variety of organizations and activities. Actually, anyone can ask to use the Center's space in order to initiate a new activity aimed to serve the interests and welfare of gay, lesbian, bisexual, and transgendered people. The annual report for 1996, for example, listed about 120 groups that met on its premises. In addition, the Center promotes many public events, discussions, lectures, exhibitions, parties, dances, and more. The website indicates that "established in 1983 the Center has grown to become the second largest LGBT community center in the world" as of 2010.

My diverse cohort was composed of seniors, bisexuals, Radical Fairies, sexual compulsives, men attracted across race, Leathermen, Bears, Gay Fathers, men engaging in nonsexual physical affection (Gentle Men), and Positive Body (engaging in safe-sex education, advertising its meetings as "Sex Talk"). At this time I also extended my research on the gay community beyond the Center to churches active in the city, offshoots of various denominations: Protestant—the Metropolitan Community Church (MCC); Catholic—Dignity; and the Unity Fellowship Church—a black, Baptist-style congregation. Taken together, this diverse group of sites afforded the opportunity to observe a wide section of the gay community across ethnic, cultural, and social divides. It also provided a chance to become acquainted with individuals from a variety of backgrounds, a number of whom have become close friends and trusted informants. My engagement with these institutions continued in later years (until 2010) on subsequent longer and shorter visits.

Many social scientists—beginning, most famously, with de Tocqueville (1956 [1835])—have observed what has often been deemed a unique characteristic of American society: the propensity to form voluntary associations and civic organizations (e.g., Huizinga 1972 [1927]; Schlesinger 1944; Bellah et al. 1985; Ginsburg 1989; Wuthnow 1994; Sanjek 1998; Gamm and Putnam 1999; Curtis, Baer, and Grabb 2001). None of these studies, however, have encompassed the gay and lesbian community. Instead, ethnographic work on gay life in the United States, mostly by American scholars, has typically taken one of two directions. The first, much affected in later years by the AIDS epidemic, is the study of sites and institutions that offer a safe space for social interaction, in particular, for anonymous sex (e.g., Humphreys 1970; Delph 1978; Style, 1979; Brodsky 1993; Newton 1993; Bolton 1995; Levine 1998; Leap 1999; Hennen 2008). The other is the study of specific social issues, such as the construction of gay and lesbian identity, history, family relationships, community life, parenthood, patterns of conjugal bonding, youth, language, race, and AIDS (e.g., Newton 1972; Altman 1986; Feldman 1990; Weston 1991, 1993; Herdt 1992; Kennedy and Davis, 1993; Leap 1996; Lewin 1996, 2009; Cameron and Kulick 2003; Faima-Silva 2004; Boelstorff 2007; Valentine 2007; Lewin and Leap 2009).

To redress this omission, I propose to expand the social science interest in voluntary associations to those of the gay community, drawing together observations I have made in a number of its diverse groups mostly in New

York City. My aim is thus to reveal yet another facet of cultural creativity representing gay and lesbian life in the United States. However, my research on the Yordim and on CBST, which seemed closer to the tradition of single-site community studies, ultimately resulted in full-fledged ethnographies on both. In contrast, some of my observations at the Center have been published thus far only as separate articles introducing specific organizations. The present volume incorporates that work, adapted to the leading motif of my account along with additional material introducing my long-term observations in other organizations, the churches and synagogue included.

I present those groups whose meetings I regularly attended for at least six months (except for the Bears) and in which I had the opportunity to develop close relationships with a few or more participants. I continued to communicate with some of my close "informants" and friends who are presented in the following pages through phone conversations, e-mail exchanges, and meetings on my frequent visits to New York. I also occasionally visited some of these groups in later years to observe changes in the population and in their style of activities. Alongside the six chapters that report on group meetings, I include a chapter that represents my observations at the gay religious venues. I incorporate two chapters that explore issues in gay men's lives: one on the challenge of being HIV positive and its impact on the relationship with the researcher (Chapter 2), the other on the search for partners for love and sex (Chapter 10). These two chapters transcend the individual groups reported on but nevertheless deal with matters given voice in their meetings. They draw on the detailed accounts of a few friends and acquaintances made in my research. However, I begin this ethnography with an introduction on the history, theory, and method of my work (my engagement in the research of sexuality in particular), and end with concluding remarks offering an integrated, analytical frame for the project. I also add some comparative observations on the social reality among gay people in Israel.

I admit at the outset that my work cannot be classified in the genre of queer theory or cultural studies. For better or worse, I am a mainstream anthropologist trained in Manchester, UK, a disciple of the "extended case-method" of ethnographic analysis (e.g., Gluckman 1959 [1940]; Van Velsen 1967; Burawoy 1991), and addicted to intensive fieldwork projects. I share the position of Stein and Plummer that "there is a dangerous tendency for the new queer theorists to ignore 'real' queer life as it is materially experienced across the world, while they play with the free-floating signifiers of texts" (1996: 137–38). A similar argument has been recently made by

Lewin and Leap: "The primary data sources informing queer theory have been literary or philosophical texts, rather than ethnographic ones" (2009: 6). Instead, this volume is rooted in the ethnographic tradition that aims to present life in vivo.

My position finds support from another quarter: David Halperin, who claimed that queer studies avoided the topic of gay male subjectivity—"the inner life of male homosexuality, what it is that gay men want" (2007: 1). Halperin, however, was probing gay men's motives for sexual risk-taking (having unprotected sexual encounters—"bareback sex") in the context of the HIV epidemic. His search employed, in particular, the personal evidence confessed by another gay intellectual (Warner 1995) who tried to answer: "What makes some men fuck without protection when they know about the dangers, when they have access to condoms, when they have practiced safe sex for years, even when they have long involvement in AIDS activism—in short, when they 'know better'"? (quoted in Halperin 2007: 159).[1]

I believe my observations have enabled me to penetrate deeper into the motivation that drives gay people (men in particular) from different walks of life and sexual proclivities to invest time and other resources in meeting regularly in the company of strangers away from the apparently more promising and often nearby venues for instant sociability, entertainment, and sexual opportunities.

It is not my intention to denigrate the contribution of queer theory and its practitioners to our perception of the position of gay people and their role in contemporary Western culture (Boellstorff 2007). The questions and discourse they raise are quintessential also for the work of anthropologists. An example is Powell's opening query: assuming there is "a gay culture" different from mainstream culture, "do we all share the same cultural experiences?" (2008: viii). However, the topic of gay subjectivity is a major undercurrent in the following chapters.

I believe there is no need to expand on my position in the present-day discourse about anthropologists' search for their professional identity, purpose, and practice. That ongoing torturous self-examination was first triggered by anthropologists' critical view of their research methodology and the ethnographic authority they command to uphold their presentation of the "natives out there." It was further affected by the gradual loss of the Third World fieldwork sites as well as the crumbling of the professional borders with the "outsourcing" of the ethnographic method to other disciplines. That process followed the surrender of the anthropologists' monopoly over the study of culture to neighboring fields of inquiry and to new academic contenders claiming to represent specific social constituencies (e.g., Rabinow et al. 2008).

I find a kindred orientation in Borneman and Hamoudi's protest against the retreat from the "Malinowskian-inspired notions of fieldwork.... The insistence that all translations are partial, all truths relational and perspectival—sound ideas and assumptions with which we agree—often becomes an excuse for offering superficial translations that prefer surface over depth" (2009: 3–5). Actually, I wrestle with that issue, considering the ethnographer's comportment when engaged in the study of sexual behavior (Chapter 1) and the reliability of the records presenting the most intimate zones of our subjects' lives. Thus, Chapter 2 deals with the pressing dilemma relating to a basic element of the ethnographic project—its "authority": how confident we can be about the "making of truth": observing and later interpreting our fieldwork material?

I have not discovered a new road to respond to the yearning for a gratifying and sin-free ethnographic authority under the auspices of what is often called contemporary anthropology. I believe I have been doing "relevant anthropology" from the very beginning of my career, changing my research strategies with ongoing transformations in the professional scene (Shokeid 2007). The circumstances of my apprenticeship impelled me to study social groups close to home (Moroccan Jewish immigrants and Arabs in Israel); later projects in the United States were similarly relevant to my social and intellectual interests (Israeli émigrés in New York and gay Jews). Ironically, however, my work among LGBT people and institutions in the Village Center, and in the churches in particular, has granted me the "classical" role of the anthropologist who sailed to a site away from home to study "another culture."

I am inclined, however, to adopt an outsider's perspective (Westbrook 2008) on the present situation of ethnographic work and consider my role in the LGBT field in terms of a "navigator." Reflecting on the abandonment of the ethnographer's long-term study in one remote site, Westbrook, a scholar of law who carried on a fruitful dialogue with George Marcus, claims that anthropologists are often engaged in the creation of "research circumstances," and their major effort is to convince the subjects they meet on their trail to share with them their world outlook and their social and personal narratives. Therefore, he concludes, the present day ethnographic encounter—while navigating research circumstances—is "thin" compared with the past tradition of "thick description." Although not an anthropologist, Westbrook seems to have grasped some evolutionary developments in the craft of his academic neighbors. This line of thought, which seems to reflect my present project and theoretical agenda, has also been pinpointed by other anthropologists who shared similar experiences (e.g., Hannerz 2010).

As an Israeli's report on a segment of U.S. society, my work, I trust, fits within the long history of "foreign-travelers" writing on America. Notable in this tradition is also *Society in America* (1994 [1837]) by Harriet Martineau, who, while sailing across the Atlantic to begin her research, drafted a guide to the study of foreign cultures: *How to Observe Manners and Morals* (1838). Lipset described that work as "perhaps, the first book on the methodology of social research in the then still unborn disciplines of sociology and anthropology" (1994: 7).

If early visitors to America, bringing their outsider perspective, were struck by the egalitarian ethos and propensity for voluntary association (the "frequency of groups" perceived by the visiting Dutch historian Huizinga as "illusionsgemeinschaft," 1972 [1927]: 275–80), what struck me most in the groups I observed was how freely their members divulged to strangers the intimacies, physical and emotional, of their daily lives. Notable as well was the therapeutic language they employed narrating their feelings and experiences.

The mode of discourse I treat as characteristic of the "therapeutic culture in America" has a long tradition in writings exploring the early success of Freudian psychoanalytic theories and therapy. As suggested by Rieff (1990 [1960]), Freud is *America's great teacher* who introduced the *psychological* man of the twentieth century (8). As a movement, he claimed, psychoanalysis was fortunate enough to achieve a counterrevolution in America. And in daily life, "to become a psychological man is thus to become kinder to the whole self, the private parts as well as the public, the formerly inferior as well as the formerly superior" (5). Or as suggested by Steadman Rice (2004: 113): "the therapeutic ethic constructed around the conviction that human nature is intrinsically benevolent, positive, and constructive." Another outsider, Illouz (2008), commented recently: "Psychoanalysis [in America] enjoyed not only the authority of a prestigious medical profession but also the popularity among the 'lay' public" (35); "the therapeutic discourse has become a cultural form, shaping and organizing experience, as well as a cultural resource with which to make sense of the self and social relations" (56), "making private selfhood a narrative told and consumed publicly" (239).

I hope my subject of interest is not associated with the staged shows on television, those displaying the stripping of the inner personal lives of volunteers in front of innumerable one-night anonymous spectators in the studio theater and beyond, such as on Oprah Winfrey's programs. I consider these staged performances a new form of the old freak shows that paraded on stage unfortunate disfigured humans such as the Elephant Man. Kaminer (1992) and Plummer (1995) have critically reviewed the confessional television talk shows as well as the American culture of recovery groups as centers of sexual storytellers offering "instant" therapies.

Perhaps paradoxically, the smaller, closer-knit, and far more communal Israeli society does not foster, even among close friends, the confessional-intimate atmosphere I witnessed. Although Israelis are assumed to have no inhibitions about inquiring into the lives of others and are well known for their straight-talk (*dugri*) style of conversation (Katriel 1986), nevertheless, they are reluctant to expose personal intimate matters. This hesitancy extends to the professional realm as well. The ethos that promotes both individual self-assertion and enduring social commitments (e.g., Dominguez 1989; Furman 1994; Illouz 2008) operates against Israelis seeking therapeutic help by way of revealing their true selves and as a strategy to improve their social skills.

Given this background, I wondered what explained the free sharing of personal information and the moving expressions of empathy that I witnessed in all the groups observed. Did the common sexual orientation connect the participants and heighten the emotional resonance of their disclosures? It seemed so. But still, one ponders over what it is that leads mature, educated, and frequently quite successful people to seek trust and friendship in the company of strangers gathered at often run-down buildings for lay-led meetings conducted without professional direction. I wondered, like Umberto Eco (1986) in Disney World, what the visitor takes away from these experiences. Is it fantasy, or is it something real? And if the latter, what is the reality produced in these meetings? In sum, I repeat Halperin's archetypal query, "what do gay men want?" albeit addressing a field of behavior that only marginally involves intense sexual activity.

My purpose is to reveal a missing block in the vast corpus of research in the "house of anthropological queer studies" (Boellstorff 2007). I consider my observations and interpretation of affective relationships displayed in voluntary fellowships, in specific issue-oriented groups composed of strangers, or among circles of close friends as essential components of the dynamics that impact gay identity and constitute gay community life. I develop a perspective on modern intimacies (Plummer 2003), more specifically on affective solidarity, also explored by feminist and lesbian researchers (J. Dean 1996; Cvetkovich 2003). It exposes a powerful notion of spontaneous fraternity—*communitas* experiences, in anthropological parlance—among people who express a notion of solidarity and mutual trust without the constraints of earlier acquaintance and regardless of socioeconomic markers dividing them in daily life. This journey among the various gay arenas of mostly dialogical sociability offers a deep entry into gay subjectivity.

I consider that fraternity endeavor a vehicle for specific gay selfhood confirmation beyond a general accommodation with one's gay/lesbian identity. That deep-felt personal impact distinguishes the groups I present from most other "small groups" popular in American society. Based on a vast national survey, Wuthnow (1994: 4) concluded that following the tradition of voluntary associations, four out of every ten Americans belong to a small group that meets regularly and provides caring and support for its members. Nearly two-thirds of all small groups have some connection to the quest for spirituality, and the rest are geared to more specific needs, such as helping individuals cope with addictions

I hope my observations might illuminate some essential issues affecting contemporary gay life. Whatever the answers, however, given the direction of globalization, it is to be expected that the phenomena I recorded will find their way to Israel. A cross-cultural study of social activities in Tel Aviv as compared with our observations at the New York Center might suggest whether, and to what extent, this is actually happening. I have already made a tentative assessment of that trend (2003, 2010).

I believe my portrayals and reflections will be of interest to both gay and nongay audiences, offering a wider view of the urban gay experience—with its alternative spaces and novel patterns of sociability—than the more familiar and limited ethnographic exploration of the gay scene of sex and recreation. It extends and elaborates on Bech's (1997) rendering of the existential conditions and opportunities for sociability emerging in contemporary urban gay life.

A final comment: most of the chapters present my observations in groups that brought together gay men. Naturally, I could not attend all-women/lesbian meetings. But in three chapters, which introduce the association of bisexuals, sexual compulsives, and religious congregations, lesbians are strongly represented among the participants and occupy prominent leadership roles. In order to maintain anonymity, all names and identifying features of the participants mentioned in the book, except for the well-known religious leaders at CBST and MCC, have been changed.

A Personal Note

I assume that some colleagues among my cohort in academia who are familiar with the work in earlier stages of my career have been puzzled by my attraction in the last two decades to gay studies. However, I am not connected in any serious way, professional or social, to the network of "queer anthropologists." As I remember, I expressed a lone opposing voice at the meeting of the Anthropology Research Group on Homosexuality (ARGOH) when it was decided to change its name to SOLGA (Society of Lesbian and Gay Anthropologists). I thought the decision might deter other researchers uncomfortable with that personal "tribal" designation. I have been equally unhappy with other AAA sections and networks that represent "minorities" and "identities" of all sorts (Jewish included).

Nevertheless, I did not relinquish my association with that group of researchers (in 2010 renamed again: AQA—Association for Queer Anthropology). A few among its leading figures have favorably reviewed my CBST ethnography and support my positions in other academic venues. However, my work has not entered the "official," though unwritten, list of "texts of the tribe" (usually recipients of the Benedict Prize), and I remain an outsider in that socioacademic ambience of identity politics. So in a similar vein as my query in the above pages "what do gay people want?" I try to explain, not to excuse or legitimate, what made me depart from the "mainstream" research venues of my earlier projects and immerse myself in a subject that has become a field strongly associated with the researcher's own personal identity and political agenda.

As I mentioned earlier, my engagement in the gay field started with the chance invitation to attend a CBST service. As had happened to me before, and to many other anthropologists in their unplanned choice of fieldwork sites, I was "hooked," "enchanted," by what became a "fatal attraction" to that group of people who stood against the Jewish establishment and its organs of all shades at that time. I assume I also came gradually to enjoy my own position of a somewhat "radical" character in the Israeli academic milieu. But mostly, I felt comfortable in the company of American gay men and women of a similar socio-economic-cultural background, with whom I developed warm relationships of a sort I rarely experienced in my ordinary daily life and academic environment. It was that generous openness—the main theme of this book—that continued to appeal to me and made me move on to study other gay venues. At the same time, however, I was not drawn to extend my research among gay people in Israel. Why not? Too close to home? As fellow Israelis—not representing the ethnographic "other" in the real sense of the term? Was I worried about an intimate involvement among my "own" people? And last, I started my ethnographic work by conducting research at home. In recent years, however, I have preferred to keep my professional engagements separate from subjects that are inevitably related to my daily life, politics, and obligations as an Israeli citizen.

CHAPTER 1

The Anthropologist in the Field of Sexuality

The study of gay people inevitably involves a consideration of the ethnographer's engagement with issues of sexuality, the major indicator of his/her subjects' social identity. Moreover, it calls attention to the observer's own comportment in this field of behavior. That topic naturally reminds us of the turmoil raised among anthropologists with the discovery of Malinowski's diaries (1967). His confessions touched on various sensitive issues. Particularly embarrassing seemed the revelation of his sexual frustration during his work among the Trobrianders. Nevertheless, it took another twenty-five years for that issue to arouse more serious interest in professional forums.[1] The discourse of reflexivity in ethnographic texts, which has continuously expanded in recent decades, has finally penetrated the most intimate sphere of the ethnographer's life during fieldwork: his/her own sexuality.

Since the early 1990s, conference sessions, articles, ethnographies, and edited volumes have removed the veil of secrecy[2] and the taboo that surrounded the sexual demeanor of anthropologists (e.g., Newton 1993; Wade 1993; Kulick and Willson 1995; Bolton 1995, 1996; Carrier 1995; Lewin and Leap 1996; Markowitz and Ashkenazi 1999; Haller 2001; Goode 2002). While gay and lesbian anthropologists seemed to be more aware and open about that dimension in their professional life, heterosexual anthropologists gradually shared revelations similar to those of their homosexual colleagues.

By and large, the ethnographers mentioned above contested the old code that desexualized anthropologists during fieldwork and taught them to hide any sexual involvement with their informants. The reformist ethnographers considered these implanted guidelines seriously wrong, both professionally and ethically. The lone anthropologist, they argued, whether a man or a woman, is "a human being" also during fieldwork, and as such, not devoid of a sexual drive or of a sexual persona. By abstaining from sex, ethnographers are apparently observed by their informants as strange, if not deficient, people. Consequently, this behavior has shut them out of a major dimension of their subjects' lives.

Not surprisingly, for many decades anthropologists have studied "family and kinship" but only rarely dealt with the sexual lives of the people they studied (e.g., Vance 1991; Tuzin 1991; Friedl 1994). The pioneers, Malinowski and Mead, proved to be far less prudent (and prudish) than later generations of anthropologists who left the field of sexual behavior to the monopoly of other academic disciplines and the mercy of therapists. This narrowing of the ethnographer's domain of competence also legitimized the ethos that taught older and younger practitioners to refrain from any breach of morality engaging them in a sexual alliance with their informants.

Not only were anthropologists careful to refrain from studying sexuality and concerned about any sexual distraction in the field, they were also anxious to keep their distance from activities and groups defined by a stigmatized sexuality. In particular, they avoided any association that might mark them with the stigma of homosexuality. Observations of homoerotic interaction were rarely reported in ethnographic texts since the anthropologist's reputation was at stake (e.g., Read 1980: 184–85; Shokeid 2003, 1995: 22–27; Markowitz and Ashkenazi 1999). Read's confession is particularly illuminating. In *Other Voices* (1980: 184), he returned to his New Guinea ethnography of 1955: "The gaps in my record of the Gahuku cannot be retrieved now and I advise skepticism in accepting my statement that homosexual practices did not exist. . . . As a 'legitimate' study, homosexuality remained the 'vice without a name'."

More radical, and still largely controversial, has been the claim by a few "maverick" anthropologists, both heterosexuals and homosexuals, that having sex with one's informants is beneficial for fieldwork. Anthropologists who are sexually involved with their informants, they argue, are better integrated into the community they wish to study.

Heterosexual Anthropologists Reveal Sexual Secrets

Peter Wade (1993), Fran Markowitz (1999), and Erich Goode (2002), all heterosexuals, described the path that had led them to have sex with close informants. Wade, who studied black Colombians, had two romantic/sexual affairs during his two fieldwork projects, the first in a small village and the second in Medellin (one of the largest cities in Colombia). He claims that his intimate affairs affected his standing with both men and women: "My position in both Unguia and Medellin was consolidated and legitimized by virtue of my relationships with Marcela and Roberta. . . . As a result, many people saw me as part of the community: the relationship implied some commitment to Colombian, especially black, society" (208).

In her study of Soviet immigrants in New York, Markowitz describes an encounter with a male informant to whom she said that her professional ethics inhibited her from having sex with men she interviewed. "'What?!' he exclaimed with incredulity 'Aren't you a human being?!'" Eventually, as she dropped her celibacy, it "brought with it a great deal of advantages that last into the present" (168). She claims also that her female informants expected and supported her sexual involvement with Soviet men. Nevertheless, Markowitz ponders her standing within the conventions of the discipline: "My biggest problem, however, remained the nagging thought that I was doing something wrong that went against the ethical foundations of the discipline" (168).

Goode, who conducted research on the National Association for the Advancement of Fat Acceptance (NAAFA), recounted a number of sexual liaisons, including one that resulted in the birth of a daughter. Although his research was not a story of great success, he nevertheless assumes that sex between social scientists and their informants cannot be avoided in certain circumstances: "And pretending that it doesn't take place and that it isn't a fit topic for discussion, strikes me as a variety of collective insanity" (2002: 529).

Gay Men's Sexuality and Gay Anthropologists

The Hidden Observer

The ethnographic work available on sexual behavior in Western society has been mostly carried out in the field of anonymous gay sex. However, for many years, the ethnographers who conducted that research performed their task as unidentified observers (e.g., Humphreys 1970; Delph 1978; Style 1979; Leap 1999). Such studies have been relatively easy to conduct without developing close relationships with the "natives." That trend won methodological and theoretical support from the school of symbolic interaction (as represented by Goffman in particular).

Laud Humphreys was probably the first researcher who conducted intensive ethnographic work among gay men. His *Tearoom Trade* (1970) remains a landmark not only for its methodological innovation and sociological revelation, but also for its ensuing scandal. Humphreys observed men having sex in public restrooms in the parks of an American city. He conducted his observations by adopting the role of a "watch queen," warning the participants of the approach of the police and unidentified visitors. Humphreys could take notes about the participants' visible, though silent, sexual communication, but he had almost no additional knowledge about their lives outside these meeting sites. The men were quick to depart and had no wish to carry on conversations that might have revealed their identity. They would have certainly left immediately had they suspected the presence of a researcher on the premises.

In order to obtain additional information about his subjects, Humphreys employed another unconventional method. He wrote down the registration numbers of the cars of his subjects parked nearby; he then used his connections at the relevant license administration offices to track down their addresses. He visited them at their homes about a year later, somewhat disguised and under the pretext of another survey. This was obviously a most serious breach of privacy, as well as a violation of professional ethics.

Against the fierce wave of criticism about the flawed ethics of his work, Humphreys defended his methods. He claimed, first, that he took all the measures necessary to protect the confidentiality of the men he observed. Second, he argued that his research proved that men who participate in this stigmatized activity were good citizens who might happen to be the readers' next-door neighbors or close relatives. He believed he contributed to the obliteration of the myth and prejudice about the apparently deviant characters who associate in the sites of sleazy anonymous sex. He did not regret the first part of his observations but admitted he would not have repeated the second stage of his research, in which he interviewed his unsuspecting subjects at their homes. He believed, however, that no other alternative method could produce equivalent reliable data (1975: 223–32).

Since Humphreys published his pioneering research, many studies of close observations have been carried out in the field of anonymous sex, including in saunas, bars, public parks, and parking areas (e.g., Leap 1999). Most observers, who remained incognito at the sites of their research, employed the ideas and tools of symbolic interaction. This was long the method adopted to describe the "discourse" that maintains the intimate communication between silent bodies, as well as the strategies practiced by the participants to conceal their use of public spaces for "forbidden" behavior. Observers suggested contrasting opinions about the pros and cons of public "anonymous" sex. Were these sites the crucible for the development of gay supportive communities (e.g., Altman 1986), or were they the scene of brutal competition and depressing alienation (e.g., Bersani 1998)?

The Active Observer

In recent years, however, the methodology in the field of gay men's sexuality took a new direction, propagated by openly gay anthropologists. This generation of scholars conducted their research equipped with a new professional conviction, which was combined with the urgency of a social mission. Their work was stimulated by their efforts to prevent the spread of AIDS.

Ralph Bolton, an American anthropologist, worked in rural Peru for many years. Only later in his career, in the 1980s, did he come out as a gay man and become one of the most active medical anthropologists engaged in gay issues. He undertook research on anonymous sex as part of a project that sought to reveal habits that might facilitate or curtail the spread of AIDS. His method of studying anonymous sex abandoned the old tradition of participant observation, which left the researcher in the safe position of a detached voyeur. Instead, he claimed, it was an advantage for the researcher to take full part in the activity under study. Employing this strategy in his research of gay saunas in Brussels, Bolton believed he could thus obtain more reliable information, far superior to that obtained through the "voyeuristic" tradition or through the methods of survey and interview.

Bolton's active participation raised doubts and sometimes disdain in professional circles. He noted his mainstream colleagues' ambivalent reception of his method and sadly concluded: "Real ethnography was not to be tolerated; distance must be replaced through the use of data-collecting techniques that keep informants at bay" (1996: 162).

That method was also reported in ethnographic work done elsewhere, such as that of Carrier (1995) in his many years among gay men in Mexico. Carrier reported extensively on his observations at sites of anonymous sex, his experiences of long-standing intimate friendships with individuals, and his continuing association with networks of Mexican gay men. His ethnography probably presents the most uninhibited report on the sex life of an anthropologist in the field. However, his conclusions raised some doubts among other gay anthropologists, though not for ethical reasons.

Murray's (1996) critique of Carrier's observations, supported by his own work in South America, is of particular importance. Although Murray also admitted he had sex with local men, he argued that the anthropologist who believes he uncovered "true" evidence because he had sex with his subjects may end up with information invented for the researcher. For example, an American ethnographer in a Latin American country might truly believe that local men indeed willingly take part as "passive" partners in anal and oral sex, despite their ethos that "manly men" would never do that. But Murray suggested that men in Guatemala might consent to adopt the recipient role in anal or oral sex with the American visitor, who is a privileged outsider, something they would not countenance with their compatriots. Therefore, Murray concluded, the anthropologist might be seriously wrong assuming that his shared gay identity and engagement in sex with his informants endowed him with inside knowledge and with an important lesson to teach the personnel involved in AIDS prevention: "The relationship between such data and native intra-cultural behavior and thought is far from obvious. Having sex with the natives is not the royal road to insight about alien sexualities" (1996: 250).

The fully participatory research strategy took an even more controversial turn when it was adopted for a project in Sweden. Benny Henriksson (1995) studied porno video clubs in Stockholm catering to a gay men clientele. He identified these establishments as substitute commercial sites for the gay baths, which had been banned in 1987 as part of the official battle against AIDS. However, an article in a local newspaper revealed that Henriksson did not conduct the observations himself. Instead he employed five assistants, who were not discouraged from having sex with the men they observed. They were told to avoid unsafe sex but otherwise were expected to report in detail on the verbal negotiations and actual erotic activities they observed or joined in.

A public scandal soon erupted. The sites studied by Henriksson's assistants were raided by the police, and the institutions that funded the research were severely criticized. In the final report, Henriksson rejected the accusations leveled at his work by officials, professional groups, and gay organizations. He contended that his unorthodox use of participant observers was legitimate (relying on Bolton's arguments in particular) and caused no harm to his research assistants, who had engaged in these activities prior to their recruitment to the project. He promised that the identity of anyone observed in the clubs would remain strictly confidential. Moreover, he believed that the participants' ignorance of being observed was justified in terms already stated in previous studies of anonymous sex: "The use of participant observation gave me an in-depth understanding, of what "the devil was going on" in different erotic oases, to paraphrase Geertz" (1995: 78).

In defense of his work, Henriksson advocated his research findings in particular. He claimed that gay men cruising these video clubs for anonymous sex had mostly abstained from unsafe sex. The latter, he concluded, was more likely to take place in the sanctity of private homes of both homosexuals and heterosexuals. It was through the intimate relationships and participant observations conducted by his assistants in these stigmatized territories, he insisted, that his team was able to discover these were not hotbed sites for the spread of AIDS. Thus, Henriksson's view was similar to that expressed long before by Humphreys. In sum, a method considered unethical by colleagues and other observers seemed, in the eyes of its practitioners, to be redeemed by findings that offered a new understanding of a publicly condemned behavior.[3]

Bolton's strategy was also employed by Lunsing (1999), in a study of gay men in Japan. Lunsing admitted he had sex with ten informants. However, a warning about uncritical celebrations of the advantages of the openly gay researcher engaging in intimate relationships with his gay subjects was raised again by Haller (2001) who studied homosexuals in Seville: "Insiders can become berufsblind: they miss out on phenomena obvious to outsiders because they interpret the world from a similar perspective as the people they study" (125).

My review of the history of research in anonymous male sex thus reached the same conclusions regarding the behavior observed and produced the same legitimization suggested by those criticized for their breach of ethical norms, as well as for their full participation in the "natives'" culture. From *Tearoom Trade* in 1970 to Henriksson's 1995 report, the claim was made that gay and bisexual men who participate in anonymous sex activities are not a minority of deviants—sick, isolated, and dangerous men who might propagate disease into mainstream society. This finding seems to override all hesitations about the violation of both the participants' privacy and the professional ethos of "don't touch me" observations.

The Ethnography of Lesbian Sexuality

My review of the literature has been dedicated primarily to the study of gay men's sexuality, leaving one to wonder if this again is a case of a male bias. However, as documented in Kennedy and Davis's ethnography (1993) on the lesbian community in Buffalo, New York, until very recently women had not developed their own institutions, particularly bars, nor could they use public spaces for an open search of female partners for sex and love. The whole phenomenon of cruising, so basic to the life experiences of gay men, is almost absent in lesbian history. Baths, bars, and parks, for example, have been available for gay men in New York and other metropolitan cities for at least a century (e.g., Chauncey 1994). In those decades women could never stroll alone in public spaces, such as parks, without immediate risk to lives and reputation. Moreover, they lacked the money or freedom to entertain on their own outside their homes.

Only since World War II have women been able to claim their own space in certain bars. On the whole, therefore, the sexual life of lesbians has been less visible and has not attracted the interest of professional observers. Karla Jay, editor of a volume on lesbian erotic life, made an opening statement that seems most relevant: "As we come to the end of the twentieth century, the question of whether or not lesbians have sex is still a hotly contested issue" (1995: 1). I assume that a cultural ethos concerning the "sanctity" of women's sexuality also inhibited the study of lesbians' sexuality. That avoidance on the part of researchers was also evident in other domains of lesbian lives unrelated to the display of sexuality. Lewin (1996b) reported the pressures imposed on her by research funding agencies to change the outline of her research project and cloak her interest in the lives of lesbian mothers. Blackwood, a pioneering researcher in gay studies, pointed out the lesser position afforded to research on lesbian practices during the formative years of the anthropology of homosexuality in the 1970s, following the rise of the gay rights movement (2002: 77).

But there are signs of a new trend. A few among the leading cohort of anthropologists engaged in gay and lesbian studies have in recent years conducted research on some of the formerly invisible facets of lesbians' sexuality. I refer here to Newton (1996) and Kennedy Lapovsky (1996), who offered their descriptions of the lives of major informants and of their own relationships with them. Amory reported on a lesbian dance club in San Francisco that survived for about three years, until 1992: "An important part of the celebration of sexuality involved cruising for girls, cruising other women's bodies and striking a pose while others cruised you" (1996: 153). The author claims Club Q catered to a new generation of lesbians, whose sexual boldness could be intimidating for other women. Thus, cruising is no longer the exclusive domain of males' behavior and observation.

Away from the United States, however, Sinnott presented a different perspective on female same-sex sexuality regarding the use of space in the formation of identity, sexual relationships, and community. Reporting from Thailand, she claimed that "masculinist or 'western' discursive patterns impose the linkage between 'public' spaces, cultural norms regarding men's use of space, and the 'liberating' practice of same-sex sexuality" (2009: 228). For example, same-sex dormitory spaces (at school, college, factory, etc.) were found as one of the most productive sites for networks and sexual liaisons of same-sex relationships among women.

Observing Gay Institutions in New York

In the following presentation I will describe the experiences I went through when I came to study communities of gay men and was directly confronted with some of the issues discussed above. The field situations, the strategies I adopted as an observer, and my response to unexpected circumstances demonstrate the complexity of the issues involved in the research of sexual behavior beyond the dilemma of "partaking or not" in sexual activities.

During the 1990s and early 2000s, I carried out research at two gay institutions in Greenwich Village. I first studied Congregation Beth Simchat Torah (the gay and lesbian synagogue), and later the Lesbian and Gay Community Services Center. These are very different organizations. I will not expand here on the characteristics that distinguish them but mention only one major feature that also affected my position and my work. CBST, a lay-led congregation at the time of my fieldwork,[4] offered its members an opportunity to get together during the weekly (Friday) and festival services. The congregants could also meet and socialize at various committee meetings and other activities. I could attend most events, observe, and be observed in a community of people who were not an anonymous crowd, the growing number of participants notwithstanding. The Center, in contrast, was led by professionals, and its activities catered to numerous special interests and social groups. The 1995–1996 annual report presented a list of

120 organizations and groups associated with the Center. I could regularly attend only a small number of the activities and engage with but a few of the groups that met on its premises. Only rarely did I meet participants who regularly attended the activities of more than one or two groups. Naturally, in the synagogue my network of friends and acquaintances was wider and my relationships with them were closer.

I tackle now my own response as I confronted two major problems that emerged in my review of previous works in the field of sexual minorities:

(1) The ethnographer's unannounced presence at the site of his research.
(2) The ethnographer's sexual comportment during fieldwork.

I emphasize: I was not guided beforehand by an ideological or professional conviction as to the pros and cons of the anthropologist's mode of active participation in erotic activities. Nor had I endured during fieldwork a personal crisis of any sort. I believe, however, that reporting the hesitations, decisions, moral dilemmas, and mistakes I made might add a more balanced perspective to issues of fieldwork that cannot be dismissed any longer.

In my previous ethnographic projects I often engaged in the subjects of family, kinship, and gender, but I did not initiate research in the field of sexuality. Moreover, I was careful to avoid any erotic entanglement with informants. For example, in my study of Moroccan immigrants in an Israeli village, I dealt with the changing division of labor between men and women (particularly in consequence of the engagement of women in farming). But that interest did not lead me to study issues of sexuality.

An exception was my work among Muslims in a mixed-population Israeli town. In a discussion of the Arab code of honor, a subject that seemed to dominate my informants' worldview, I introduced the discourse of masculinity. My observations revealed the growing consumption of opium as a strategy by some men to prolong erection. I interpreted the recourse of young men to artificially strengthened sexual potency as a response to a prevalent notion of social insecurity that affected their sense of manhood (Shokeid 1980). My Arab friends often complained about conflicts with their wives, who seemed to imitate their far more emancipated female Jewish neighbors. However, in particular, their gossip about adulterous women made me aware of that issue. Nevertheless, I was not engaged in a direct study of sexuality.

Conducting Fieldwork in a Gay Synagogue

I was studying Israeli emigrants in New York (1982–1984) when a colleague at a local university asked me to help him supervise a student who was struggling with a Ph.D. dissertation based on his work at CBST. Never before had I heard of that type of institution. However, since the manuscript the student handed me lacked a clear description of the synagogue and its crowd, I suggested (in a telephone conversation) that I visit the synagogue to get a feeling for the place.

I had to make a decision about how to comport myself before setting foot in this "unconventional" field. How does one dress for a Friday night service in a gay synagogue? Need I wear a jacket and tie, as one often does in a mainstream synagogue? Or should I choose more casual attire, as fitting for a synagogue of radical Jews? I decided to take the middle ground and put on corduroys and a casual jacket, similar to what I would wear on campus. I was on time for the meeting with my student-guide at a bookstore on Sixth Avenue in Greenwich Village. However, I saw no one waiting there who looked "gay." Actually, I noticed somebody standing nearby, but I thought he "couldn't be gay," since he was too conservative looking. Eventually, I approached him and asked if he had seen anyone else waiting. He was embarrassed to discover it was me he was waiting for. It became evident he expected me to come in somber (professorial) attire, just as I expected a more radical looking young man. In retrospect, it was partly an inability to disappear in the crowd that probably handicapped my guide's own work.

I was greatly surprised when we got to the synagogue to find a big crowd of many men and a smaller number of women who seemed to me so . . . ordinary! They looked very different from what I had expected. My encounter with the gay synagogue raised my doubts about the frequent portrayal of gay male society in the anthropological literature. Why only, or mostly, was their depiction in the field of anonymous sex? I thought that anthropologists who for many years refrained altogether from the study of a group that might have affected their own status in mainstream professional life had by default helped direct the belated interest in gay people to the restricted issues around sexual demeanor. They thereby also called public attention to a further stigmatizing type of behavior. The outbreak of AIDS undoubtedly strengthened the trend of research on issues of men's sexual behavior. However, I do not blame anthropologists. I assume I would not have dared engage myself and "compromise" my reputation with the study of gay people had I been at an earlier stage of my career.

On my return to New York in 1989, planning to conduct research at CBST, I did not intend to concentrate on issues of sexuality. Nevertheless, I expected some difficulties on entering the field of gay society. A dilemma I immediately confronted was, how do I go about introducing myself? I have already discussed this issue in my ethnography (2003 [1995]: 7–10); however, I should emphasize that the dilemma of the anthropologist's role during field-work—the information he or she offers the subjects about the researcher's identity and the goals of research—are not unique to fieldwork with sexual minorities. These issues are equally relevant to most other fields of study that are no longer conducted among "other" people, those who are visibly differ-ent from the researcher's ethnic and social identity.

I had faced a similar problem during my study of Israeli immigrants in New York (Shokeid 1988b). For many years they have been disparaged by their compatriots and nicknamed Yordim. Since I was not studying my fellow Israelis through the more formal techniques of survey and interviews, was I supposed, according to professional ethics, to inform any Israeli I spoke to that I was not a Yored and that I was planning to write about the Israelis in America? Actually, a previous research project initiated at Queens College to study the various immigrant groups in the Borough of Queens had failed with the Israelis. They refused to cooperate with the interviewers. Similarly, was I supposed to inform my new acquaintances at the gay synagogue, on first meeting each man and woman, of my sexual identity and that I might write about them?

For nearly a hundred years, the position of Euro/American fieldworkers has been mostly visible and clear. They usually came from another continent or racial/ethnic group and retained the status of guests who only rarely could and did "go native." But when an Israeli citizen comes to study other Israelis in America, or when an Israeli-Jewish anthropologist shows up at a gay syna-gogue, he/she is not immediately categorized in the role of alien observer. The "otherness," a major characteristic of the anthropologist's social encounter during fieldwork, as well as a theoretical mainstay in the ethnographic text, is thus immediately lost. The anthropologist's own "otherness" is now far more subtle and a matter for gradual revelation and negotiation—for example, the "true" national identity of the Israeli ethnographer on a sabbatical stay in New York versus that of the Israeli immigrants (Yordim) in his study. Similarly, the assessment of the "true" sexual identity of the Israeli anthropologist, versus that of his gay American coreligionist congregants, is now a matter of gradual discovery rather than a clearly marked characteristic identified immediately on the ethnographer's arrival.[5]

Attending Sexual Activities

I soon discovered that the gay synagogue was not a cruising site. Obviously, I had no need to consider Bolton's strategy. I might even suggest that my unannounced sexual orientation was somewhat advantageous. I learned to be "physical" with friends, men and women, something foreign to the culture of Israelis of my generation, who do not habitually kiss and hug, a common habit in the United States and in gay society in particular. Still, I never had sex with a congregant. On one embarrassing occasion I learned how easily one can lose one's position of sexual "otherness." I decided to visit a gay sauna that was mentioned to me as one of the last surviving institutions of this type in Manhattan. I assumed that in the early afternoon hours I would not meet any of my acquaintances there. I was naturally embarrassed when one of the few attendees at this slow business hour told me I was familiar to him from his visits to services at CBST. It now became clear that I had not considered the possibility I was not the only academic in town free of a strict work schedule. In any case, it was not the problem of being discovered at that place but the anxiety of how to decline his advances without incurring personal offense.

Later I learned that one could observe a site of sexual activity without necessarily engaging in the activity and without violating the participants' privacy. Jeff, who was among my close friends at CBST (see Chapters 2 and 10), felt secure enough to share with me some details of his sexual adventures. The mutual exchange of feelings and information sustained our intimate relationship. He once told me that he was a member of the GSA (Golden Shower Association). I must admit, I was puzzled about the "obscene" pleasure he found in getting soaked in urine. What I had in mind was a very surrealistic image of that phenomenon. In a casual manner I told Jeff I was "curious" about that activity. As I later realized, my expression of curiosity left him with the impression I would like to see the scene for myself. I had forgotten all about it when, a few months later, Jeff suggested I join him at the next GSA monthly meeting. For a long time, he told me, he had hesitated to invite me, mostly because of the embarrassment of having me watch him during a sexual activity. But eventually, he concluded that at most, he would not enjoy for once the complete freedom to "do his thing." He considered this a minor sacrifice.

It was now my turn to hesitate and consider my forthcoming voyeuristic role in a notorious sexual activity. I decided to go along, and to my great relief, I soon discovered my presence was not as embarrassing as I had thought it would be. I was not obliged to strip but remained in jeans. Nor was I obliged to participate in the ongoing activities. Benefiting from the introduction by Jeff, I could stroll around and talk to friendly members. Also, contrary to my worry, the place did not smell of urine.[6] Most important, I did not feel I was violating the privacy of the participants. I came as Jeff's friend. Jeff could rely on my code of confidentiality and feel assured that my observations, if ever published, would not harm his friends.

My visit to the Golden Shower event seemed to cement our friendship. As we all exited, relieved that all had gone well, Jeff told me that when the lights went out for a few seconds, he thought it was a police raid and was worried about my being caught in an embarrassing situation. He then told me another reason that had initially made him unwilling to take me along to the event: he did not wish to feel like an "organism under a microscope." But since then he had read my CBST book and had no worries about my way of portraying the people I observed. He liked his own presentation in my narrative, although his identity remained disguised to anyone else.

As for my mood about this event and my evaluation of my own behavior as "participant observer," I felt that I had undergone one of the most daring experiences in my career. Not because I witnessed a Bruegel picture—a chaotic, fantastic, and in some way forbidden scene—but because I did not shy away from a social setting, one that prior to my participation seemed somewhat obscene and threatening to my reputation.

I again experienced the difficult choices that confront the observer in this field when I was encouraged to join a group of men for the annual Bear Pride Convention in Chicago. This time I was fully aware that once I decided to participate it would be far more difficult to retreat into the "don't touch me" position. I assumed that being away from my home territory might make it more difficult to leave the scene before I got entangled in an embarrassing situation. I felt the same hesitations that had beset me when Jeff invited me to attend the Golden Shower event. Yet I thought that not participating would be cowardly on my part and another lost research opportunity. I had avoided attending all previous annual and regional conventions and weekend retreats that were advertised by the groups I studied. I knew these were opportunities for more intense social activities and for the experience of communitas that nourished these groups for a long time afterward; nevertheless, I worried about the implications of that intensified engagement with my subjects.

The Bear Pride convention took place at a major Chicago hotel. While there, I was supposed to share a room with three other occupants. I decided to go along and let myself be immersed in the event with no preconditions. I was only slightly acquainted with a few of the participants, who were vaguely aware of my professional interests (see Chapter 8).

It was a lively event, with many activities in the hotel (receptions, lectures parties) and in other locations (the major bars in town in particular). An estimated 1,400 men attended the convention. The participants were constantly meeting old buddies and making new friends. My roommates expressed much mutual affection with each other and showed no inhibition about sex play with either old or new acquaintances or in the presence of others. I let go once and joined a sexual activity with a roommate. I was shocked at first at my own loss of "guard" and its possible implications for my research position, reputation, and self-perception. Had I, at last, "gone native"? But I soon dismissed that notion of guilt and adopted instead a sort of fatalistic approach to these "bourgeois-mainstream" conventions and worries. Was it my "advanced age" that made me develop a more opportunistic approach? I will save the reader my own self-analysis and other defenses. But more important for the subject of my presentation: had I gained, due to that intensified participation, a deeper inner understanding of the phenomenon observed?

Although somewhat disappointingly, I must admit, my "active" participation did not endow me with any special hermeneutic revelation. That conclusion reminds me of Murray's and Haller's critiques about the privileged knowledge the anthropologist must gain through participating in sex with informants. At the same time, however, I felt afterward—or perhaps only consoled myself—that I had gained some better credibility with my roommates and their friends. At last I was "normal." Recalling Markowitz's report (1999: 167), I proved to the people I wished to observe that I was "a sexual human being." It allowed me, I believe, to observe later instances of sexual encounters in an unobtrusive manner, as much as to excuse myself without offense when invited to participate. Nevertheless, I have no proof that I might have been treated differently had I not shared in a sexual activity. In any case, I wish to emphasize, I had not consciously employed at that event the strategy suggested by Bolton. I reacted to the circumstances of the event I attended and to a sensual excitement surrounding me. I cannot claim that I was responding to an ideological or a professional conviction.

The Unannounced Observer

Although unrelated to sexual behavior, a more distressing situation arose during my observations of another group at the gay community center in Greenwich Village. I regularly attended the weekly meetings of a few SCA (Sexual Compulsives Anonymous) social groups (see Chapter 4). These meetings, similar in structure to those of Alcoholics Anonymous, are open to everybody, although the discussions are presumed to be confidential (e.g., Plummer 1995: 103–4). I never concealed my professional identity, but as at most other activities I attended at the Center I did not publicly announce my research interests. The presentation of my "true" identity, sexual and professional, seemed a difficult task at the Center. The lack of a single main focus of activity there (in contrast to the gay synagogue) made my persona far more obscure among its visitors.

Actually, I was not concerned at that time about the way I would ever use my field notes from the SCA meetings. For the time being, it was a natural extension of my work at the Center, since for my research I tried to attend as many group meetings there as possible. The issues the participants raised at the SCA meetings seemed particularly relevant to the work and literature dealing with anonymous sex and, in retrospect, to the issue of gay men's subjectivity (Halperin 2007). Many of the male participants described painful experiences caused by their attraction to the various "oases" of anonymous sex. Never satisfied sexually and emotionally, they could not stop going back to these sites, which by their account seemed to ruin their lives. I became familiar with a few participants of one particular SCA group.

One participant, also engaged in the social sciences, was especially friendly to me. I believed that our mutual sympathy was stimulated by our professional kinship. However, to my great surprise (I assumed he was acquainted with my CBST ethnography), it took him a few months to comprehend that I was doing research. One day, as he saw me inquiring about a particular issue, he burst out in a tone of dismay: "Are you doing research?" To my matter-of-fact response he reacted with words I cannot forget: "I feel violated." I believe he was offended, in particular, because his late revelation of my professional interest shattered the notion of a shared struggle that had sustained our relationship. He must have assumed that I experienced the same existential predicament that seemed to ruin his life.[7] I was shocked and deeply moved by this expression of painful revelation and never went back to meetings at that particular group or to other SCA gatherings.

Could I justify my SCA observations in terms suggested, for example, by Humphreys (1975) and Henriksson (1995)? Would my findings redeem these people, as much as the other presumably "unethical" studies had done before? But as I was pondering that dilemma, I considered a more heretical quandary: had not anthropologists, all along, employed an ethically flawed method? After all, the "natives" in most conventional field sites, although they welcomed the foreign anthropologists, nevertheless rarely maintained a clear idea of the anthropologists' craft or their forthcoming writings. Why privilege Western people, heterosexuals or homosexuals, when they happen to inhabit the ethnographer's field? These, I assume, are partly naive and probably unanswerable questions.

Responding to Circumstances

Returning to the two major queries I posed earlier, what can I suggest from my own experience?

First, I gradually made my role and identity known to a growing number of congregants at the gay synagogue.[8] In contrast, my role and identity remained far more obscure at the Community Center. The research situation and the constraints I experienced at the two different gay institutions (albeit in the same neighborhood) have underwritten the strategy of my presentation of self in each.

Second, I remained totally "chaste" during my fieldwork at the synagogue. I also remained uninvolved in the apparently "wild" Golden Shower party. But I did engage in sexual activity at a social event initiated by one of the organizations associated with the Center. However, it was neither a change of methodology motivated by new professional convictions nor an ideological transformation that made me adopt a more active type of participant observation at the Chicago convention. Again, I reacted to specific situational provocations and personal incitement.

Certainly, two anthropologists may be affected differently under similar conditions and make other choices. In real life, "circumstances" are not objectively defined and perceived as indicated by the term. Also, the same individual, when confronting similar circumstances, may adopt different modes of accommodation conditioned, for example, by changes of his/her personal status (as a younger or an older person, etc.).

I believe there is no prerequisite to be gay or lesbian in order to study gay people. Anthropologists have usually studied "other" societies. Gay and lesbian anthropologists can offer an insider's perspective, but that is true for "native anthropologists" in all other fields. However, neither the insider nor the outsider anthropologist is privileged with the one definitive perspective. There are advantages and disadvantages to both practitioners.[9]

Anthropologists may find themselves becoming engaged with their subjects in intimate relationships that are unorthodox in terms taught at school or unexpected before departure for the field. I opened my discussion by presenting the experiences and conclusions volunteered by both heterosexual and homosexual ethnographers. My own experience suggests a more pragmatic approach than that advocated in some recent works presented earlier. The method of conducting my observations and my response to specific trials during fieldwork represent the consequences of sound or poor acts of judgment taken at a particular moment. The ethnographic project is dependent on the instant decisions made by anthropologists engaged in various sensitive domains of behavior and relates to both the researcher and his/her subjects. The history of ethnographic work proves that we mostly rely on the wisdom of its practitioners and that we have no way of scrutinizing the outcome of their actions. I can now better comprehend the old Jewish saying "Don't judge your friend until you share his position."

CHAPTER 2

Concealments and Revelations
in Ethnographic Research

I wrote this chapter in a state of emotional anxiety, but also one of great relief. It relates to the relationship with one of my closest informants/friends, Jeff, whom I had met at CBST twenty years earlier. He assumed the role of a dedicated guide and taught me about the inner life of gay men and their popular sex venues. Although in a very different ethnographic world, I could compare him with Mochuna, Victor Turner's admirable teacher of Ndembu society and culture (1967b). Jeff's personal history, his demeanor, and his ideas about gay life are presented in other chapters (Chapters 1 and 10 in particular). The following quotes suggest the complexity of research engagements in what seems to be a common phenomenon of secrets and revelations that anthropologists confront in their work:

> This is the inner life of the individual with whom we interact. He may, intentionally either reveal the truth about himself to us, or deceive us by lie and concealment. (Simmel 1969 [1908]: 310)

> In much ethnographical writing, the treatment of secrets constitutes a criterion for how the text and the ethnographic work behind it will be evaluated. The ethnographer's ability to penetrate the secrets of his or her objects becomes a major stake in the ethnographic quest. (Lovell 2007: 57)

> Secrets and silences operate, and are made, through all relational contexts and interactions. How is one to write about them, then, if they are so ubiquitous and of the ordinary? (Nast 2008: 395)

Anthropologists: Decoders of Secrets

From a young age we learn the art of keeping and sharing personal, family, and communal secrets. That skill is among the elementary assets of sociability that children acquire in most societies (Taussig 1999: 267–71). Since anthropologists try to penetrate the lives and culture of their subjects in societies both far and near, one might define ethnographic fieldwork as the art of secret-decoding.

Anthropologists long ago studied cultures of secrecy, men's secret societies in particular (Morgan 1851). I mention Herdt's more recent studies (1981, 2003) of male secret initiation rituals in precolonial New Guinea. Pitt-Rivers, in his study of the Sierra people, represented a different category of a cultural ethos of secrecy and deception: "Andalusians are the most accomplished liars I have ever encountered" (1971: xvi). But as suggested above by Lovell, beyond gaining entry into institutionalized secret societies or cracking the cultural codes of deception, anthropologists believe it is their special skill and privilege to penetrate the personal inner-life territory of the individuals they study and breach their sealed areas of behavior, beliefs, and sentiments. This assertion certainly calls for a measure of caution lest mainstream anthropologists be seen as stepping into the role of psychotherapists.

Particularly famous are the practitioners whose ethnographies revealed sensitive intimate details of sexual, spiritual, or mental health conditions. Examples include Oscar Lewis's (1967) portrayal of the life of Fernanda, a Puerto Rican prostitute, and her close family members, as well as Crapanzano's (1980) rendering of Tuhami, a Moroccan tilemaker who believed himself married to a camel-footed she-demon. We know, however, of a few cases of mutual antipathy that tainted the relationship of ethnographers with their subjects, the latter resentful of the researcher's intrusion or offended by the manner in which the published text revealed their private lives (e.g., Turnbull 1973; Scheper-Hughes 2000).

I usually considered myself lucky to enjoy the collaboration and often the liking of my subjects at the various field sites of my research. My conviction about that advantage was reinforced in particular during my study of gay people, who shared with me many intimate details of their personal lives. Actually, I came to believe that gay people were exceptionally open in exposing intimate life experiences not only in the company of close friends, but also when participating in groups wherein they engaged with many strangers, as evinced in the chapters of this book.

My present discourse does not relate to the more usual situation of first entry into a new field site, when the ethnographer might confront subjects' objections to efforts to infiltrate their public and private spaces and their withholding of sensitive information from his intrusive gaze (e.g., Geertz 1973; Godelier 1999; Kalir 2006). I intend in this context to expose the gray areas in our endeavor, the "shadow side of fieldwork,"[1] when we may not comprehend the reluctance of the apparently welcoming subjects to share with us some confidential information. The observer might reach this embarrassing realization long after assuming he/she had won the confidence of close informants who surely considered the ethnographer a safe haven for their happy or painful secrets.

Just recently the belief about my privileged position as ethnographer, one who could confidently rely on his subjects' true reports about their life experiences, was shaken. This embarrassing discovery involved an informant whom I considered open to me and trustworthy beyond doubt. As the story of deception unraveled before me over a period of several months, I also learned the reason for and feeling behind the concealment of some sensitive information and the conditions under which secrecy is maintained even among intimates, the ethnographer included. My discussion, which seems to highlight a major issue of ethnographic methodology, is deeply interwoven with the existential conditions and predicaments of gay life. However, the ethnographer is not immune to the pains and stigma that affect his gay informants or invulnerable to the strategies of concealment they employ in their relationships with other people.

The question and professional dilemma I tackle stir up a broader issue than this specific ethnographer's "trauma": whatever the excuses for particular concealments, how does the discovery of a close informant's hiding a major piece of personal information reflect on the quality of the ethnographer's work? I remind the reader of Lovell's assessment quoted above: "The ethnographer's ability to penetrate the secrets of his or her objects becomes a major stake in the ethnographic quest." Are anthropologists nowadays expected to prove a level of "truthfulness" in their fieldwork journey and their later reporting on their subjects' lives, comparable, for example, to the thorough documentation of a lawsuit? A similar quandary concerning the ethnographer's authority at presenting her data from the field, assumed by her readers to be guided by certain rules of evidence, was raised by Wolf (1992) comparing the construction of ethnographic portrayals with the writer of fiction, who is in total control of the "information" presented.

Except for a few famous cases, such as the Redfield-Lewis and Mead-Freeman debates or the Yanomami controversy, the issue of truthfulness or the
reliability of ethnographic accounts has rarely been addressed in ordinary
professional public discourse.[2] It has become a nonissue, particularly since
anthropologists have given up the positivist framework of earlier generations.
True, one occasionally hears rumors about the shallow or dubious fieldwork
venture conducted by colleagues or their students, but only under exceptional
circumstances might a controversial ethnographic report necessitate official
scrutiny. However, the lone anthropologist is usually the single witness to
report to readers on his/her performance in the field, ascribing full authority
to the accumulated field notes and the published text. Although the position
of the subjects as readers and commentators has been enhanced in recent
years (as expressed in writings on reflexivity in anthropology), they have not
yet assumed the role of public critics in the real sense of the term (see, for
example, Brettel 1993). Moreover, the subjects are not necessarily in a better
position to know about sensitive issues related to all individuals in their own
community. But whatever the lesson learned for ethnographic work, that particular case offered me a deeper comprehension of the existential conditions
of gay life under the impact of the HIV/AIDS epidemic.

Jeffrey—The Ethnographer's Informant/Friend

Jeffrey remained my close friend from the early days of my 1989–1990
observations at CBST. I had a few other intimate CBST friends (whom
anthropologists usually define as informants); however, many of that cohort
of congregants died of AIDS.[3] Other close acquaintances moved away from
New York. With some, I lost interest in their affairs or the contact faded,
as often happens with acquaintances and friends in daily life. But I never
returned to New York, even for a short visit, without meeting Jeff for dinner
and a long schmooze at a Village restaurant. We kept up that close bond
even after he retired and moved from Manhattan to a new residence on Long
Island.

My relationship with Jeff was cemented years ago when he invited me to
join him at a monthly meeting of the Golden Shower Association, a group of
gay men who shared erotic experiences together (see Chapter 1). It was a sign
he considered me an intimate friend from whom he had no need to hide his
most private sexual preferences. During the many years of our acquaintance,

Jeff told me numerous details about his life—his early childhood, parents, introduction to gay life, employment history, past boyfriends, and continuing search for mates for love and sex (see Chapter 10). Jeff was acquainted with my writings, and we had many a good laugh about my use of the invented name for him, Jeffrey, as presented in my texts, when I called him or when I left a message on his machine. This was one of our shared secrets.

A Secret Revealed

In June 2008 I arrived in New York for a few days' stay to participate in a professional meeting at New York University. I called Jeff and suggested that we meet when he got to Manhattan. Jeff responded enthusiastically and told me he planned to combine that visit with some other engagements he had in town. When he asked to stay at my place for one night, I willingly agreed to host him at the apartment I rented in Chelsea. Jeff showed up in the late afternoon and we enjoyed our dinner at a nearby Italian restaurant. He told me about his recent affairs, starting a new part-time job, and getting involved in a promising romantic relationship, a man he had met at a party in the company of local affluent gay neighbors.

I had to leave the apartment early the next day, scheduled to present a paper at a morning conference session. However, by around 5:30 a.m. Jeff was already awake, complaining of acute stomach or kidney pains. He could hardly stand up. I realized I must take him immediately to an emergency room. I helped him get dressed, stopped a cab, and headed to St. Vincent's Hospital, nearby on Seventh Avenue.

I stood close to Jeff as he answered the questions needed for registration and reporting on his medical status. He was listing his past treatments and medications as he extracted from his bag a large container of pills. Suddenly, Jeff raised his eyes to me and said, "You'll not like this," and continued his report: "I'm HIV." I was stunned but remained impassive. I knew that in recent years Jeff had suffered a series of medical problems. He had also gone through a period of depression. But I never suspected he was infected with HIV. I remembered a story he told me years before about a moment when his late mother's voice had stopped him on the way to the Mineshaft, a sex club later identified as a major site of HIV transmission.

I was in no way uncomfortable with the discovery of having been in close social contact with a man infected with the dreadful virus. I was not embarrassed thinking that the paramedic who took notes of Jeff's medical history might assume I was the cheated-upon partner in a gay relationship. But I felt betrayed at not being informed by a friend I strongly believed had no secrets hidden from me. I was conscious of the deep disappointment and the notion of failure of the mutual relationship we both experienced before the seemingly disinterested stranger. In Goffman's terms, one might suggest that shame was not only Jeff's share (1967: 106): "by the standards of the little social system maintained through the interaction, the discreditor is just as guilty as the person he discredits [through the unexpected revelation in our case]."

I refrained from any verbal comment and busied myself looking around as if curious about the hectic commotion in the crowded emergency room. In the meantime, however, Jeff managed to contact his family doctor on his cell phone and inform him of the situation. As soon as Jeff was put in a bed to await further examination, I left for the apartment to prepare for my long day at the conference. I managed to get to my session at NYU on time. I called Jeff a few hours later and discovered he was on the bus going home after being treated for his pains and discharged; he had been informed it was a nerve infection of some sort with no further complication. I called him again before my departure the next day, and he seemed to have returned to his normal affairs.

I soon got over my surprise, disappointment, and feeling of being deceived by a close friend. When I called Jeff a few weeks later from Tel Aviv, he told me the details of his infection, tracing it back to the late 1990s or even earlier. I did not probe his lack of disclosure about that misfortune, leaving it to be discussed on a future occasion. I came to believe anthropologists sometimes develop a distorted perception of reality, assuming their close informants are uniquely open to them, with no untold stories intentionally left hidden behind.

However, as it soon turned out, another chapter was waiting for me to complete my story. In late November 2008, I returned to New York for a few days en route to the American Anthropological Association meeting in San Francisco. I called Jeff sometime before my departure and made a date to meet him for dinner on my last evening in New York. Looking forward to seeing him, I thought I must find a way to access that untold story, which had left me wary of a relationship I had considered so trustworthy. How could I rely on Jeff's other stories which I believed truthful? I called him soon after my arrival in New York to confirm our meeting. He told me he would come to my place accompanied by his boyfriend. As much as I wanted to meet Jeff's new partner, I was disappointed since I assumed that in his presence I would not be able to return to the last disturbing incident of his collapse in my apartment and the HIV revelation.

I was surprised beyond all expectations. Martin, the boyfriend, a young-looking blond man in his late forties (though not a Latino—Jeff's preferred type), seemed eager to meet me. The two arrived in good spirits, and even before they had seated themselves on the sofa, Jeff announced, "You see here two survivors!" Clearly, he was referring to the last embarrassing story that had taken place in the same apartment. Actually, I already knew that Martin, who had been with a partner for the prior twenty-five years, was also HIV positive. He seemed very relaxed and open and soon became the dominant participant in our long conversation.

In that cozy atmosphere I made my move, asking Jeff directly why he had kept his HIV infection situation secret from me. He and Martin responded almost in unison, claiming that gay men normally keep that information secret even among themselves. Martin was angry in his reaction as he expressed his dismay over the way gay men handle the disclosure of another gay man's HIV status. He first experienced this disturbing response when he witnessed the enthusiastic reception of a good-looking man who entered a gay bar in their Long Island neighborhood. The man was immediately swamped by admirers. But then somebody must have whispered that the guy was HIV positive; he was abruptly left on his own. At that moment Martin realized what his own position might be in this company. He regretted divulging his medical condition without reservation.

Consequently, when he met Jeff he was too scared to tell him he was HIV positive. He was afraid he might lose a man he loved more than anyone in the previous twenty years (his relationship with his domestic partner was no longer one of loving companionship). He waited a few months before deciding he could no longer deceive Jeff and took the risk of revealing his status. Jeff did not desert him, but to Martin's surprise, he resisted Martin's insistence on having protected sex. It took a few more months until one day, Jeff went down on his knees in a dramatic gesture and told Martin he had something important to tell him. Martin could never understand why Jeff had clung to his own secret long after he himself had disclosed his condition.

It was now my turn to ask Jeff why he had kept that secret from Martin, to which he responded: "I was afraid to be left alone!" At that moment he revealed that he had been "afraid" that I would also stay away from him after learning his medical condition. He had been so relieved when I called him from Tel Aviv. It was a moment of relief also on my part. What could better indicate the anxiety and the concealment strategy employed by gay men than what was exposed in the relationship of this pair of lovers? Shame, fear of loneliness and secrecy, among the fundamental existential experiences of gay life (e.g., Love 2007), seem to have shaped Jeff's treatment of both his lover and his close friend the ethnographer.

As made evident by Jeff and Martin, the individual gay man cannot unconditionally rely on the empathy of the men who share his erotic lifestyle. When the stigmatizing misfortune befalls the unprepared gay man, he is left alone, segregated by his own people. As suggested by Simmel: "The purpose of secrecy is, above all, protection" (1969 [1908]: 345).

Martin continued to complain about the habits of gay men who also conceal their specific sexual preferences. In particular, they would not admit they were "bottoms" (in the sexual act). Instead, they would usually claim they were "flexible" on the ladder of sexual orientation between the extremes (from full bottoms to full tops), depending on the partner they met. Martin was somewhat unusual in his openness, admitting he was a "100% bottom" despite originating from a masculine, macho, small-town in Texas. However, he stressed, it was stigmatizing to admit being a bottom, even though it was so much a part of gay sexuality. The stigma of HIV, he claimed, was also associated with the assumption that its victims were mostly bottoms.

At this moment of intimate revelations, Jeff repeated in detail the history of his health condition and the side effects of the medication regime he had experienced in the foregoing ten years. I could now comprehend the source of the ailments I knew already, the periods of depression, and the role of the therapist Jeff so admired.

Martin could not stay for dinner, which allowed Jeff and me to discuss other personal issues. I also learned, as in past meetings, the story of his current relationship with Martin, which had started as a wild sexual encounter at a party in the country residence Martin shared with his partner of many years. It developed into a complex though difficult threesome. For a long time, Martin had had no sexual relations with his partner who continued to dominate him due to his superior financial position in their comfortable home economics. Jeff, who was afraid of remaining alone, expressed his wish to work out a full conjugal relationship with Martin. But for Martin, to separate from his partner would entail a severe loss of his affluent lifestyle. So we were back at our usual intimate communication, as I also contributed from my own life and work experiences.

On my next visit to New York a few months later, in April 2009, we returned to the same subject, which bonded us more than ever before. As suggested by Lynd, "The very fact that shame is an isolating experience also means that if one can find ways of sharing and communicating it, this communication can bring about particular closeness with other persons and with other groups" (1958: 66). Jeff again planned to stay overnight at my place, an opportunity that also allowed him to meet with Martin (at his nearby town residence) for a few hours on the days of arrival and departure. During our phone conversation I commented jokingly that I hoped he was not planning to drag me again in the early morning to the nearby emergency room.

He arrived at my place in the late afternoon in the company of Martin. They were visibly cheerful, having already spent together a few hours at Martin's apartment enjoying the absence of his partner. Martin soon left for home, and Jeff complained to me about their situation. He felt he was lonely. Martin appeared unable to terminate his unhappy lifelong partnership with his abusive mate, and Jeff had no other close relatives to rely on. Sadly, he realized he could not depend on close friends either (as related in Chapter 10, Jeff and Martin later moved to Florida together).

That comment, however, reopened a wound of painful memories related to the discovery of his HIV status. Jeff reminisced about the time in 1995 when he volunteered to participate in an epidemiological research project on health conditions affecting gay men; it was then that he was identified as carrying HIV. It was a terrible day. He felt the ground trembling under his feet. He tried to find out how it had happened: who had infected him with that disastrous disease?

Jeff soon discovered the heavy social price of HIV. He started a romantic relationship with a man to whom he felt he should be open about the virus. They had dinner at a Village restaurant when he told him about his medical condition. Without uttering a word the man stood up and left the table. Jeff remained totally devastated and ashamed, feeling he was "a piece of dirt." He often asked himself, "What have I done to be punished so cruelly? I didn't drink alcohol, didn't take drugs—I just wanted to enjoy good ordinary sex!"

Still, only in 1998 was his immune system seriously weakened. He was ordered by his doctor to start a rigorous medication regime. He then endured another unexpected humiliation as he approached a close gay friend, a scientist employed at a pharmaceutical company. In a phone conversation he asked him about the side effects of the medication prescribed to him. Instead of a friendly, soothing piece of advice, he received an irate response: "'Get used to it!' he yelled at me." As Jeff repeated the response that left him shattered, his face was flushed with anger. I was acquainted with this friend and his partner, whom I had met at CBST many years before. It was at their home at a Yom Kippur (Day of Atonement) dinner breaking the fast that I had first met Jeff. This couple was often mentioned in our conversations. Yet despite that friend's heartless reaction, when Jeff moved to Long Island he looked for an apartment in a neighborhood close to their residence. But since that episode Jeff had avoided mentioning his medical state in their presence, aware it was not a welcome subject in their exclusive Long Island neighborhood.

However, another blow awaited him from the same couple a few years later. They were planning to register for domestic partnership, a status granted to gay couples by the state. The medical expert's partner indicated to Jeff that he would be invited as one of the two witnesses needed for the event at the mayor's office. Jeff responded enthusiastically to the prospective invitation, which symbolized close friendship as well as a major political achievement for gay people. But as the scheduled date of the event approached, the partner tried to dissuade Jeff from attending, assuming it might oblige him to set out for the occasion too early in the morning. Jeff responded he would stay awake the night before to be on time for that great moment in his friends' lives.

On the day of the happy occasion, Jeff arrived in good time, wearing his best suit, and waited in the corridor outside the mayor's office. He now recognized two other acquaintances ready to attend the ceremony. Then, waiting to be called as a witness, he realized to his embarrassment that he was not one of the two witnesses invited to sign for his friends to confirm the legal procedure. Deeply hurt, he spent a few days in bed depressed and humiliated as never before. He felt he was not respectable enough for his "decent" affluent friends. They must have considered him a lower-class, sleazy, irresponsible, HIV-polluting gay man. As he tried to understand why he had not been told about the change of the appointed witnesses, the partner grew angry and asked him to stop nagging him on the subject. With no excuse forthcoming on their part, Jeff abandoned that friendship of many years. It was now a year since he had seen them last.

Jeff now returned to our own story. With tears in his eyes, he told me about the predicament he experienced whenever we got together: "I thought, here is my friend, an anthropologist who writes about the life of gay men. I should have told him about the suffering I go through and that of many others." But he could not bring himself to confront another loss, which seemed inevitable in view of his observations of the frightened and brutal reactions of many gay men. Naturally, he was relieved when I accepted the embarrassing revelation with no overt sign of panic or disappointment. Moreover, he now suggested helping me connect to other HIV patients among his acquaintances, who might share with me their stories of infection and the ways they had accommodated their unhappy circumstances.

Obviously, I was relieved I had no need to employ my own devices to dig up what seemed to be the full story of Jeff's HIV affliction and the reasons he had hidden it from his anthropologist friend. But would I have ever gotten to know that story if Jeff had not suffered a health crisis in my presence? Does this impromptu "happy ending" to my story diminish my own uncertainty about the accuracy of ethnographic reports? Have I to reconsider other descriptions and quotes related to Jeff? More generally, how much deception and naïve assumptions about the truth of our informants' reports enter our scientific writings? On the other hand, are ethnographers as open and honest with their subjects as they expect them to be in return? Do we, in our "nonprofessional" daily life, always encounter 100 percent truth as presented to us by our family, colleagues, and friends? Simmel warned us long ago about that basic element in social relationships.

The Ethnographer's Own Gray Behavior

I now turn my introspective observation onto my own assumed trustworthy treatment of my informants. I remember the long period I kept secret from another close informant the fact that I knew his ex-boyfriend. I met Nigel, a black engineer, at a lecture we both attended in 2003 at the LGBT Center in Greenwich Village. We developed a friendship that continues to this day (see Chapter 10). Early in our acquaintance he told me in detail about the painful separation from his boyfriend, a relationship that had lasted some two years. However, about a year later I got together with Peter, a black academic I had met a few years earlier at another Center group, SAGE (see Chapter 3), that I observed for a few months. When we first met in 1999, we developed a strong mutual interest and thereafter met regularly at the Center and other places. However, in spite of my deep empathy with Peter's position on various issues under discussion, I felt I was unable to accommodate his expectation for a more intimate relationship, which might have eliminated the researcher-informant distance separating us. Not having seen him for a long time, I told Peter about the sites of my present observation engagement. He immediately suggested that I might be familiar with Nigel, his ex-boyfriend. I was amazed by the coincidence of my close acquaintance with these two separated lovers. I answered that I did know him but then made an unwise promise, at Peter's emphatic request, not to tell Nigel about that discovery.

Peter was still infatuated with Nigel, and at our renewed association, he spoke endlessly about their life together and expressed his longing for his lost love. I soon realized that Peter needed my company as a link to Nigel and as a sort of pseudo-therapeutic treatment. At this stage, it was not my close friendship he wished to regain, although he went out of his way to spark my interest and often invited me to join him at meetings of various social groups. What started as part of my role as ethnographer turned into my new task of analyst of sorts. To my embarrassment, I found myself telling Peter he should forget Nigel, free himself from a hopeless love obsession, and look forward to meeting new partners for a gratifying relationship.

Nigel likewise had often related to me the story of his life with Peter and the reasons that made him give up that relationship. I believed there was no hope of Nigel resuming his relationship with Peter. In fact, he made every effort to avoid any contact with him. I was careful not to divulge to Peter any sensitive information about Nigel. Nevertheless, I deeply regretted my promise to Peter not to tell Nigel about our acquaintance. This was not the common situation of ethnographers avoiding passing any information among subjects they communicate with in the field. Instead, I felt that I was playing the part of a double agent, dividing loyalties and betraying a close friend, talking about him behind his back.

Moreover, I was worried that eventually Nigel might discover my secret anyway, and would accuse me of treachery. I was afraid of losing Nigel's friendship and trust, particularly as he had become a major link for me to an organization that I was observing at that time. But it seemed too late to inform Nigel about my close acquaintance with Peter. I often imagined Nigel's angry reaction and my sordid disgrace once he discovered my hidden friendship with Peter.

I wrestled with that discomfort for a few more months. But gradually the idea of maintaining the secret became easier to endure as I was meeting with Peter less frequently. The timing and the trigger of its revelation came unexpectedly, just before I exited a train that Nigel and I had taken back from a Sunday afternoon stroll through a street market. I do not remember the exact reason he mentioned Peter, but I admitted in a neutral tone that I had met him some time earlier at another group meeting. Since Nigel was staying on the train while I was getting off at the next stop, there was no time to discuss my sudden announcement. To my surprise and relief, he did not mention my sudden confession when we met a week later.

I did not delve any deeper into Nigel's unexpected lack of interest in my acquaintance with Peter. I told him much later that I was pleased he was not concerned about my omission of that piece of information. I assume that he considered my silence part of my discreet manner of avoiding gossip about my local acquaintances. I consoled myself for my poor ethics with a comment made by the late Rachel Eytan, an Israeli writer of whom I am fond. Her major, moving novel, *The Fifth Heaven*, tells the story of a girl abandoned in orphanages by her divorced parents. At a public lecture, intimating the autobiographical elements in her book, she said, "The author is a traitor who trades in his family secrets." Without prior planning I had become an invisible partner in, and betrayer of, Nigel's and Peter's most intimate life experiences and romantic fantasies.

Discussion

Ethnographers and their subjects, like all human beings, have secrets hidden from close relatives and friends. On occasion they also experience unexpected revelations that their interlocutors and close partners inspire. Our informants might conceal personal or other sensitive information not necessarily because of manipulative calculations or for gain of any kind. As the cases I have presented above tell us, these concealments often result from fear of damaging social relationships and losing the respect, affection, and love of significant others.

I find support for my observations in the work of scholars from various disciplines; an example is Helen Lewis, a psychologist, who in her work focused on shame and analyzed transcripts of psychotherapy sessions (1971). Lewis proposed that shame arises when there is a threat to the social bond. Every person, she argued, fears social disconnection from others. Jeff's reluctance to expose his HIV status had its roots in his painful experience with close friends. He described his feelings of degradation and fear of being perceived "like dirt." Jeff's memories of the traumatic experiences of revealing his medical condition to close friends remind us of the sociologist Lynd's terms on the circumstances of shame: "Finding oneself in a position of incongruity, not being accepted as the person one thought one was" (1958: 37).

Like many others of his generation of gay men afflicted with HIV and its later development into full-blown AIDS, Jeff was totally unprepared for the physical and social devastation that threatened to ravage his life. It was not in the category of the well-known and somewhat "legitimized" medical epidemics and life-threatening diseases, such as cancer. It was not among the embarrassing but easily treated sexually transmitted diseases that are also shared by heterosexual men and women. It was a shocking realization that one is struck with an incurable, debilitating, and stigmatizing infection. No empathy was in store for HIV/AIDS victims, in contrast to victims of cancer or other life-threatening diseases (e.g., Altman 1986; Bersani 1988).

Jeff recalled that he once visited a medical clinic for treatment of an STD (a syphilis infection). He was struck by the number of good-looking men who must have shared the symptoms. They were treated with penicillin, a simple medical procedure, making the STD seem like a sort of a flu infection. But now he felt he was all alone, treated by the media, the gay community, and even close friends as if stricken by a defiling disease. In his agony he believed that he was seen even in gay society as a sex addict who must have satisfied his erotic drive in sleazy venues and turned himself into a receptacle of tainted fluids. In common with other writers at the peak of the epidemic, Bateson and Goldsby argued that "Homosexuality, extramarital sex, and IV drugs are still stigmatized as antisocial or sinful behavior by many, and the health problems that accompany them are sometimes seen as divine punishment. Moreover, internalized homophobia and low self-esteem make individuals value their own lives and health less, leave them with less hope for the future" (1994: 128).

During the early years of the epidemic many patients developed AIDS-associated Kaposi's sarcoma, with ugly skin lesions. They made efforts to hide these marks of the disease and often avoided going out in public. The reaction of mainstream and many gay men to the victims of HIV/AIDS was reminiscent of the treatment of lepers, the outcasts of earlier generations. Ralph Bolton, a leading ethnographer of gay life, made a compelling defense of the gay society lifestyle, blamed by both heterosexuals and homosexuals for the spread of AIDS. He commented that "AIDS is about promiscuity. In the voluminous material on this epidemic, promiscuity stands out as the key concept, dominating and linking together diverse genres of thought and discourse about AIDS" (1992: 145). A similar position was taken a few years later by Murray: "Blaming victims is a leitmotif of public discussion of AIDS, derived directly from the view that "promiscuity" is an invariant, defining characteristic of gay men" (1996: 108). He also highlighted "the predisposition to equate the outbreak of unexpected diseases among gay men with anal transmission" (106). This statement implies the guilt of the receptive role ("bottoms") in gay sexual intercourse, a theme angrily raised during my first meeting with Martin.

The situation of both HIV-positive men and those with full-blown AIDS has greatly changed since the discovery of new drugs that prolong life and erase the visible physical marks of the disease. This has not diminished the binary position and the worries of stigmatization between HIV-positive and HIV-negative men (Munoz 2009: 46–47). Jeff, a survivor of an earlier generation, was still experiencing the trauma of devastation and social stigma that its victims endured. I remember the public excitement caused by the late Mel Rosen, president of CBST, who revealed in *Jewish Week* (February 3, 1989) his medical condition as an AIDS patient. About the same time, he also announced his disease at a public event at B'nai Jeshurun, a major mainstream Conservative synagogue in New York. It needed a leading figure in the New York State health administration and a man of considerable personal charisma to come out with that stigmatizing secret. Mel Rosen was also endowed with a robust masculine appearance (he was the tallest man at any gathering), which made his appearance contradict popular stereotypes about the looks and demeanor of gay men. His statements, both written and spoken and to both homosexual and heterosexual audiences, displayed a forceful protest, as expressed by Bolton, against the "fact that people do lie about their sexual histories, about their drug habits, and about their HIV status" (1992: 177).

Jeff admired Mel Rosen, but he could not imitate his heroic example. Jeff was masculine in appearance and demeanor, presenting himself as a "top" in the sexual act. His somewhat macho clothing style and his comportment projected the image of an easily identifiable type of gay New Yorker. However, he lacked the extraordinary personal and social capital that made Mel Rosen a quintessential advocate of gay rights and helped him publicly admit his medical condition. Rosen was virtually fearless in that sphere of his personal life. Jeff, however, was afraid of losing my friendship and respect, as well as jeopardizing Martin's love.

Albeit in a different social situation, I too had my fears. I was afraid of losing Nigel's friendship, which would have also positioned my work in a new fieldwork site at risk. Without doubt, Jeff's worries and my own were exaggerated or even completely misguided. But we had no way to predict the reaction of our buddies and mates once they discovered the secrets that threatened to expose us to shame and stigma. Certainly, the comparison covers two very different personal circumstances. Jeff's revelation about his medical situation came about by default. In contrast, I volunteered the information about my deception. But the pain and the risk of the revelation must have been far more severe for Jeff.

"True Reports"

In retrospect, the unexpected circumstances that prompted the discovery of Jeff's medical situation offered me a better understanding of the painful existential condition of a close friend and "informant" in the professional terminology. However, it presented an example of the exceptional experiences in daily life that might engage "ordinary" people—researchers and their subjects included (Shokeid 1992). Jeff's case exposed the risk and the discomfort entailed in concealing sensitive personal information from one's significant others. It also displayed the emotions and the calculation that might compel the individual to continue concealing his/her secrets. That suppression of personal information appears less threatening and less painful than the potential consequences of confronting close relatives and friends with damaging revelations. The study of sexuality and of the life of a sexual minority presents the ethnographer with additional difficulties. Few other subjects in social life exhibit similar issues of shame and secrecy.

I believe my report reflects on an old tradition in ethnographic writing: narrating a captivating account from the field and its interpretation in terms relevant to broader issues in the anthropological repertoire. My discussion is not intended to introduce yet another convincing proof of the faults of the positivist approach in ethnographic research. We have long since lost the "innocence" of the founders of anthropology. "Have your data right ... shut your mouth and open your ears"—these were the farewell warnings and blessings my supervisor, the late Max Gluckman, offered novices on their way to the field. These methodological prescriptions have become part of our professional folklore and the stuff of nostalgia for a lost golden age and its promise of "reliable" ethnographic testimonies. We are convinced there is no "true report" from the field in the legal or scientific meanings of the term.

The case that instigated this thesis serves as a mirror image of the constraints that might hinder the efforts to gain "true" observations and "valid" reports in research conducted by ethnographers who are committed to a rigorous fieldwork methodology.[4] However, unlike earlier critiques of the theoretically misconstrued, ethnocentric, or distorted colonialist perception of the native's behavior, my discourse exposes the human condition of the subjects of the research, and sometimes of the researchers themselves, which might handicap the ethnographer's mission designed to realize the Malinowskian vision.

In this light, a symposium I attended at the packed annual AAA meeting grand ballroom session, in the late 1980s, dedicated to the Mead-Freeman controversy, seems now a grotesque show. It needed a dead tribal chief and a vengeful maverick to expose the poor quality of field research and the lack of good supervision that might have forestalled a presumably shabby ethnographic work. My supervisors at Manchester, avowed fieldworkers and propagators of the "extended case-method," never inquired about my field experiences or asked to see my field notes. They were ignorant about my field site, the language, and the local culture, as Franz Boas was equally nescient about Samoa half a century earlier. Yet they could evince some unkind reactions when they felt that the novice anthropologist was displaying personal weaknesses adjusting to his/her designated field site. The "human condition" in its various manifestations was not part of the constraints condoned by the propagators of that research project.

For better or worse, we continue to rely on the anthropologist's personal integrity, dedication, and creative ethnographic imagination. Despite the doubts often expressed about the quintessential position of fieldwork in the craft of anthropology,[5] I assume that the method will stay with us as a major identifying disciplinary marker for many years to come.[6] A growing awareness of our subjects' sensitivities, as well as of our own role in their social and moral world, might enhance the authority of ethnographic work—more particularly when anthropologists move away from the "classic" field sites in Third World countries.

In conclusion, I gained this "educational" revelation through the agency of a close friend who also took on the role of a master teacher in my entry into the field of gay life. As mentioned earlier, Jeff and Martin moved to Florida in 2010; although we call each other occasionally, we may never meet again. I feel like Victor Turner, among my models for ethnographic writings, on the day he parted from Mochuna. We anthropologists owe so much of our professional gains and our emotional well-being to the natives, in an African village or in metropolitan New York, who open their hearts and unlock the gates to let us penetrate their personal and social worlds.

CHAPTER 3

The Regretless Seniors

I begin my presentation of the organizations I observed at the Center with the SAGE group (Senior Action in Gay Environment). They appeared on the list of the daily activities I saw at the reception desk when I first entered the building and began my regular observations at that site. The participants defined themselves as the younger membership cohort of that organization, so I thought I would not appear conspicuous in any way among them.[1] They received me very warmly and, as it turned out, were the subject of the first paper I wrote about my work at the Center. I introduce them first in this volume because the discourse they carried on at the meetings seemed to encapsulate some of the major issues of gay men's life that came to occupy my project in its later phase. I believe that had I left my notes on that group as data for analysis by somebody else, he or she might not have concluded that they represented people who defined themselves as "seniors." The stories, complaints, and experiences related by the participants could often be told and listened to in the company of their "juniors" in gay men's society.

Studies of older gay men have yielded contradictory results. Some, like Lee (1989), supported the traditional assumption that having lost their physical attractiveness in a youth-oriented gay society, their lives are characterized by isolation and invisibility. But others, Berger's (1996 [1982]) in particular, found that older gay men are no less adjusted than older heterosexuals. Furthermore, his respondents reported a level of sexual activity that belied the stereotype of the sexless life of older gay men. But whatever their major perspective, all studies emphasized the importance of involvement in close social networks and organizations for successful aging in gay society (e.g., Simon and Gagnon 1969; Berger 1996 [1982]; Slusher, Mayer, and Dunkle 1996). The expansion of gay and lesbian institutions in recent years has brought with it the development of organizations specializing in the needs of older lesbians and gay men in the urban environment in particular. Among the first and most successful of these is SAGE.

The Circle's Meetings

The SAGE group met every week; regular participants rarely missed a meeting. The fact that they were always held in the same homey room contributed to the feeling of familiarity. I was not the only new attendee at my first SAGE meeting. All present introduced themselves, and the newcomers explained their reasons for joining the group. I presented myself as an Israeli anthropologist on sabbatical who was interested in gay life and mentioned my book on the gay synagogue. This information did not prompt any questions or comments, so I never again raised the subject. While members were sometimes interested in my experiences as an Israeli, they never inquired about my occupational life. I felt that emphasizing my professional interests would detract from the feeling of comradeship.

As indicated in Chapter 2, the anthropologist conducting research in a Western urban setting resides on a different ethical plateau and may find himself/herself acting somewhat clandestinely. Much later, during a stay in New York in 1999, I was more explicit to the group about my research intentions. Again, this disclosure prompted no demurral on their part. Only one participant, Peter (among the few blacks and who is also encountered in Chapters 2 and 10) approached me after the meeting and showed interest in my work. I was a full participant in the group meetings, in discussions and "sharings," but avoided revealing intimate details of my life. More than once it was suggested that I take the role of facilitator, but I was careful not to take any leading position. When I returned after a six-month absence, I was welcomed by the old-timers and immediately felt comfortable regardless of the many new faces.

A meeting usually drew about fifteen to twenty members, among whom I gradually identified a core of six to eight men who knew each other well (during my visits in 1999 attendance expanded to nearly thirty participants). Most of the core had been attending for over a year—some for several years. A few, however, had joined the group only shortly before my arrival and soon became regulars. Most attendees were in their late forties to early sixties; only a few infrequent visitors were much younger or older. All were "single," though many had been involved in longstanding relationships that had ended in death, or more often "divorce." Almost all regulars were college educated. Most were—or had been before retirement—successfully employed in a wide range of white-collar and professional occupations that included therapy, social work, teaching, sales, administration, and art, among others. With the exception of one churchgoing core member, the others were mostly not actively involved in their religion, including gay congregations. The family background of the participants was Italian, Jewish, and other whites. One regular was African American. I was the only foreigner attending. Rarely did participants mention their ethnic background as part of their presentation of self. During discussions, however, a reference might sometimes be made to an Italian family tradition, for instance. Jewish identity was typically revealed indirectly through joking or using Yiddish terms.

The meetings started at 7:30 p.m. and ended by 9:30, after which all in attendance were invited to adjourn to a nearby diner for drinks or food. Only the regulars, or newcomers who had an interest in future attendance, joined that fellowship, which lasted about an hour. An area at the back of the restaurant was rearranged to enable the group to sit together around one table. While the two-hour meeting at the Center was a structured event led by a facilitator (from among the regular participants), the discussions at the diner were more freewheeling. These late gatherings often included gossip about regulars who did not attend and newcomers who did, as well as personal stories volunteered by those present. This was also an opportunity for core group members to arrange weekend outings to a movie or an exhibition, or plan activities for upcoming holidays. In my observation, these social activities only rarely entailed romantic involvement. Except for a few fleeting encounters—and one regular being suspected of importuning newcomers—I did not hear of dating within the group.

What I proffer in this chapter as well as those following is a second, or perhaps a third, stage in the process of ethnographic construction of the life of the group. I was inevitably selective in the first round, as I wrote down my field notes. I was selective again during the phase of writing the major part of this chapter. However, these leading themes, even if chosen and magnified through my subjective perception, nevertheless introduce an important component of the discussion and events that took place during the many evenings I spent in the company of the SAGE membership.[2] A few of the major participants, as well as a "sample" of the stories and issues they shared with their veteran and newly arrived colleagues at the weekly meetings, are introduced next.

Love, Sex, and Discontent

The meetings usually started with a go-around. Each participant introduced himself by name and mentioned what had affected him most during the week since they had last met. For the regulars, this represented an updating of the group on key themes in their life histories. The facilitator summed up the major issues raised during the introductions and suggested probing more deeply into one or two themes that seemed most fruitful for a group discussion. One could describe these two-hour meetings as weekly oral diary sessions, filled out and expanded with the help of questions and comments raised by sympathetic listeners.

The participants consistently objected to defining their weekly gatherings as a "support group" or even as "meetings," a term they associated with Alcoholics Anonymous (AA) or other organizations with a therapeutic element. "This is not a support group, though it isn't not a support group. We are here in an undefined territory," Paul, a veteran member, once explained to newcomers. "A good rap group" was the definition preferred by some. Most participants did not consider their meetings as a substitute for therapy, which many were, or had been, in. They sometimes complimented members who had missed therapy in order to attend the group, boosting the group's morale.

Michael was the facilitator at most meetings he attended. In his mid-forties, he was among the group's younger members. He was muscular, trim, casually but well dressed, projecting self-assurance. He had a good sense of humor and a pleasant demeanor. He worked in a pharmaceutical laboratory. As I soon learned, he regularly updated the group on his frequent travels abroad, trips that often engaged him in romantic adventures. One weekend trip to Paris was particularly memorable. Soon after settling into his hotel, he made his way to a nearby sauna. There he immediately noticed a good-looking young man. They retired to a private room and had "great sex." Only then did the young man ask him if he spoke English. To their mutual surprise and fun, it turned out they were both from New York, where they were almost next-door neighbors. They had a date the same evening at a popular club. The next day Michael checked out of his hotel and spent the last night with his new mate in his luxurious company-provided residence. By the same extraordinary coincidence, they were booked on the same flight to New York, and Michael was dropped off at his doorstep by the limousine that awaited his new friend at JFK—ending a dreamlike sexual and emotional weekend affair.

That was the good part of the story. The bad news Michael had already been aware of: his weekend date was in a nearly ten-year relationship with an older man. The couple had problems and seemed on the brink of separation, but even so, his date would not let Michael call him at home and gave him only his office number. Michael told him he was available for a serious relationship and the "ball was now in his court."

Michael, who was himself now involved with a "part time" lover in Seattle whom he had met in New York through mutual friends, cheerfully summed up his love life: "I have two part-timers: 50 percent in Seattle and [referring to his Paris partner], 25 percent in New York." It raised laughter and sympathetic metaphors reminiscent of old melodramas such as *Back Street*.

One of the most committed regulars in the group observed that Michael always initiated his love affairs as a tourist or with tourists from out of town, which, he concluded, indicated self-inflicted failure. "Why is it that we meet men we desire in remote places?" and "Aren't there nice men in New York?" were comments reiterated by a few listeners. Michael responded by quoting a friend's conclusion that "all the nice men are married." Others took issue: "Is it true?" "After all, all the men in our own group are single!"

Michael then related another friend's suggestion—rejecting it resentfully—that he should not be too choosy and pick up the first reasonably suitable man he could find because it would be more and more difficult for him to meet an attractive mate. Tony, an artist in his early sixties who had recently joined the group, reacted strongly against that "defeatist idea." He cited his own recent decision to leave his lover of two years, a very good-looking and much younger man. His friends were astonished to see him make that move, but he claimed there was no evidence that older men could not be passionately loved by younger men. Jack, a core member in his late fifties, seconded this view: his two former lovers were both ten years younger. Tony then declared: "There are thousands of men out there. Everyday we come across many new men. Why should we settle for less than we deserve?" It was mostly a matter of the way "we see ourselves," he concluded.

A few weeks later Michael reported he was preparing for a trip to Greece. He had had a difficult week. He was torn again by the dilemma of whether to make a career change. He had decided to separate from his part-time Seattle lover and had not heard lately from the young man he met in Paris. Jack reacted with emotion. He lamented Michael's decision to give up his Seattle lover. He had hoped, instead, that one or the other would eventually "move his ass" to New York or Seattle.

Michael's trip to Greece ended without a new romantic encounter to report. He declared he wasn't going to settle for half a loaf. He had given up on the man from Paris and spoke critically of those who could not go on with their lives without some sort of a mate, even if evidently unsatisfactory. He also voiced a complaint about people who come to their meetings, look around, and leave immediately or attend once and never come back because they do not find anyone they are attracted to. Picking up on the theme, Henry, a newcomer in his late forties, a divorced lawyer I had met before at the Gay Fathers Forum, argued that the men he observed in other groups were always desperately looking for Mr. Right. He thought they should instead just get together to discuss issues of shared interest. Inevitably, they would meet Mr. Right. He was out there, but one had to have the right attitude and patience. Tony, the artist, cited his own motivation for becoming a SAGE Circle regular: he found the meetings enjoyable. Considering Tony's good looks, extrovert manner, and successful career, one could accept the implication that he had other opportunities and was not attending in order to meet a partner.

Paul, in his early sixties, frequently acted as facilitator in Michael's absence. He was far less revealing about himself except for the endless minor calamities in his household affairs—leaking pipes, loss of keys, and computer crashes. He sometimes mentioned some details from his past life and lovers, but only as comments on other participants' stories. A man of somewhat distinguished appearance who now lived alone, he had no regrets about his earlier years. In his retirement he was engaged in a late career in musical composition and was active in organizing occasional weekend and holiday outings to museums or the movies, which included some of the veteran participants. I also occasionally met him at other Center activities. Although he spoke little and avoided emotional outbursts, his comments, offered in a very restrained tone, were often instrumental in facilitating a smooth continuation of meetings that lacked an evocative theme for a more lively discussion, and thus saved the gathering from early dispersal. Reserved and analytical, he would have been a good candidate had the group required a professional facilitator.

In his late fifties, Jack was a dedicated regular for whom SAGE was his only gay circle in New York. He divided his life, as well as his public identity, between gay and straight. He considered himself gay but was closeted at work, at home, in his church, and in his community. He was in the thirtieth year of a happy marriage to a woman who had long ago discovered his other life but remained with him after he promised never to "shame" her. Their two sons were unaware of their father's secret life, and although married, they remained very close to their parents. Jack's robust, extrovert manner, his avowed loyalty to his church, and his conservative attitudes in various spheres gave no clue—stereotypically—to his homosexuality. But for many years, apart for the SAGE weekly participation, Jack acted out his gay identity also at his cottage on the New Jersey shore. His family and friends tolerated his dedication to his beach retreat as a special addiction that did no harm. Here Jack enjoyed complete freedom to express his sexual orientation. He sometimes invited friends and new acquaintances from SAGE meetings out to his house, but more often he looked for male company at the bars and beaches in his Jersey community. Over the years, he had shared the house with two lovers, with each of whom he had had long partnerships before separating. He still lamented the loss of his partners who left him as they looked for full-time lovers.

At most meetings Jack related experiences from the preceding weekend stay at his cottage. He had a reputation in the group as an incurable romantic and a relentless seeker of a love-based relationship. He was convinced he had no desire for one-night stands. Nevertheless, he experimented with occasional dates, particularly since most patrons at gay establishments located around his weekend retreat represented a more reliable clientele, well off and older than the bar regulars in New York City. He felt close to the old-timers, including those who were not really "his cup of tea." He was particularly happy with the arrival of Tony, whose Italian ethnic tradition soon made him a close pal.

A large but unprepossessing man in his mid-fifties, John seemed less educated than most other regulars. He was often described as a tireless cruiser and was once reprimanded by Michael, who noticed him leaving a meeting for a long break, which he assumed John spent at another Center activity checking out the men there. John apologized, embarrassed as a schoolboy caught doing something naughty. At one meeting he spoke of his recent vacation in Mexico. Once there, he confessed, he had wasted no time in searching for sex and had a good time with young local men whom he soon met at the nearby plaza. His sexual adventures were safe and inexpensive but left him no time to visit the ancient ruins he wished to see. John was open about his attraction to young men, a desire he could not easily satisfy in New York. Someone in the group asked John why he didn't invite one of these accommodating "boys" home with him to New York.

Sam, a college administrator in his mid-fifties, was a prominent regular whose follies nevertheless commanded respect. He was a man of striking physical presence, tall and heavy, with a generous and humorous manner. At the first meeting I saw him, he was edgy and related the troubles of the day—noisy neighbors who incessantly made his life intolerable and his closest friend's arrest for causing a public disturbance due to his alcoholism. About a month later Sam happily told the group that he had invited a gorgeous heterosexual young man he met at an AA meeting to stay at his apartment rent-free. His adoring description was confirmed later the same evening when the charming houseguest joined Sam at the post-meeting get-together.

Sam happily indulged his new friend. He had already spent a few thousand dollars on him. A member of the group hearing this jokingly complained: "You gave me only $5 for a blow job, but you showered this heterosexual with $3,000!" Sam replied: "Yes, but I have love." Sam rented a luxury car and gave it to his new friend to drive them around. Together they saw the sights outside New York. But Sam's happiness was short-lived. A few weeks later he was deep in trouble. His handsome friend had disappeared with the car, and Sam was accountable for its loss. He now discovered that his dream boy had already ripped off others, men and women alike, who were victims of his charms. Sometime later, after the man turned himself in to the police and was awaiting trial for a long list of other felonies, Sam told us his heart was hurting. He wished he could have him released from jail. He had enjoyed so much opening his heart to the young man, who gratified him with affection, calling him "Dad." His listeners reacted with a mixture of amazement and empathy.

Irving, a sixty-year-old university history professor, a regular, prominent not for his physical bearing but for his sagacity, humor, and sharp analyses of his colleagues' behavior, seemed less sympathetic to Sam's plight. In a critical tone he told Sam he should have exerted more self-control against this irrational and destructive attraction. Sam reacted angrily to Irving's reprimand: "You should allow people to show their feelings and let others listen to them." Paul defended Sam, referring to the themes of irrationality, chaos, and the incompatibility of reason and emotion in his own musical compositions. For myself, I was ambivalent. I was appalled by Sam's self-inflicted injury but felt empathy for his predicament. I offered support for Sam, likening his compulsive attraction to a charming heterosexual—and a crook at that—to the aging professor's pathetic attraction to the handsome young boy in *Death in Venice*.

From their interaction at the meeting, I assumed Irving and Sam represented two fundamentally contradictory personalities with little to breach their contrasting temperaments. Yet I soon had an opportunity to discover I was wrong. As we walked together after the meeting to the nearby diner we saw a group of transsexuals who had just left the Center. I was surprised to overhear Irving joke with Sam about the *miyeskeyts* (Yiddish for "uglies"). Cooling off from their heated exchange, they enjoyed a campy conversation that made use of a shared ethnic vocabulary. Sam and Irving, in fact, had a far warmer relationship than I first assumed. At the diner following the meetings, they often entertained the crowd with their campy impersonations of Carmen Miranda and other gay icons.

The group was less delicate in the case of Frank, a man in his late forties engaged in retail sales, who in his manner, speech, and dress seemed less sophisticated than the others. He attended occasionally but typically contributed little to the discussion. At one meeting, however, he informed the group that he was going on a date with an attractive man he often bumped into in business but who had never before shown any interest in him. To Frank's great surprise, the guy had approached him recently and suggested that they go out together for a drink the next weekend. At the next meeting's go-around, Frank detailed the date he had so anticipated. It had started quite pleasantly—they had a couple of drinks—but ended in great disappointment once they went to his date's apartment. Unwilling to go into more detail, he only commented that "the sex was horrible." Michael, the facilitator, and a few of the members, insisted that he give more information to enable them to help him understand what had gone wrong. After all, he still admitted the man was very attractive, behaved in a civil manner, and was affectionate. Someone suggested Frank's companion was drunk by the time they got home. No, that was not really the case, Frank reluctantly reported. Under growing pressure and an inquisitiveness I rarely observed at these meetings, he confessed that the guy had immediately insisted to be served with a blow job and then lost interest. It was a humiliating experience and a disappointment for Frank who was so romantically attracted to him.

Some tried to encourage the frustrated Frank about the prospects for a relationship with the same man. However, that was the last time I saw Frank. He did not attend any of the meetings I observed in the following months. Was he embarrassed by having to publicly reveal his humiliation? Did his romantic dream come true despite its poor start?

A businessman with an impressive bearing in his mid-fifties, Andrew began attending meetings early in my research and soon became a prominent regular. He had divorced his wife of many years and was determined to compensate for having subordinated his personal needs—including sexual—to his family obligations. He was overwhelmed with the possibilities of gay life and eager to find a mate. He exchanged phone numbers with James, the only black participant at that time, whom he complimented on his trim appearance.

After some weeks of attendance, an unexpected crisis erupted. To the group's surprise, Andrew suddenly became agitated. He claimed that he had been treated in an unfriendly manner at the prior meeting. When he had raised a question about dating, he felt he had been "put on the spot" and lectured to. Andrew complained that he didn't need that; if he wanted counseling he could go to a therapist and get professional advice. As he saw it, the group should share their intimate experiences but not tell each other what to do.

Paul and Michael immediately tried to pacify Andrew. Paul emphasized that "this room and our meetings must be a safe space." Anyone who felt threatened was right to speak out. Jack reminded the group of difficult situations they had experienced at past meetings, including his own three-month walkout after someone (Sam, I later learned) called him a Nazi for being closeted at work. Andrew was not appeased. He stopped listening and whispered something to James, who was also trying to calm him down. Jack then chided Andrew, telling him it was offensive to whisper at meetings. Andrew responded angrily that he "had had enough" and left the room. A few participants reminded the group of Andrew's late divorce and his nervous effort to make up for lost time. Andrew never showed up again.

What was the cause of Andrew's departure? Had he really been angered by something that happened at the meeting, or was he—new to gay life—disappointed with the group as a pool from which to draw a suitable mate? Most of the regulars had a longer history of gay life, of relationships and their predicaments, and seemed less inclined to assess the group in terms of its dating prospects. Andrew was ultimately dismissed as the type of visitor interested in meeting either fleeting sex partners or potential mates and who showed up only once or twice. A chance encounter with Andrew at another Center activity allowed me to ask what had triggered his angry departure, but he offered no clearer explanation (see Chapter 7). Jack told me he made an effort during their meetings to steer the discussion away from the mantra of the newcomers: "I am forty. I came out recently. I want to find a lover. How do I do it?" He continued in a tired tone: "If I had an answer to that I wouldn't have come to meetings for the last twenty years."

The upcoming Valentine's Day was the theme of the meeting when Michael, now bereft of his two "part-time" lovers, told the group how he had phoned a friend at work and gotten a recorded message that the friend was off for Valentine's Day. Michael envied this gay friend, who could publicly announce he had a lover to spend the day with. For Michael this was the fulfillment of a dream he believed they all shared: to have a lover and to feel free to be public about it.[3]

Most revealing was Willie, a newcomer in his late fifties—but younger in looks and demeanor—who was usually in a good mood, smiling throughout the meeting. A month earlier, he had retired from his job as a salesman in a large bookstore, finally giving himself the time to join social activities. He told us he had recently undergone a prostate operation, which caused the loss of ejaculation and limited his sexual pleasure. He did, however, occasionally have sex with a friend, whom he characterized as a "fuck buddy," a compromise he accepted until something better came along. Irving responded in his characteristically realistic way. Recognizing how difficult it was for them to find mates, he claimed he was ready to buy love, if he could find a nice, "clean" young man, asking "who should I leave my money to? My nephews already have more than enough!"

While participants did not typically detail their sex lives, an erotic atmosphere often did prevail at the meetings. This occurred mainly through the medium of jokes and humor. Jack, for example, reported on a recent colonoscopy performed by a gorgeous young physician. When Jack asked the doctor how long the instrument was, he replied, "Twenty-two inches." "Jesus," Jack exploded, "I've never taken more than eleven inches!" Irving told us he got a Valentine's Day card from a female friend. On the outside was a picture of a fat woman and the question: "What's the difference between 'Ooo' and 'Aaa'?" Inside was the answer: "3 inches!" The audience almost wept with laughter, and the atmosphere warmed up.

Old Age and Other Troubles

The lives and destinies of gays versus straights were often compared at the SAGE Circle meetings. Conflicting views were expressed. Jack and Tony, for example, lamented the lives of their married male relatives who were burdened with the pressing obligations of an "Italian family." Their sex lives with their spouses were long over: they were confined to their homes watching television or babysitting their numerous grandchildren. In contrast, Jack and Tony claimed, gay men took care of themselves, had sex, and met many interesting people. Irving disagreed. Gay men were lonely compared with the heterosexual couples he knew, who, though they had given up sex with each other, nevertheless remained close friends. They also had children to love and observe growing up. Like a few others in the group, Irving claimed that most gay men missed not having children. He concluded: "I would not recommend gay life to anyone." Sam reacted angrily: "Who said you could choose gay life? Who wishes to be in the minority?" Paul intervened: "True, I am an aging lonely gay man, but I don't regret having been gay." He argued that he would not have had his career if not for his first lover of many years and other talented gay men. He also referred to their meetings, which were so gratifying that Sam for instance would travel a good distance at the end of a long and tiring day to get there. Michael added angrily, "We wanted to discuss what is good about being gay, but now we only hear good things about heterosexuals, and that gays are selfish and miss not having children." He reassured the others that he was happy to be gay, never wished to be a father, and thought that men were beautiful and knew better than women how to satisfy men. The issue remained unresolved.

One might expect a SAGE group often to deal with issues related to the reality of aging and associated problems. But only rarely, as described below, did aging figure directly as a major subject of the meeting. Soon after the Gay Pride Parade, the members reported their impressions of the event. Some had stayed home but felt isolated and alone. Some were critical of the more outrageous displays they had seen. Others found no group they felt comfortable marching with. Irving and Michael had been among the few who had marched, having joined the SAGE contingent. Irving chided those members whose failure to march he interpreted as reluctance to associate themselves publicly with a "senior" group. For Irving, the march represented the full cycle of gay life. He was happy to take credit for his generation's contribution to gay liberation. He ended triumphantly: "You walk with SAGE and young beautiful men on the sidewalks applaud proudly. They see what they are going to become."

At another meeting, a newcomer, who appeared agitated, confessed that he had come because he needed to talk about a recent experience: this was his sudden "discovery" that he was getting old. He had just turned fifty-eight and had become afraid of death. For the first time in my association with the SAGE Circle, the issue of aging and death dominated the meeting. The urgency of his concern, however, was seen as excessive, if not bizarre, to his audience. In a relaxed manner, a few spoke of their own recent turning fifty-eight, noting no ill or depressing results. The newcomer then went on to explain that he had happily retired at fifty-five with enough means to enjoy the years to come in comfort and be free to pursue his neglected interests. But soon after, a growth was discovered. He worried that had it been malignant it would have left him disfigured. More recently he was put on a device to aid breathing during sleep. He was miserable with it but was afraid not to use it. He also had other worries: to whom should he leave his estate? To his aging mother and aunt? To another remote relative?

During the ensuing discussion, most speakers expressed their surprise at the newcomer's obsession with death. Irving suggested that the issue of aging might be more difficult for gays, who are often single and separated from their families. But another participant commented that today many heterosexuals shared this situation. Willie, who a week earlier had revealed his predicament caused by the prostate operation, made a brief reference to his own physical handicap and concluded that one must become reconciled to the ravages of aging: "You have to swallow it." This caused much laughter, reminding the group of Willie's spermless situation, and allowed a relaxed departure from the gloomy subject. The discussion continued on the way to the diner. Michael commented resentfully on the visitor: "They come, pour out their shit, and disappear." In fact, the newcomer never returned.

More than anything else, the meetings I attended offered an outlet for stories about the daily difficulties and frustrations at home or at work. There was Sam's continuing problem with his noisy neighbors; Paul's troubles with his apartment's plumbing repairs or computer mishaps; John's difficulties with his boss; Jack's aggravation with his coworkers; Irving's confrontation with his department chair over whether to teach a crowded introductory course; Michael's frustration with junior members of his lab team; and Willie's financial troubles. No issue raised, by a veteran or a newcomer, was considered too unimportant or tiring to listen to. This attitude was consistent with that observed by Wuthnow in other small groups: "Small groups nurture our self-esteem, at least in small ways, because the other people in the group take us seriously. They listen, they accept, they empathize, they support" (1994: 187).

The core members saw the SAGE Circle as more than an ordinary rap group. They took pride in the group's longevity, despite the fact that it had no professional facilitator, no written charter, no formal leadership, and no registered membership. Not surprisingly, at one meeting the conversation turned to the group itself. Irving complimented the group by contrasting it to gay venues where cruising was paramount and communication free of sexual interest was avoided: "Heterosexuals will strike up a conversation with people they meet, but gay people won't speak to you when you bump into them in a gay bar." When Michael and Paul complained about the burden on them of being facilitators, Sam argued that the job could be shared with any of the participants. The group did not depend on the guidance of a leader. Sam triumphantly exclaimed, "The group has a life of its own!"

When I returned to the SAGE Circle after a six-month absence, I was surprised to see so many new faces. About a third of the group were the old crowd (these included Paul, Michael, Jack, John, and Irving); Sam, I was told, was so busy with other Center groups he decided to take a break from SAGE; James had left town; Henry was recuperating from a recent operation; and Tony was busy and had apparently been fed up with Sam's offensive remarks. Those present at the meeting, I learned, kept in touch with others in the group. Among the "new" faces were returnees who had attended prior to the beginning of my research. Some of these, as well as the actual newcomers, were now regularly attending and taking leading roles, including serving as facilitators. Despite these changes, the agenda of the meetings did not seem to have changed much.

On meeting Sam a few years later, attending the same SAGE group, I expressed my astonishment at the survival and even expansion of the group membership. He replied in his typical ironic style: "What do you expect? These are all lonely faggots. Where else would they go to!?"

The Group Has a Life of Its Own

As reported above, the major theme that dominated most meetings was the search for Mr. Right. I opened with the story of Michael, the traveler, whose well-planned trips always involved an erotic/romantic element. These stories evoked familiar experiences and expectations shared by most attendees. John was less romantic on his travels but more direct in his search for sexual gratification. Jack never lost the hope of meeting a third lover to fill the gap left by the first two, who for many years had accommodated his closeted life in New York. Sam's search for love was far more disastrous even though he was ready to accept love without sex. Tony, Henry, and others believed Mr. Right was waiting for those who were emotionally and mentally prepared for that meeting, without the desperate search that invites disappointment and injury as Andrew and Frank seemed to exemplify. Without tears, Irving was ready to pay for love in order to avoid celibacy or the humiliation of rejection. Willie and Paul reconciled themselves to the loss that age and deteriorating health had inflicted upon them and compromised by accepting a smaller slice of their romantic and sexual dreams. When not relating their pains, successes, and failures in the field of love and romance, they often joked about sex.

Their preoccupation with a search for love and stable intimate relationships—both an ideal and a program adopted as a life's quest—seemed to integrate them far more than frequently assumed into the mainstream American cultural ethos (e.g., Bellah et al. 1985; Seidman 1991; Illouz 1997). As Varenne, another foreign observer, commented: "for Americans, the search for love, and all that it implies, has to be actualized to be fully appropriate. Acts cannot be merely symbolic. They must not only express love, they must also work for it" (1977: 208).[4]

Although the authors of *Habits of the Heart* did not include gays in their study, their observation could well apply to the SAGE Circle: "Americans believe in love as the basis for enduring relationships" (Bellah et al. 1985: 86). Not only did this observation apply to the SAGE Circle, in some respects the circle exceeded it. At a time when most heterosexuals of similar age and social characteristics had given up the quest for an all-absorbing love and sexual relationship, these gay men were still deeply engaged in the fervent pursuit of romance and sex as major means for happiness, self-esteem, and the affirmation of their true selves.

Another frequent theme of SAGE Circle discussions was the comparison of the fortunes of gays and straights. Are gays the losers, destined to loneliness? Are they the lucky ones who enjoy leisure, affluence, love, and sex? Do gays miss having children? Are they, on the whole, a happy or an unhappy "tribe"? The group remained undecided. While many members tended to stake out fixed positions, the mood of the group would swing back and forth. Were they worried about aging as gay men? Not particularly. They were more worried about daily troubles: inconveniences at home and work, health problems, and so on. In sum, in the company mostly of those they had met only recently—if not that same evening—but of some whom they had been meeting with regularly for weeks, months, or even years, they shared their most inner feelings, their pains, hopes, plans, and everyday worries.

I was first surprised but then also deeply moved by that unrestrained openness among strangers as well as by the generosity displayed by the attendees, who listened patiently and offered genuine empathy and good advice. They did not conceal a sometimes critical view, but their response was always meant to help the others take a better line of action. Never before, in my mainstream Israeli environment, had I witnessed or been informed about that type of social relationship. Israelis are apparently embedded in close networks of friends often going back to their early years at school, army, and university. They might joke or gossip about sexual matters or vaguely hint at a romantic liaison, but they never seriously relate their emotional and sexual cravings. They meet regularly, on weekends in particular, and are engaged in daily-life gossip and current politics. But they are usually reluctant to involve their friends, let alone strangers, in their more intimate experiences and feelings. Very rarely would Israelis inform their acquaintances about an appointment with an analyst, which might imply "psychological problems."

I was soon integrated into these weekly gatherings and treated as an old friend. There was no need in this company to hide the losses of age and health, setbacks at work, disappointments with family, lovers, and friends. In a poetic vein I would claim the SAGE meeting room was enveloped in a spirit of affectionate relationships.

I conclude with Sam's words, "the group has a life of its own," a reflexive metaphor for a social product and a mirror of collective consciousness. It was molded and sustained by the continuous investment of its evolving membership. That sense of communitas revealed an underlying awareness of a shared identity of older gay men as evocatively expressed on one occasion by Irving: "You walk with SAGE [in the gay parade] and young beautiful men on the sidewalks applaud proudly. They see what they are going to become!"

CHAPTER 4

Attending Meetings of Sexual
Compulsives Anonymous

The idea of strangers gathering to share their sexual difficulties and help each other reform their "distorted" sexual behavior might seem bizarre to the mainstream person. Surprise often meets my mention of the Sexual Compulsives Anonymous (SCA) meetings I observed in New York. Straight and gay people alike seem to assume that sexual troubles are not a matter for public schmoozing but should be addressed by a disciplined therapeutic procedure under the supervision of expert clinicians.

However, the emergence of a social problem related to "uncontrolled sexuality" has been considered part of the consequences of modernity; deeply embedded in the growth of individuality and the loss of authority by family and community over the personal life of their membership. "Blunted autonomy" was the term employed by Giddens to define this type of problem under the circumstances of modernity in which "sexual experience has become more freely available than ever before" and "where sexual identity forms a core part of the narrative of self" (1992: 77).

The issue of sexual compulsion and the social groups evolving among those identifying themselves as sharing that predicament have been studied mostly by psychologists. They were looking into the sources of that addiction and the ways to heal those afflicted. Quadland was among the first to study compulsive sexual behavior. He considered the syndrome anxiety-based (like other compulsive behaviors): "The sexual activity functions to reduce anxiety often related to issues of loneliness, low self-esteem, poor interpersonal relationships and fears of intimacy" (1985: 122). Like most other observers, he considered group psychotherapy the most effective treatment for a variety of addictive behaviors. In a two-year study of two groups ("addicts" and a control group), he found that the frequency of unwarranted sexual activity among the addicts declined considerably and their sexual behavior came close to that of the control group.

A similar study, but with gay men participants, was done a decade later by Baum and Fishman (1994). The results of their research, identifying behavioral changes, and their conclusions concerning the effect of group psychotherapy were similar to those reported by Quadland. In addition, they found that during the meetings, the majority of the participants revealed a sexual secret in their past life (sexual abuse, etc.). Baum and Fishman concluded that group participation offered the "addicts" a new framework of close relationships and a social commitment they had been deprived of. However, the authors were also aware of ongoing changes in social definitions of proper sexual behavior, which necessarily affect our perception of normative sex life. Sexual activities that during the 1970s might have been considered healthy, pleasurable, and congratulatory expressions of sexuality had become marked as notoriously dangerous behavior in the era of AIDS.

Baum and Fishman's observation of the circumstantial transformation of sexual norms of behavior was pursued far more critically, though from a sociological perspective, by Levine and Troiden. They attacked the idea of sexual addiction—an invention they attributed to Quadland—as a culturally determined definition. They were equally unimpressed by the mushrooming of SCA groups and their employment of the twelve-step recovery program[1] based on the AA (Alcoholics Anonymous) tradition: "As applied presently, these concepts merely pathologize behaviors that diverge from the erotic standards held by the wider society" (1998 [1988]: 171). They held "sexual compulsion" and "sexual addiction" to be therapeutic constructions that contradicted their own assertion of sexual conduct as a learned behavior that "expresses a person's overall lifestyle." Therefore, "the so-called sexual compulsives and addicts express and manage their sexuality in ways that violate prevailing societal expectations" (173). Moreover, they considered the invention of the concepts of sexual compulsion and addiction, which are "highly subjective and value laden," a threat to the civil liberties of sexually variant people (174).

A more recent and thorough study of sexually compulsive men was conducted by Pepper (1997), a psychologist. She began her research by attending numerous SCA meetings in New York City then selecting twenty-one self-identified sex addicts, mostly gays, who answered a detailed questionnaire and were subject to a clinical interview. In contrast to the early congratulatory studies that emphasized the effects of group therapy, Pepper's study indicated the limitations of the SCA Twelve Step rehabilitation program. Subjects unable to resolve sexual and interpersonal difficulties through the use of that method described their addiction as escalating and themselves as increasingly anxious and depressed. Pepper's conclusion does not, however, refute the positive effects reported from studies of group psychotherapy initiated by skilled clinicians.

The issue of compulsive sexuality, though not unique to gay society, bears immediate relevance to a major facet of gay life. The eruption of Gay Liberation since the late 1960s has been marked by a proliferation of commercial institutions and public spaces that offered (mostly to men) the free expression of sexuality, free of the norms and sanctions of mainstream society. Therefore, the emergence of groups that battle with excessive sexuality, in the era of AIDS in particular, appears as a profound critique of gay life.

My query and methodology were not intended to identify the sources or the process of "healing" from sexual addiction. Instead, employing the anthropological method of participant observation, I set out to investigate the dynamics of social relationships that energize these groups of strangers. I wished to identify the modes of expression, the symbolic strategies, and cultural creativity (what is probably meant by the current term "cultural text") developed in these meetings. My exploration of the metaphors and the symbols initiated by the SCA participants expands the field of gay language, a major component of gay culture (e.g., Leap 1996, 2008, 2010; Cameron and Kulick 2003; Kulick 2003). This search inevitably suggests the meaning that the SCA members attribute to their participation in these groups.

SCA, AA, and Other Groups

SCA has undoubtedly been a successful offshoot of the worldwide Alcoholics Anonymous movement. Many participants in the groups I observed told stories about what had led them to join the SCA organization, in conformity with the official narrative about how the first group was established. In an official SCA publication, Rick H., a founding member of the movement, offered a short description of his graduation as a "sober" man, following his experience with the recovery program of Alcoholics Anonymous: "When I began to see the addictive nature of my sexual activity, I wanted to stop but

I couldn't" (SCA 1990: 40). In 1982 he and two other AA friends started a sexual recovery meeting in one of their apartments in New York. At that time they called themselves Sexaholics Anonymous, following the example of SAA (Sex Addicts Anonymous), a group of heterosexuals that had originated in California. Although they later changed the name that so visibly displayed the model for their enterprise (Alcoholics Anonymous), they retained as their goal "sobriety," the term most evocative of their efforts, and they adopted AA's recovery program. They actually transformed the pattern started in California to suit their own constituency, mostly gay men. As they looked for a public space for their meetings, they approached the gay synagogue and the nearby churches. Eventually the Lesbian and Gay Community Center accommodated most of the new meetings.[2]

I learned about the history of a group that departed from the Center and met at a midtown church. It had been started four years earlier by a man who had since left New York, fed up with the groups he attended. During the break at one meeting, I was looking at the sample of SCA literature exhibited on a side table. Noticing my interest, Donna, a prominent member at the church group, advised me to purchase a copy of the book *Out of the Shadows* (Carnes 1992) as an introduction to the problems and the recovery program of sexual addiction.[3] I followed her advice and learned from Carnes about three levels of sexual addiction. The men and women I observed at the SCA meetings mostly represented the first level, that of minor addictions—the compulsive pursuit of anonymous sex, pornography, masturbation, and the like. The second and third levels represent more serious addictions prevalent among heterosexuals, including exhibitionism, incest, child molestation, and rape.

The very acknowledgment of the first level of sexual addiction, which characterized most SCA participants, seems to support Levine and Troiden's (1998 [1988]) complaint about the cultural definition of sexual behavior. These men in particular were patrons of the commercial sex institutions and the public spaces for male sexual bonding considered havens of gay freedom only a decade earlier. But whatever cultural constraints and social changes seem to have spoiled the happy consumption of that freedom, these men, and the minority of women at these meetings, felt they had lost control over their sexual desires and modes of gratification. They assumed that other gay people had reached a far more satisfactory balance between desire and its acting out.

I will not delve into the research about the AA curing strategy and membership. Only rarely had anthropologists considered these groups a field suitable for ethnographic research. However, employing an anthropological perspective, Antze's (1987) analysis of the AA texts seems pertinent to my observations of behavior at SCA meetings. Both the AA and the SCA movements draw participants into a community that reorders their lives. Both groups offer their members a new understanding of themselves and their motives and grant them a new identity. They use a series of similar symbols and practices that produce new patterns of action and a revised worldview. Both refer the participants to a "higher power," which might present itself in various forms of deity: the individual himself, the group, God. I also concur with Antze's interpretation of AA's strategy of transformation in terms of "a cult of affliction," borrowed from Victor Turner's (1968) perception of Ndembu society religious and ritual life, a method of responding to specific calamities besieging individual Africans.

But SCA differs profoundly from AA's major orientation and consequences. AA members do not aspire to return to "normality" in the sense of becoming regular consumers of alcohol. For the rest of their lives, AA members must abstain completely from alcohol and remain indefinitely in the category "alcoholics." In contrast, SCA members are not expected to abstain from sex. They strive to learn the meaning and joy of a stable, loving relationship as a major component of a sexual relationship. While there is no way for AA participants to differentiate "good" alcohol from "bad" alcohol, SCA members develop an ethos of good versus bad sex.

The relationships between the participants at SCA also constitute an element mostly absent at AA meetings. While the substance of danger that unites the AA membership is "out there," the SCA gay participants are surrounded by potential objects for their addiction—mostly attractive men who could easily become the targets of their addictive fantasies and actual cruising. Yet participants are trained to change their habits of indiscriminate "sexualizing" and maintain a new "normal" lifestyle of sexual demeanor. But whatever the differences, many participants reported a past association with the AA Twelve-Step rehabilitation program. Their testimony of battling another uncontrolled behavior strengthened their sense of a shared experience, often in gay bars where excessive consumption of alcohol is a frequent feature.

Despite being organized around a specific goal, SCA meetings engaged in a wide range of activities, relationships, and commitments in the lives of its membership, who shared the most intimate details about their families, work, and sexual lives. Whereas members of other organizations I observed at the Center met mostly once a week, many SCA participants met each other several times, if not on a daily basis, because they often attended several SCA groups. Moreover, many also related to each other as sponsors (guides in a personal program of recovery) and sponsored. In addition they communicated with a wide network of participants as phone-call pals. The SCA membership probably represented the largest multifunctional subcommunity hosted at the Center.

While the SCA agenda and the continuing discourse among its participants seemed mostly engaged with sexual behavior, other groups I observed at the Center sometimes displayed a far more erotic atmosphere. Obviously, their members didn't consider themselves addicts who were supposed to curtail their sexual drive. Although not a few among them sometimes engaged in anonymous sex at sites that had become "battlefields" for many SCA members, they did not consider themselves victims of an uncontrolled compulsion. Like many other visitors to these sites, they often hoped they would meet Mr. Right there. Giddens argued that addictions can be described as a frustrated search for self-identity and suggested that the leitmotif of addiction recovery groups is "a rewriting of the narrative of self" (1992: 69, 75). I assume that the various groups I observed were also engaged in a project of transforming their participants' "narratives of self." They certainly differed greatly in their directions and goals. While some still strove to liberate their members from self- or socially imposed restrictions on their sexuality, the SCA people wished to bring under control sexuality that in their eyes, for whatever reasons, blunted its mission. However, as my following observations might illustrate, the SCA participants nourished and manifested a shared advocated identity against the popular perception among both straight and gay audiences of a stigmatized behavior and an infamous gay identification.

Integrating into the Field

On my early visits to the Lesbian and Gay Community Services Center in Greenwich Village, I noticed a list of a few SCA meetings advertised in the daily schedules. I had no prior knowledge of these events, and when I finally made a hesitant visit on a Saturday evening, I was surprised to discover a room crowded with more than fifty attendees, mostly men and a few women. I arrived a few minutes late and was relieved to find a vacant seat in a remote corner. The crowd was composed of young and older people, mostly white, who were casually dressed except for several in formal office attire. Almost immediately I was treated in a friendly manner. Colin, a pleasant looking man in his early forties, was seated next to me. I asked him about the schedule of the meeting, and he told me he attended SCA meetings almost every day. He gave me his telephone number, saying I could call him if I needed any more information. I could contact him any time and should not hesitate if I suddenly felt I needed somebody to talk to, even if I were in the street at a late hour. There was no sexual innuendo in his tone.

I called Colin a few days later and discovered that he himself had joined the group only four months earlier but that he was already experienced with the AA program, which he had attended for a few years. He joined the SCA because he wished to discover his true inner self "instead of running around like an addict always hungry for sex." He hoped to retrieve his ability to love. He promised me that if I raised my hand at meetings, joined in the "sharing," and related my problem, people would get to know me and open up to me. He knew of many participants who dated nice men and made close friends among the SCA participants. He also suggested that I join another SCA group that he particularly liked, which met regularly at a midtown church. All SCA groups met weekly for a session of ninety minutes. For those who joined the fellowship for a meal or snack afterward, and many did, the meeting lasted about three hours.

Thus began my observations of a group I soon discovered was open to newcomers and most congenial for the development of close relationships. However, I was uncomfortable about the promise I made with all others at the beginning of every meeting—to keep the content of the meeting confidential: "The things you have heard here are given and spoken in confidence and should be treated as confidential." After all, much of what I observed and heard in other groups that met at the Center was equally private. I believed I was well experienced with the issue of preserving the anonymity and reputation of the people I observed. At the start, I told the individuals who approached me about my book on CBST, the gay synagogue. I assumed the information would present me as a serious scholar and sympathetic to gay issues. However, I immediately realized that mentioning my previous work and the implication of my present endeavor changed the hospitable attitude. Faces turned stern, and I was told that I was welcome as long as I shared with the group a problem of sexual compulsiveness.

Some participants, both regular and casual, were already familiar faces to me from the Center and elsewhere, Larry and Sam in particular. Larry was among my close acquaintances at CBST. In his early fifties, he was a veteran congregant who had joined the synagogue in the 1970s and remained among its most dedicated members. I was surprised when I first noticed him in a front seat at an SCA meeting and was worried about his reaction. Would he be embarrassed or resentful to see me there? My worries were soon relieved. Cheerful as ever, as I greeted him, Larry asked: "Are you going to write another book?" He went on to say he had helped found the first SCA group in New York twelve years earlier. At that point they hadn't yet developed the literature and rules specific to the present SCA organization. He told me he attended seven meetings a week in various parts of the city. He added he was glad to see another CBST member attending the meeting, whom he recognized as a regular visitor at "all those sex places."

I now perceived Larry through a very different personal configuration: not so much a proud "gay Jew," but nonetheless a self-assured, sexually compulsive gay man closely associated with other "addicts" of various denominations.

Encouraged by seeing a few SCA attendees who were also my acquaintances from CBST, I assumed that my presence at meetings, and the ethnographic method of presentation, would have no effect on the participants. However, as discussed in Chapter 1, I stopped attending SCA meetings after a dedicated participant, also a social scientist, who befriended me expressed personal offense on discovering my "true identity" as a researcher. That one painful encounter was enough to dissuade me there and then of my deep conviction about the potential contribution of my work to the welfare and reputation of SCA participants. In any case, I invoke Humphreys's (1975) justification of his own project of unannounced observations in the field of anonymous sex. Naturally, it raises professional issues and ethical dilemmas demanding further investigation.[4]

My presentation reports on the thirty meetings I attended during four months, from mid-February to mid-June 1995; however, I attended meetings sporadically in later years as well.[5] I describe fifteen meetings with two groups that met once a week at the Center on Saturday and Sunday and fifteen weekly meetings with a group that met at a church in Manhattan. My continuing attendance at the weekly church meeting throughout this period familiarized me with its participants in particular. The style of meeting and the atmosphere at these events differed greatly from group to group. For example, the meetings on Saturday and Sunday always started with one regular member or a guest who presented his/her experiences ("qualified" in the official SCA terminology) for about twenty minutes or more and then opened the floor for other participants to react and briefly share their own. This type of meeting was confessional and attained a level of emotional reaction rarely displayed at the church meetings, where the dominant pattern of sharing was related to the list of "tools" used by the program (including the means of education and communication, like prayer and meditation, the telephone, meetings, socializing, service, sponsorship, dating, literature, slogans, etc.). Here the participants described their recent experience with the efficacy of each tool. Actually, during my stay, members suggested that the pattern be changed to allow for more than three "sharings" for each tool. It was argued that the tradition of three equal shares for every tool limited the expression of experiences, since not all tools raised the same level of response. The participants voted to allow any number of sharings for each tool.

A new SCA group at the Center that started during my stay, which I attended only once, adopted a pattern of equally allocating four minutes of sharing for each participant, which allowed many members to take part at each session. Participants were not encouraged to develop a confessional style there either.

Gradually, I identified two sets of participants. At each weekly group I observed those who attended meetings regularly and took on the duties that kept the group going. I also came to identify quite a few who, although attending the church meetings regularly, for example, also often went to other groups. I was greeted by my church acquaintances when we met at the Center's SCA meeting on Saturdays and Sundays. I assume that the overlap of participation was far more frequent and also involved groups I never attended at the Center or at other places around the city. Meeting the same individuals at various groups visibly strengthened my feeling of camaraderie. People from the church group who identified me as a regular (though silent) participant reacted to me when they saw me at other meetings as though I were a close acquaintance and hugged me warmly. This was typical of their meetings with other regulars who revealed more about themselves.

I assume I was perceived by many participants as an actor simply waiting for the right moment to strut onto the stage. I had held a similar position in my earlier study of Israeli immigrants in New York. Many of my Israeli acquaintances assumed I would finally stay on in the United States and join their community. They had already observed that process with other Israeli residents they had met, who first arrived in America as temporary visitors (Shokeid 1988b).

I encountered another problem at the SCA meetings. Although the participants usually expressed their emotional predicaments and daily experiences in a very clear and eloquent style, when I got home and started to write down my observations, I had difficulty reconstructing their individual narratives. It reminded me of my earlier experience attending meetings of Israeli immigrants in New York with teachers from Chabad (a Jewish Hassidic movement). At first I could not remember the specific contents of the teachers' lectures. However, I solved that difficulty when I obtained permission to record the meetings. I then discovered that the source of my handicap lay in the almost identical style employed by different teachers as much as in the repetitive nature of the messages designed to convey a very specific moral lesson (1988b: 145). But now I could not ask to record the meetings, and I never entertained the idea of recording without permission. Why couldn't I more clearly remember the specific narratives, the reactions, and other expressions I witnessed at the SCA meetings?

Compared with the Chabad lectures and discussions, the SCA regular sharings and discourses were far more captivating and emotionally moving. I assume that my "memory loss" was not a self-censoring strategy I adopted to accommodate the ethos of confidentiality imposed on the SCA attendants. More likely, it reflected the similar experiences that the majority of the membership divulged during meetings. One listened fully absorbed and sympathetic to the stories of pain, frustration, disappointment, betrayal, and abuse from young and older people whose promising lives were seriously disrupted by bad luck and addiction. Many could blame, for example, their parents for betraying them: neglectful, sexually abusive alcoholics who denied them love and affection or underestimated their talents. A common history of early deprivation curtailed their opportunities for love and success and consequently caused them to resolve their unhappiness in sexual addiction. Many others had no one in particular to blame for their misfortune. Regardless of the roots of their problem, they all gravitated toward behavior they came to consider self-destructive, an endless pursuit of "loveless sex"— mostly at the various sites of anonymous sex—humiliating, dangerous, and life-threatening in the era of AIDS. For some this involved serial romantic infatuations, attraction to unattainable or abusive partners, compulsive masturbation, and addiction to pornographic literature or films. These predicaments were generally interpreted as symptomatic of the inability to love. In many cases, sexual compulsiveness was preceded by or coexisted with the detrimental experience of alcoholism. Similar in content and emotional tone, these public presentations were difficult to remember as individual narratives.

The Scripts of "Acting Out" on the Stage of SCA Meetings

After attending a meeting one night, I joined the fellowship for dinner at a nearby restaurant. One of the men told me immediately on sitting down that he had already been with the program for four years. Actually, he added, he recently rejoined after finding he was back at his old "disastrous habits." He spent all his nights at one of the surviving gay saunas and yet was never satisfied. "We know we are addicts and we are not going to give up our sexual compulsion," he explained, "but we help each other, listening and sharing. We have many friends here and have a great time together." "I like you already," he assured me. Contemplating the disruption of intimacy in a small therapeutic group, I asked the naive question "What happens when participants are attracted to each other?" His answer was, "Of course we are attracted to some of the men around, and I often see good-looking guys here I wish I could go to bed with!" He went on to explain, "We sexualize each other; we don't want to stop our sexuality. What we look for is the power to control our lives. Instead of letting our sexuality control our lives, we try to control our sexuality." As proof, he told me that that day he had wanted to "act out"—have sex at some site of anonymous interaction, a tearoom, sauna, pornographic movie theater, etc.—but had decided to attend our meeting instead. Colin then joined our conversation, adding that, compared with the AA program and activities, the SCA offered a special challenge: the AA people fight an addiction together "out there," but with the SCA, the addiction is "right here"; namely, presented by the participants themselves to each other. However, he went on, even if some participants did act out an immediate attraction, the circumstances here were much different from at a site of anonymous sex.

One member of the church core group, Rick, was among those people I met at other meetings. He never missed an opportunity to share his problems, and his story was among those I have never forgotten. He was in his late thirties, good-looking; he had a college education but was often agitated about his situation of unemployment yet hopeful of getting a job. A few times he arrived dressed up in a suit, shortly after an interview with a prospective employer. Later he told me he had been with SCA for seven years, where he made many friends who helped each other "to handle the shit." He also informed the group he had received his test results confirming he was HIV negative. Sounding astonished, he added that having had sex with "thousands of men" he was supposed to be dead already (from AIDS) or murdered (because he used to cruise the park at two in the morning). But, he claimed, he was not going to places like bars, saunas, or tearooms anymore. I listened to Rick's sharing a few more times over the following months. He was angry and unhappy with the government, his potential employers, and even his sponsor in the SCA, who he felt was too strict with him. At one meeting, as we related to the telephone as tool of support, he said that he had used it recently to call on many friends from the group, and they had saved him from a breakdown. Sometime later, Rick told us he had a new sponsor who had suggested a new recovery program that seemed to work for him. He also made it a rule to pray before he left home for an interview. "I am flying," he ended happily. Rick was always allowed to express his predicaments, despite the very limited time for sharing at the meetings.

Richard, a social worker in his early forties, was also an angry man, though he was more articulate than some other members. He emphasized the egalitarian AA and SCA tradition, which he believed had its origins in the American Indian circle meetings with their sacred nature. We had only just met when I expressed my astonishment at how intimate even the large meetings felt. He responded firmly, "We are all gays. We know we are here together surrounded by homophobia. This is our community; these are our synagogues!!" (He was not Jewish, but he once told me he had attended a dance at CBST.) He also suggested that I attend a Friday SCA meeting at the Center that was particularly crowded and hectic. I gradually recognized Richard's deep despair. Referring to the tool of dating, he shared with us his inability to establish a love relationship. He was either bored by the second date or hopelessly infatuated with men who would not reciprocate. He there-fore ended up "acting out" at a site of anonymous sex. He concluded that his addictions had ruined his life and career. At one meeting he told us he tried not to "act out" as much as he wanted, because if he "slipped" too often, he wouldn't be able to go on attending meetings. But he couldn't afford to lose his friends here. In the next meeting he admitted that he hated attending because he realized he would never attain the goal they all strived for. Still, he repeated his message from the previous week, namely he could not give up the fellowship he shared with the group.

Richard's delivery usually lacked the high emotionality of Rick's and a few others'. Instead, it was characteristic of other sophisticated sharings—funny and self-mocking. Sometime later, Richard's despair reached a new nadir. Repeating his loss of hope in ever getting "sober," he also publicly expressed his disappointment with the SCA participants. They kissed and hugged him, and told him "We love you," he said, but he knew deep down they did not really care about him, since they did not call or invite him anywhere; they saw him only during the meetings. This statement seemed to contradict his previous claim, "These are our synagogues." No one reacted publicly to Richard's accusation. A few days later, I met Vincent at a Sunday Center meeting. He asked me about the church meetings he had missed in previous weeks, when he was out of town. I told him about Richard's complaint. Vincent responded, "True, not all participants feel close to all others. It is not always a loving relationship." But he insisted there were some who became really close. He assumed Richard expected far more than that. He himself, he told me, had called on Richard a few days before. Richard continued to attend meetings and seemed to forget his severe attack on his colleagues.

Saul was another participant whose story remained stuck in my memory. A youthful looking man in his mid-twenties, he described himself as a "Jewish boy from the suburbs," though not a "nice" one, as suggested by the stereotype. He often shared his painful predicaments, first emphasizing that he was not the victim of incest, child abuse, or neglect. He did, however, suffer from being less talented than his older brother. His addiction, he believed, handicapped his chances for a successful career, which also made him relatively poor and always short of money to spend freely. Although he knew he should head home, he couldn't resist staying on in the bars, just hanging around. This often ended in trouble. "I'm miserable and I don't know what to do about it," he frequently concluded. In spite of his pathetic presentation of self, Saul inspired sympathy with his somewhat humorous, self-mocking style and his streak of optimism. Once he claimed, to the amusement of his listeners, that stools should be removed from tearooms (public restrooms). He hated tearooms, he said; they were boring, but celibacy was even more boring and consequently he couldn't keep away from these boring places. Many laughed at this self-mockery, which touched upon their own sense of degradation and waste. Not a few among the participants approached him later in a warm manner. One day later, Saul shared again in another group I attended at the Center. He confessed he was disgusted with his own compulsion to have predictably humiliating sex, ending on his knees in a dark room begging for affection from men who were "shut off" from any emotion. If he couldn't get off at one of these places, he ended up masturbating at home. "I am probably crazy," he concluded, "but I am happy I can share the shit with you." Saul volunteered "to service" the group (as a tool), taking care of the SCA literature.

During my stay, George and Vincent, both good-looking men in their late thirties, played leading roles in the group, acting as chairman and treasurer.

George made us all laugh when he shared his wish that men would stop using the subway. He explained he didn't need a porno theater or a notorious gay bar to get aroused since he was so readily attracted to men on any train or in the nearest street. A few weeks later, George informed the group he had taken the HIV test. He was worried since he had "slipped" and "acted out" a few times recently. Taking the test as part of his participation in a research project, he was asked as it was being administered whether he had some guilt feelings. The macho-looking George told us he had answered that it wasn't a matter of guilt but of face-saving: "You can't save your face and ass at the same time!" His audience reacted with a big laugh. I was present when George shared again a month later. He sounded desperate though still humorous. He told us that while he had managed to avoid any form of casual sex, it had not improved his life at work or in the love department. "So, what's the achievement?" he asked his listeners. The last time he shared during my stay, he related how much he had changed since first joining SCA, when he was attracted to many in the fellowship because he sexualized any connection. He even sexualized men who didn't fit into his preferred type, including those completely incompatible because of age or other reasons. But then "I discovered they're all as fucked up as myself," and he gave these attractions up. It was still difficult for him, he told us, to ride the subway, because he was desperately attracted to so many riders. Again, George admitted he could not claim a considerable improvement; nevertheless, he was grateful to the fellowship for his new ability to differentiate among various relationships.

Vincent, the treasurer, always arrived in elegant, formal clothes and always appeared relaxed and pleasantly serious. He reflected the image of a successful businessman, a real estate agent, or a lawyer. I was surprised when he first told the group he had "slipped". He knew he was not allowed to visit "that place" (probably a bar), but he made himself a deal to go there for only fifteen minutes. However, four hours and five places later, he finally reached his train and had to ask himself: "What is going on?" Later, as he approached me during the break and asked for my name, which is somewhat difficult to remember because of the Hebrew intonation, he seemed like the same relaxed and composed man. As he hugged me before we left, he explained that he needed to recognize all participants in order to be able to announce those who made progress with their program. A few weeks later Vincent experienced another relapse, for which he had no explanation. "I slipped last Wednesday," he told the group, acting out and coming home at nearly 5 a.m. Vincent was always careful to avoid details about the sites and his activities when he relapsed. He told us he had already shared that experience at another meeting over the weekend. Relating to the telephone as a tool, he told us he had already had many phone calls from friends from that meeting.

When Larry, my CBST acquaintance, qualified (opened a meeting with a personal presentation) at a weekend Center meeting, he told his life story in a campy style that combined pain with laughter. To the delight of his listeners, Larry related his reaction when his mother discovered a photo of a nude man in his bag: "How did it get there?" he had asked her, astonished. Discovering at twenty-three that he was desperately attracted to men, he believed one could have sex only with hustlers, which meant having quick sex and going on immediately with one's other tasks. He remembered leaving one quick sex encounter to attend a family wedding. Fearful he smelled badly, he stopped to wash his face before entering the hall packed with his elegantly dressed relatives. Later he discovered the saunas. It was often humiliating, but he didn't know anything better. At first he refused to join AA, but twelve years earlier he had finally committed himself, and there he met the man who started SCA. Larry was currently celebrating eight years in the program that had brought an end to his humiliating lifestyle.

Sam was in his late fifties. I first met him at a weekly SAGE group meeting at the Center (see Chapter 3). At a weekend SCA Center meeting he was a guest qualifier who told his listeners how ten years before he had started attending AA meetings, where he learned about the SCA organization. Sam's cosmopolitan experience and professional education had not stopped him from drinking heavily and dragging himself to bars and other places where he had indiscriminate sex. Eventually he ruined his health. Sam admitted his disastrous attractions. He was attracted to unattainable men, young Irish policemen and firefighters in particular. He was attracted to his clients at work as much as to the good-looking guys attending the SCA meetings.

Sam also expressed his gratitude to SCA in other forums. For instance, at a SAGE meeting, he attacked another leading member who seemed bored and edgy about listening to a participant's complaints. He suggested that he attend an SCA meeting and learn how to allow other people to express their feelings and learn the skill of listening. It was an opportunity to tell SAGE people about the SCA agenda, because most attendees were not familiar with the organization.

The attraction to impossible or wrong candidates for a love relationship remained a major theme for the subsequent speakers. Carl, in his early sixties, was the oldest active member I met and among the leaders of the church meetings. He attended Sam's qualification at the Center and was also moved to share. He commented that he was well aware that the drive for unattainable or wrong targeted sexual partners would always be there, as "sober" as he might be. But the goal was not to be "cured" of his addiction; rather, it was to be able to control it, to be aware of its dangerous presence. At a later church meeting, Carl told us he had managed to remain celibate for a long time despite of the potential urge to "act out." Carl, who had been with SCA for seven years, emphatically stated that living without his recovery program was pointless: "This fellowship is very important for me. Some of my dearest friends are here."

Howard's immaculate and formal appearance might have misled an outside observer. He was in his early thirties, impressive in his good looks, and always wore a suit and tie. Early in my visits he approached me, asking for my name and other details. Later, I often saw him approach newcomers to facilitate their entry into the group. Once during the discussion about the tool of "service" he commented: "I am doing services [for the group] for my own sake. If I have to take care of others, I must keep sober. I approach newcomers as if I am a welcoming committee, which I am not! I do it even if I go to a meeting I haven't been to before. I know everyone. I write down the names of newcomers so I can remember them." This was a man who later confessed that he had been very uncomfortable when he first joined SCA: "I felt so ashamed when I first came to a SCA meeting, as if everyone looking at me knew my shameful behavior and tried to cruise me." Another participant agreed, commenting that service made him speak to other people, which allowed other participants to approach him because they now knew him. Otherwise, he would have been sitting quietly not speaking to anyone. When he shared a few weeks later, Howard emphasized again that welcoming the newcomers and immersing himself into their reports kept him from "acting out" and, as he later told me, kept him sane. He looked intensely into my eyes as we spoke during the break. I couldn't avoid telling him that I saw a deep sadness in his eyes. He responded it was a sign he wanted to "act out." I regretted I didn't know what a committed SCA member would have done at that moment; I let him go.

Alfred, a man in his early fifties, always took the same seat at the front, close to the facilitator. He never gave up his right to share, despite the large size of the group. He had been a member for ten years but seemed unable to resist his attraction to men who didn't want him and to dangerous situations that could lead to brutal beatings or even death. Alfred initially irritated me by his stern look and what seemed like an authoritative and intimidating demeanor. I changed my attitude once he served as major qualifier, where I could listen to his story more carefully and intently. He began by saying that somebody had told him that he looked sober but lacking in serenity. True, he had celebrated three years of sobriety in his program, he told us, but he believed that he lacked serenity out of not yet having accepted himself. He attributed this to the way he had been raised. His parents had taught him to keep his problems secret. Only here had he learned to open up and "take the stuff out."

Alfred was open about his hopeless and dangerous attraction to younger men. He knew the problem would only get worse with age. He was equally open about his relationships in the group. He admitted he didn't like everybody in the room, although he had learned to control his feelings. He also understood that his unfriendly attitude was the outcome of his tendency to control. Things had to go his way. In any case, Alfred was grateful to the group and the program that helped him to keep away from "acting out." Instead of an arrogant and intimidating man, I now saw the suffering under his irritating facade. Reacting to Alfred's sharing, a man in his late thirties thanked him for his honest presentation. On one occasion Alfred had told him quite angrily that "Gay men miss the good old days."[6] Alfred's words now came back to this man as he thought about his last experience of "acting out." He had spent eight hours at a place he did not name. Eventually the manager ejected him in a humiliating way. The speaker hated how the manager had shined a flashlight in his face to identify him and told him he would never be admitted again. He could now comprehend Alfred's discontent: had the good old days ever existed?

I became aware of a conflict between messages. The idea that the SCA meetings were not effective as a "cure" seemed a common perception, though many expressed their disappointment that they had slipped in spite of their continuing attendance. Early in my visits, a man in his mid-thirties told me that he attended as many meetings as he could. He compared the idea of a mutual help group to taking vitamins in abundance. He also used the example of diabetics who inject themselves with insulin; it does not cure them, but it helps them survive. To him this meant delaying or controlling, though not preventing, the urge to act out. Less optimistic was Len, one of the very few black participants. While having a good experience as an AA member, recently at SCA meetings he found himself in trouble again. The company of attractive men at the SCA meetings made it more difficult for him to deal with sex. He had started drinking and spending his evenings watching pornography and masturbating.

Women on the SCA Stage

Although women were a minority among SCA participants—there were never more than five female attendees, and often only one or two—they played important roles in many meetings I attended. A few women also seemed to belong to the core of more prominent members. Donna, a good-looking woman in her late thirties, qualified a few times and became chair of her group. She had been married for nearly ten years before she met a woman who dominated her life for several years. The trouble had started when Donna realized that her own son couldn't tolerate her lover's domineering style. She felt she was losing her son when her lover, because of her own resentment toward the boy, tried to drive him out of their home. Donna finally decided to regain control of her life and gave up her lover. She later discovered her problem: she became immediately infatuated with women she had sex with, believing it was true love. Her predicament was not much different from those related by the men in the group. A few months later, Donna told the group she had been offered a new job that would involve a lot of traveling. She was worried because she would be unable to attend SCA meetings regularly. However, she had called on two SCA friends who traveled a lot, and they had told her she could take the SCA literature on her trips as a way of coping with the loss of meetings.

Sue-Ellen, another female qualifier, in her mid-thirties, elegantly dressed, and articulate, told us she could not develop intimate relationships, only fleeting sexual encounters. At an early stage, she had believed that having a lot of sex with many partners was glamorous. Sue-Ellen assumed her troubles were rooted in her history as an incest survivor. She could not develop a deep love relationship because she couldn't allow anyone to "penetrate her private space." Her qualifying was analytical and restrained, lacking the emotional tone and the humor that often prevailed at these events. At a later meeting, another young woman reported on her issues, predominantly with men. Her problems had started in college, where she had been associated with a group of addicts. Often she had no idea whom she ended up in bed with. She had sex with her best friend's boyfriend, then with men at the office, and eventually with men who picked her up from anywhere. Her story shared the metaphors of "acting out" and the emotional tone of many gay male qualifications.

In Giddens's terms (1992:72), the addicted person engulfed in "time out" is in "another world" and may regard his or her activities with cynical amusement or even disdain. In our case, male and female participants' narratives of "acting out" (materialized or fantasized) formed a major symbolic vehicle for a shared identity.

The Practice of Tools

A few SCA tools raised a more emotional response than others. Sponsorship seemed particularly important. Participants often commented on their special relationships with their sponsors. I mentioned Rick, whose relationships with his sponsors were volatile. He was no less dedicated to those he sponsored himself. Dani, a good-looking man in his early thirties, once shared his problem with a certain place he had to pass through on his way home and the fantasies it always raised in his mind about what was happening there. The one thing that stopped him from going there was recalling his sponsor's uncompromising decision: he must give the place up completely. His sponsor made it absolutely clear that Dani had to choose between acting out that attraction and continuing his relationship with the sponsor. Would he give up a close friend for the sake of "acting out," as he often had previously in his life? Dani made a promise not to go there anymore. Sponsors become close friends whom one can call on any time and from whom one can expect immediate support.

Meetings, when discussed directly as a tool, inspired a special sentiment among the participants. For example, a man in his early fifties told us that he did not benefit much from the telephone as a tool, but that the meetings enabled him "to break through my unreal reality" and connect with the world out there. At meetings, participants claimed they at last found "affection." A man in his early forties proclaimed how happy he was to be with SCA, where he had discovered that his constant "acting out" stemmed from looking for affection in the wrong places. Only here had he at last found the friends and the affection he missed so much. Another man explained his past attraction to tearooms: he believed no one anywhere else would be interested in him, and he never felt cared for until he joined SCA meetings. Since then, he had made an important step in his recovery—a seven-month relationship with a very nice person, although the relationship was mostly based on sex. He believed he was finally ready to find a partner for a love relationship.

A man who admitted he had come by mistake, assuming it was an AA meeting, enthusiastically expressed his feeling that this was the place he needed more than anything else. Until now, he had been fixated on destructive activities—alcohol, drugs, sex—that made him "the receptacle of unwanted sperm," since he only sought people who didn't want him. His immune system was badly compromised, and going to a bar was the last thing he could afford. Again and again participants emphasized that their attendance at meetings kept them from going out to places where acting out was inevitable. Participants understood that their membership depended on a serious effort to curtail their addictions. But most of all, they also realized that attending meetings enabled the development of social relationships not limited to the perception of men in one context only—sex.

Participants at the SCA meetings frequently told of the death or terminal illness of relatives and close friends. They shared with the fellowship these most painful experiences, which often raised memories of unresolved animosities and lost love. For some, the meetings symbolized the end of the pre-AIDS world they could still glimpse when they visited the bars in West Village. At the same time, these gatherings were a substitute for that lost world. A man in his mid-forties shared the sadness that engulfed him during his occasional visits to those bars, which made him recall his dead friends. He considered himself a survivor. He had made a decision to accept the ending of that world and never go back there.

Many members attended meetings right after painful visits, usually entailing a trip out of town to a family reunion or to other events. When they returned too late for a meeting, contacting a sponsor immediately or getting a friend on the phone from one's list of SCA members helped stave off the impulse to act out. They looked to the meetings for consolation after acting out or for protection from its immanent threat. Before or after acting out another threatening attraction, they acted out a shared consciousness—defined by SCA teaching and practice as the tool of "meeting."

Very few blacks attended meetings, and those who did represented mostly a middle-class population. One man, for example, shared about the tool of prayer. Before he joined SCA, he told the group, he thought that God and prayer belonged only to his grandmother and her generation of women. But since then, he had learned to pray and it helped a lot. Meditation and prayer were cited as a means to stave off the temptation to act out. A young man related how he would start meditating whenever he saw an attractive guy, and how regular daily meditation enabled him to go to the steam room in the gym without getting aroused. A few who praised prayer as a means to avoid acting out associated prayer with the group. When I expressed my doubts about my ability as a secular person to start praying, I got several responses: you pray to your higher power, or (more often), you can equally pray to the group. Sometimes participants compared the effect of prayer with that of the meetings. One man eloquently expressed this in what seemed to me a Durkheimian language: "The collective is more than its parts, it is the personification of compassion!!"

Early in my visits, Richard had said of the meetings, "These are our synagogues," a metaphor that seemed to encapsulate their role in the group members' lives: the meetings promoted the shared identity of a distinct minority that also shared a collective memory; they provided sociability, knowledgeable leaders, a place to mourn the loss of close individuals, a code of normative behavior, sacred texts, and prayer. In Victor Turner's (1967a) terms, these groups offered the experience of communitas to people whose basic existential conditions were marked by a deep notion of liminality. They were all striving for a new stage in their lives that would redeem them from a long life history of opportunities lost, the burden of a stigmatized identity, emotional and physical waste, loneliness, physical danger, and the painful deprivation of love and affection. The meetings, as a social entity and as a tool, were the major theme for sharing and adulation in all SCA events I attended.

The Language of Addicts

The participants used consistently specific terms and metaphors that seemed to encapsulate their most gripping and threatening experiences. I identify this argot or linguistic code among the distinguishing features of the culture of the SCA membership. "I slipped" seemed to express the essence of their compulsive or addictive behavior. But the term sometimes preceded the more powerful phrase "acting out" (like I slipped). The concise idiom of "acting out" contained a far more expansive narrative. The attentive audience had no need to hear the precise details of the specific acting out to grasp the full script. These compact phrases struck familiar chords, leading the listeners directly to their own experiences of acting out. Therefore, each sharing of a slippage event or of acting out evoked a communal meaning that immediately raised empathy for the narrator and nourished the notion of solidarity shared by the participants.

A few additional phrases completed the concise SCA linguistic and reflexive repertoire, particularly the emphasis on the privilege to "share the shit with you" or "take the stuff out." The abstract rhetoric seemed to reflect a general existential condition and standardized types of space and sexual encounters. Slips/acting out and the shit/stuff were also often narrated in a campy style, a common element in gay culture (e.g., Newton 1972). A more direct and laconic reportage of slippage events would undoubtedly have left the listeners deeply depressed. But camp as a genre of narration, with its furious recognition of the incongruity between the public persona and the degraded compulsive self—"You can't save your face and your ass at the same time"—seemed indispensable to this culture. George expressed a wish that men would stop using the subway; Saul suggested removing the stools from tearooms. More evocatively, Saul mixed self-pity with mockery as he described ending up on his knees begging for affection from men who were shut off from emotion.

There was no need for Saul to specify the location of that humiliation, nor for Dani, who had a problem with a certain place he would not name, a place that exemplified the danger he must avoid. Was it a bar? A tearoom? A sauna? A park? A pornography shop with video booths for quick sex? The exact location was beside the point. By itself, the vague hint of dangerous or humiliating circumstances was sufficient to remind the listeners of their own chosen territories of unwarranted sexual engagements. One accidental new-comer, introduced above, found himself very soon describing his situation as "the receptacle of unwanted sperm." He left it to his listeners to add the address, the decor, the identities of the people who show up there (themselves included), and the text of the mostly silent activity that dominates these all too familiar locations.

But apart from terms that divulged their shared predicaments, a few additional expressions revealed the pleasure of their comradeship, the content of the *affection* members exchanged during and outside the meetings. It was also the substance of what they hoped to learn to get "out there."

My own difficulty with remembering and recounting these presenta-tions indicates the similarity in structure, content, style, and language of the narratives. The individual stories were absorbing but though listened to in complete silence and open empathy, they eventually seemed to represent one elementary thematic narration. From this observer's perspective, the Chabad (Hassidic) and SCA meetings were similar: each promoted a cultural text of social identity for a particular constituency that conceived of itself as a minority in American society. Each was also concerned with the production and consumption of cultural messages: the Chabad teachers repeating in concise terms and captivating stories their doctrine about the uniqueness of the "Jewish soul," and the SCA repertoire of "acting-out" scripts.

Leap (1996) discussed the importance of Gay English discourse in gay men's lives and classified its presentation into five types: Gay English as a language of desire, as a format for performative display, as a release from shame, as cooperative discourse, and as a language of risk. However, the repertoire of terms and metaphors used by SCA participants expands the language inventory for a gay discourse relevant to a most sensitive dimension of gay life. It recalls Cameron and Kulick's assertion (2003: 18–19) that language produces the categories that help organize our desires, identities, and sexual practices.

Conclusion

The SCA discourse mostly communicated a fatalistic notion that sexual destiny is fixed and almost impossible to change. Still, members continued to come, to tell their stories, and to listen to their fellow sufferers. "We know we are addicts and we are not going to give up our sexual compulsion, but we help each other, listening and sharing. We have many friends here and have a great time together." The man who told me that verdict early in my observations had no need to do long-term research in order to appreciate the consequences of SCA membership.

My experience of SCA meetings leads me to a different assessment of SCA from that suggested by either its allies or its detractors. It is not an expected cure for sexual behavior that keeps these groups going. Moreover, it seems to me that a "cure," in the clinical sense of the term, is contradictory to the production of communitas, which emerges as the major achievement of SCA group activities. My conclusion negates both the ideological charge that the notion of addiction represents submission to mainstream pressure and the clinicians' doubts that SCA cures. In my view, what cements and nurtures these gatherings and ensures their longevity is the participants' fear of a potential acting out, and their continuing failure, as much as the affectionate rewards that await "slippers." Had the participants gone instead to a professional therapeutic group, they would have indicated a far stronger commitment to change. Instead, by joining the SCA, they proclaim their voluntary association with a society of self-identified addicts, whose membership they enjoy as more rewarding or as complementary to their participation in other gay social groups. Not a few among them acknowledged their inability to change their sexual habits while emphasizing the importance of the friendship ties they developed in those meetings. SCA groups seem to have achieved one goal that other groups I observed still strove for: the promise of generous sociability and a measure of affection. Richard's complaint displayed the expectation of close relationships among SCA members. Most other groups remained far more limited in the scope of their authority to commend, commit, and compensate their membership with the resources of sociability and affection.

Levine and Troiden (1998 [1988]) resented the idea of "sexual compulsion." They considered it a mainstream invention that encouraged gay people to surrender to the doctrine of heterosexual supremacy. True, the emphasis on problematic sexual behavior might seem to other gay constituencies to reflect damaging homophobic prejudices and to confirm the stigma of indiscriminate cruising in notoriously commercialized institutions or public places. But gay sexuality in the post-Stonewall era was not an issue challenged only by mainstream society. Not a few leading gay intellectuals and scholars agonized over the future of homosexual norms and demeanor. They believed gays were destined to develop a new code and ethics for sexual behavior once oppression had ceased to be a major factor in their lives and the cup of ecstatic sexual freedom had been fully consumed (e.g., White 1983; Rotello 1997). As a response to the AIDS epidemic, the growing practice of safe sex was not imposed on gay men by outsiders. The closure of some types of sex institutions by state and municipal authorities was far less effective in changing sexual habits than was the effort of the community to regulate its own behavior.

The emphatic declaration, "These are our synagogues" was suggested to me by a participant who had given up hope for a "cure." However, Richard's perception of his affliction was not implanted by an outside agency. His futile battle against the impulse to act out did not reflect a transformed perception of sexual adventures, spoiled by the new credo of safe sex and a gentrified gay life. Richard was competent enough to comprehend the damage his "addiction" had caused him emotionally and professionally. Far more than a "cure" place, I consider the SCA a gay/lesbian social institution that engages its membership in a performative discourse on sexual behavior and lifestyle. Similar to and probably more than in other associations I attended, the SCA discourse seemed to reveal the subjectivity of gay people expressed in their continuing confrontation with the desire and the objects that define their unique identity.

What could be more gay or lesbian than an open discussion of sex life? The sexuality of modernity as introduced above in my quotations from Giddens (1992) presents some very difficult tests for most people. But how much more challenging have these circumstances been for those whose sexuality, for the first time in Judeo-Christian history, has emerged publicly, though as yet in limited territories and social contexts. We should not forget, for example, how many centuries it took European/Christian society to institutionalize heterosexual marriage and its corollary rules, sexual mores included (e.g., Ariès 1985).

My conclusions on the nature of the SCA meetings and its impact on the life of its participants seem to reflect my impressions in the previous chapter. Even more, the SCA members shared with their fellow participants a degree of intimacy we usually assume to be revealed only in a private therapeutic/medical session. They stood with no mask, emotionally naked, before a mixed crowd of acquaintances (some of whom had become friends through participation) and strangers (who might be attending for the first time). However, they had no doubt they could rely on the empathy and unconditional affection of many participants. Although reporting about an apparently degrading experience, the ambience of sharing removed the individual narrator from his/her stigmatizing private position to become a member of a constituency claiming an identity that deserved public recognition. The SCA organization gained public respect in the gay community, and its meetings seemed to resemble denominational congregations.

Finally, did I betray the privacy of the people I observed at these meetings? I reported earlier about my decision to discontinue observing SCA meetings after a participant close to me expressed his indignation on discovering I did not share the membership's predicaments. I hope that those participants who identify the places and the actors disguised in this text will forgive me for the audacity of intruding upon their meetings. I am tempted to end my presentation by trying to retrieve a feeling that often overcame me when attending these SCA gatherings. Particularly at the Center, the venue of many of these meetings, and where I first discovered these groups, one could regularly hear the applause of SCA and AA participants in packed rooms as they congratulated their members on their qualifications and announced the anniversaries of their recovery plans. That chorus of cheers constantly colored life at the Center, particularly during summer, when open windows carried it throughout the building. Striking a poetic note, I would compare it to the peal of church bells or the echo of the Amen blessings in synagogues. Richard, I believe, would like that metaphor.

CHAPTER 5

In the Company of the Bisexual Circle

I was equally attracted to the Sunday and other meetings of a group of bisexuals, men and women, who also carried out their activities at the Center. Throughout my six-month association with the bisexual group, I was continuously puzzled by the participants' "true" sexual identity. My joining in that group offered me the unexpected opportunity to employ a methodological approach I had applied in my earlier fieldwork projects, namely, the extended case method. This chapter ends with a minidrama enacted by the clique of the "sensual bisexuals," which seemed to encapsulate the sexual and emotional cravings of the wider constituency of participants who claimed a bisexual identity.

I do not consider this particular group, which started at the Center in 1988, as representative of the phenomenon of bisexuality. There were other groups dedicated to bisexuality operating in New York and advertised in the Center newsletter, including a support group at the Center that conducted its meetings also on Sunday, but was organized and facilitated by a trained psychologist. The Bisexual assembly was a social group with no pretense to any therapeutic support. However, I believe my observations add to the growing information available on this subject—a body of literature that is a long way from presenting an unequivocal position on the origins and characteristics of this "new" minority claiming a legitimate space at the table of LGBT society.

The issue of bisexuality, dormant for a very long time, has suddenly come to the fore in recent years. I discovered a growing wave of literature, but only a few social scientists have shown an interest, with not even one anthropologist among them. The discourse on the presentation and meaning of bisexuality seems to have mostly attracted scholars from the humanities (English departments in particular), women's studies, psychotherapists, journalists, and activists. I mention here, for example, the anthologies edited by Weise (1992), Tucker (1995), Hall and Pramaggiore (1996), Beemyn and Eliason (1996), Storr (1999), Williams (1999), and Fox (2004). Nevertheless, the few studies available from social scientists are comprehensive and fairly complementary: *Dual Attraction: Understanding Bisexuality*, by Weinberg, Williams, and Pryor (1994), and *Bisexuality and the Challenge to Lesbian Politics*, by Rust (1995), as well some contributions in the vast volume edited by Rust, *Bisexuality in the United States* (2000). *Dual Attraction* includes material that is closest to my own work. For a few months in 1983, the authors carried out observations of activities offered at the Bisexual Center in San Francisco, where they interviewed about one hundred men and women who defined themselves as bisexuals. They returned in 1988 and again interviewed many of those they had first studied in 1983, though the Bisexual Center itself was no longer in existence. Their project aimed at exploring in general what it was like to be "bisexual" and then at examining how the social, psychological, and sexual profiles of those who so defined themselves compared with those of people with different sexual preferences.

My project was far more limited in scope. I had no intention of studying the major characteristics of sexual preferences—the feelings and behavior— by which one might classify the various types of bisexuality or the changes over- time that individual male and female bisexuals undergo. I wished to explore the consequences and meaning that individuals, men and women, drew from their participation in this particular organization. However, as far as I can judge from the extensive report on San Francisco in *Dual Attraction*, the discussion groups and other activities offered at the Bisexual Center were mostly perceived by its "clients" as therapeutic, and it did not develop into a social center for regulars. Regarding the methodological aspect, although the team of *Dual Attraction* also carried out observations by a method similar to my own, they nevertheless maintained the formal role of researchers. I did not initiate interviews nor did I issue survey questionnaires. For better or worse, I maintained the position of an ordinary participant.

Most writers, coming from different disciplines and from bisexual activists, have emphasized the marginality and the resentment bisexuals have long experienced, ranging from their dismissal in the field of queer theory and professional knowledge to their rejection in daily life and the accusation leveled at them of spreading AIDS. Bisexuals see themselves as twice rejected: by both heterosexuals and homosexuals. Du Plessis (1996), for example, starts his discussion with the story of the bisexuals' removal from the program of the 1991 Gays and Lesbians Rutgers Conference. Pramaggiore (1996) employs the "fence sitters" metaphor to explain the ambivalence toward bisexuals, while Michel (1996) recalls Aesop's fable of the bat, the birds, and the beasts to describe their situation. The bat, who refused to take part in the war between the birds and the beasts, was finally left isolated and alone, neither bird nor beast. Garber (1995: 65–66) eloquently expresses the threat that bisexuality poses for the easy and well accepted binary perception of straight versus entirely gay or lesbian sexual orientations, as well as of its gendered reality. That binary conception serves both heterosexuals and homosexuals well, though for different reasons.

Homosexuals prefer to believe in and claim essentialism as the root of their same-sex preference, whereas heterosexuals are eager to draw clear borders between themselves and all others. The bisexuals, who blur the borders and claim continuing changes in their sexual preference, posit a "fifth column" that terrorizes the sexual and gendered order as well as the shaky status quo so bitterly constructed between straights and gays/lesbians. They seem to challenge the "ethnicity" model that served gays and lesbians in their fight for equal rights. Accepting the legitimacy of bisexuals' claims about the fluidity of the sexual orientation undermines the very basis of the ethnic model built on an assumption of the immutability of homosexual attractions. Literary publications, as well as reported evidence, have noted particular antipathy displayed by lesbians toward female bisexuals (versus the relative tolerance of gay men toward male bisexuals). That specific antagonism is related, inter alia, to the history of the intricate relation between feminism and lesbianism.

The potential antipathy, if not a sense of abhorrence, toward bisexuals, both men and women, can be perceived in classical anthropological terms, as in Mary Douglas's (1966) seminal interpretation of ritual and rules of social impurity that initiate the rejection of human beings or animals that seem to lack socially approved characteristics, in particular when these blur elementary consensual definitions. Bisexuals seem to represent "liminal creatures," in Victor Turner's (1967a) terms. Most societies have invented elaborate processes, rituals, and ceremonies to socialize their young into gendered roles and secure their survival through reproduction in strictly formalized kinship, family, and household arrangements based on clear-cut norms of sexual mating.[1] Bisexuals, however, have apparently never successfully completed that process. They are "stuck" somewhere in a never-finished process compared

with homosexuals, who have also "failed" but have come out with clear attributes of sexuality and whose position in the landscape of social life is less
upsetting because of its stable demarcation.

The emergence of bisexuality seems to challenge the most promising
sociological thesis ever suggested in this field of research, namely, the social
role of the homosexual as posited by McIntosh (1968). The claims for a bisexual identity contradict the assumed homosexual's role in confirming the
master prescription of sexuality and gender in society. Is there a role for the
bisexual beyond challenging the sexual social order? I try to regain a small
piece of that field of research left to the promoters of queer theory whose work
is based on textual analysis as well as to the psychotherapists in particular.

Bisexuals Tell Their Stories

As indicated earlier, I wished to learn how bisexuals presented their situation in a safe environment and what they looked for in the company of
other bisexuals. I was obviously curious about the characteristics of those
who adopt a bisexual identity. As I started to attend meetings regularly, I
soon identified a strong core circle of members. They were men and women
who had been with the group a long time, as well as a few new members
who joined during my own involvement and soon became part of the core.
The meetings on Sunday afternoons were often facilitated, and actually kept
going, by the endless efforts of Hazel, a woman in her mid-forties who looked
much younger. Enthusiastic, dedicated, and often emotional, she was always
on time to welcome everybody, prepare the program, start the round of introductions, collect the three-dollar contributions (to pay for renting the room
and other expenses), and persuade people to go along after the meeting for a
snack, coffee, or meal at a nearby cafeteria, Papas, on Sixth Avenue.

Starting the Sunday round of introductions, Hazel would often repeat
her story relating both to her sexual and professional situation. Although
good looking and educated, life was not easy for her in both spheres. A
trained scientist, she was underpaid in a boring technical job. Her parents
had been unusually supportive when she seemed at a young age to prefer
women, and for about twenty years she considered herself a lesbian. She had
a few longer and shorter affairs with women, but about two years before, she
met a man at work who, for the first time, made her believe she was no less
attracted to men. Hazel liked him immediately, and after a few tormented

days she responded to his persistent advances, which she believed indicated true love. The first meeting was satisfying. The man was well mannered, and they discussed intellectual issues of mutual interest. But at the next meeting the man pressed for sex. That first engagement with a man turned out to be a painful experience. In spite of this traumatic event, and although she had no other congenial sexual experiences with men, from that time Hazel considered herself bisexual. She was ready to meet Mr. or Ms. Right, whoever came first.

Phyllis, another committed participant in her early forties, quite attractive, a teacher, had been married for nearly twenty years. She was in a relationship with another man when she met the first woman she fell in love with. For a long time she thought "I am straight, but I love a woman." Phyllis was equally ready to share her story at every Sunday meeting, which added to the open and intimate atmosphere most first-time visitors appreciated. Of particular stature in the group were Barry and Nancy. They were considered founders of the group, though now they only infrequently attended its meetings. They were both active in other organizations but continued to participate as board members. In their mid- to late fifties, extremely active and friendly, and creative in their professional lives, they had a complex history of marital life and love life. Both were divorced and had children. They first met as lovers but remained close friends and comrades in shared causes. They represented the quintessential bisexuals: proud and sure of their unconventional lifestyle. Their sexual lives, as they openly narrated at most meetings they attended, left no doubt about their ability to become sexually and emotionally involved with both men and women. They served as models in a company of people whose self-presentation often reflected much uncertainty about the overlap of desire and practice, of fancy and reality.

More marginal was Kevin, a pleasant, muscular black man of a light complexion in his mid-thirties. He was dedicated to the group, but it was difficult to make out what he said due to his slight stammer. He was asked to leave the group because he seemed to force himself on a female participant. A few other black men occasionally participated; one of them, James, a young, good-looking artist, was very popular, but he showed up only every few weeks. Black women also visited occasionally but never came regularly.

At a later stage I came to know Shelly, among the founders of the group, who had stopped coming regularly since he was engaged in a disagreement with Barry and Nancy. On his first visit he immediately took a lead. In his early seventies, a self-made man, born in the Lower East Side, he made a very impressive figure—tall, firm, agile, and very persuasive in his opinions. Once one overcame the surprise of his announced age, he could not be ignored or dismissed as being too old to talk about sex. He had been married for many years and had children and grandchildren. He told us that for many years he had been controlled by the women he loved—first his mother, then his wife. But after his wife passed away, he had the freedom to pursue both women and men with whom he could share emotional and physical attachments that were free of formal responsibilities. Shelly, a respectable professional at an age when many seem more concerned with their grandchildren and failing health, treated sex as a sort of a professional analyst, but no less as a man who still acted on his desires.

With the exception of Hazel, all those described above seemed to have had some considerable sexual experience with members of the other sex. Phyllis, Barry, Nancy, and Shelly had all been married for many years. Although they had since experienced same-sex relationships that might have categorized them as gays and lesbians, they still had no doubt they could fall in love and have sex categorized as heterosexual. That claim seemed convincing to the observer.

There were, however, a few other regulars whose life stories and sexual agenda seemed noticeably different. Jim, Hank, and Bruce had all identified as gays for many years. Jim, in his late twenties, looked like the all-American boy, and he immediately attracted attention. After many years in men's company, he felt he missed women. He did not know, as he first confessed, how to approach the other sex. Would he immediately be rejected? His behavior evinced a serious effort to develop a relationship with an attractive female participant, whom he invited home for dinner, but he was equally interested in a young attractive male participant whom he wished "to nail down."

Hank, in his late thirties, was also a masculine and pleasant-looking man who had recently separated from his male lover of seventeen years, whom he had first met at school. Since they had separated, he had mostly engaged in anonymous sex, which left him humiliated and deeply starved for love. He assumed he had given up women partly because for many years he had been completely isolated by the company of his jealous lover. He, as much as Jim, was looking for a congenial place to start a sexual relationship with a woman. But Hank did not stay long with the group. He was also searching for company in other organizations. He was planning to date an attractive female he had met in the bisexual crowd, but he was soon tempted to start a relationship with an older man he met at a Friday gathering of Men of All

Colors Together (MACT, a social group of blacks and whites: see Chapter 6). That recent development was a much easier option that could immediately satisfy his emotional cravings. He soon gave up his attempt to socialize with women and never showed up again. I saw him sometime later in the company of his new lover.

Bruce, in his early forties and engaged in graduate studies for a Ph.D. in history, had been exclusively gay for many years. He attended numerous other activities at the Center. He also felt he missed female company and decided to give it a shot at the bisexual social circle, where he assumed he might learn how to start a relationship with a woman. He had dreamed of having a relationship with a man's head and a woman's body. Friendly and enthusiastic, he soon offered to entertain a group of friends at his apartment, both men and women, with whom he associated at the meetings. (I will later discuss the events leading to that invitation and the meeting at Bruce's place, with which I concluded my observations.)

Another category of participants was the men and women who defined themselves as heterosexuals but who experienced an urge to be involved with a same-sex partner. The older among these were often men and women who had suppressed a gay orientation because of social pressures and the absence of a gay community at the time and place they grew up. But not a few younger people claimed that their urge had developed at a later stage, often after they had married or divorced. Roger was particularly noticeable in this group. In his early thirties, good-looking, but very reserved and in formal attire, he had been married twice and had sex only with women. However, he claimed he felt an attraction to the company of men, but not a sexual desire. It was enough for him "to hang out with men." At a later stage, he expressed a wish for physical contact with men, though he still insisted he had no desire for a sexual affair. He considered himself bisexual even though he claimed he had never acted out a sexual desire with men.

Scott, somewhat effeminate in appearance mainly because he was over-weight, related his past involvement with women but claimed it was easier for him to meet with men. He told us he avoided the bars and other gay sites but looked for men in parking lots close to these establishments. Nevertheless, he still defined himself as heterosexual and "a top-man." At a later meeting, when we were together in a smaller circle, he confessed he was unhappy with these sexual escapades, often asking himself: "What am I doing here?" He was looking for a more congenial new start with men or women. Both Roger and Scott, to the extent that they were looking for sex with men, were reluctant to approach a gay circle and thereby also admit a gay identity. That position brings to mind William's assertion (1999: 3): "studies repeatedly indicate a frequent gap between how people behave sexually and how they identify themselves ideally."

A few men and women were presently engaged with the other sex in marriage or other domestic arrangements. Married women, in particular, occasionally attended and told their stories of discovering that hidden attraction. Sometimes they came back to report about their spouses' reactions to their visit at the Center. Apparently, their men were usually hurt, and the women did not show up much longer after that. A black woman who came only rarely told us her former husband had been jealous of her involvement with two other women, but her present mate accepted her affair with a woman. James, a flamboyant black artist, had a white female partner who was also bisexual. His previous female mates had resented his gay engagements, but his gay boyfriends did not care about his affairs with women because they did not consider sex with women as real sex. Robert, a social worker who presented himself as having a heterosexual lifestyle, told us he decided to attend a meeting "in order to explore." While we walked together after the meeting to the subway station, he told me he felt an attraction to men. He explained that he had no desire to establish a stable relationship with a man, but then qualified his statement by adding that he had not yet met a man he wished to become involved with. He told me he attended the meeting to see other people in the same position and find out how they dealt with it. He never came back.

Ruth, in her late twenties, a woman of striking looks, had been involved with both men and women. She was aware that on the occasions she went out with a man, people often reacted with "What a gorgeous couple!" but when she went out with a woman, she felt they were looked down on as "sleazy." Ruth became very active and initiated a separate group for bisexual women. When questioned about a step that could cause a division between the men and women who seemed to manage so well in the integrated bisexual group, she claimed that women also deserved their own space because men have always dominated women. The poster she prepared to advertise for the new organization showed two women in panties, but no hint of men could be identified in the flier addressed to bisexual women.

At a few Sunday meetings, I observed a young heterosexual couple who had been dating about two years and were planning to move out of their separate apartments and live together. They came now because the woman felt she was also attracted to women. Although she first told us she had never acted out that fantasy, they were both aware that as long as she did not test her true feelings their relationship might eventually suffer. At that stage her boyfriend preferred that she find a woman he knew as well, instead of her exploring with strangers, which might arouse his jealousy. Of course there were other problems potentially threatening their bond; for example, what would they do if the woman she got involved with would wish to live with them or if he disliked the woman? The next Sunday, however, the young man told us that since his girlfriend expressed her sexual fantasies and hesitations, he had also started to question his own relationships with men. He discovered that he had actually given up most of his friends, the gay men in particular, whom he felt were mostly interested in sleazy sex. He now realized that he missed a serious and intimate relationship with men. He wished he could find a good male friend. In any case, he argued, he never jumped immediately into bed even with women—it took him a few months of developing an intimate relationship before he was ready for sex with a woman. His girlfriend then told us she had actually once started a relationship with a woman but that they had broken up because of class disparities. This story, implying the potential influence of economic gaps between people who start a relationship with strangers, raised many comments and shared experiences from other participants. We were now actually discussing the American class structure.

The couple's story, as it concerned bisexual urges, was not unique. I attended another meeting when a very eloquent female Ph.D. student at a leading university told us she was dating a man and they wanted to get married. However, knowing that she was also occasionally attracted to women, she looked for advice. What was best to do? Wouldn't the attraction show up one day in force and destroy her forthcoming family relationship?

At most meetings there were also less congruous stories or surprising confessions introduced by newcomers, some of whom attended more regularly for a while. There were disclosures by men, in particular, who had never had sex; they had remained celibate because of the AIDS scare or because of other strange experiences. No one ever displayed intolerance, even when the speaker seemed somewhat odd and incoherent. The veteran regulars seemed particularly attuned to the feelings of newcomers. Just as they were ready to repeat their own stories, which must have been too boringly familiar to their close friends, they were ready to listen to the visitors' stories. Nancy once told me how essential it was to attend the meetings regularly: "It is critically important for people who come for the first time and who need to meet guys

in a similar situation that there be those around who can welcome and understand them." The veteran regulars enjoyed the meetings that offered them an
opportunity to see old friends, establish new friendships, and probably find
lovers. They were curious at meeting other people who shared the difficulties
and the pleasures of bisexuality, but they also had a mission of their own
making. That sense of mission often seemed to override other intentions and
gratifications, but it also seemed to buttress their own convictions about the
bisexual identity.

In addition to the great variety in the history of their sexual lives, the participants were also widely diverse in age. Even though the majority seemed
to be in their thirties and forties, some were younger, some older. Most participants were whites, although Latino and black men and women were often
present and a few became more regular attendees. The proportion of Jews
was considerable, sometimes amounting to nearly half the participants. The
population profile of the San Francisco group, as reported in *Dual Attraction*,
contained more Protestants and was almost exclusively white.

The great variety of existential situations and presentation of self that were
encountered at every meeting seemed to fascinate the more perceptive participants, who expressed their astonishment and satisfaction with the group.
Phyllis said: "How wonderful to come here. Everyone has his story—where
he came to us from—the gay world, the heterosexual world, whatever." These
expressions followed the weekly round of introductions, as well as the discussions that had mostly centered on the nature and the main presentations
of bisexuality in daily life. A basic question familiar to gays and lesbians had
been the classic one, as if inherited from the old anthropological Boasian theoretical discourse about the roots of social behavior: "Is bisexuality the product of 'nature or nurture'?" However, while in my previous experience most
gays insisted it was nature that made people homosexuals, opinions were
divided in the bisexual group. Kevin once expressed a position supported by
many: there is an innate potential designed by nature, but its realization is
conditioned by circumstances.

To my direct question about a definition of bisexuality, Barry responded
that he had a definition only for the two extremes of the scale, which actually
described a minority: the fully heterosexuals and homosexuals. All others
were more or less between these extremes and were attracted also to their own
sex but would not admit it. He used as an example the Israeli kibbutz, where
apparently there are no homosexuals. He believed that this apparent nonex-
istence displayed only the power of society to enforce its plans and ethos on

its members. He told me he had given up all his heterosexual friends who were unable to comprehend his sexual orientation. Later, during the ongoing discussion, Barry, supported by Nancy, argued: "There is no one definition for bisexuality, and in this room everyone is different!"

But the issue of a definition was never laid to rest. When a newcomer, a young woman seated next to me, burst out, clearly agitated, "Why all that endless pondering with a definition?" Hazel responded that society was forcing labels on everything, therefore the group was also engaged in a search for definition, but, she went on, "We are the most flexible group on the Kinsey scale." At that point, Rose, a veteran member who showed up infrequently, told her story. She had never been monogamous, although she had had long-standing relationships with men. Now she was trying out a monogamous relationship with a woman (who actually perceived herself as heterosexual). How should she identify herself? She returned to Hazel's argument as she announced: "I have moved along the Kinsey scale from heterosexuality to lesbianism, back and forth. What is the definition fitting me!?"

Another frequent discussion evolved as somebody new would ask: "Can one have relationships with a man and a woman at the same time?" Nancy once responded: "It is the potential, not the practice," and she went on: "You can love both Chinese and Indian food, but does it mean you have to eat Chinese and Indian dishes at the same meal?" Roger offered another example: a man who keeps the rules of kosher food but is attracted to bacon and sometimes succumbs to his temptation and eats pork can still return to his kosher food. Roger's metaphor suggested bisexuality as a sideline, not as a permanent state of mind and sexuality. At another meeting, Roger raised the question whether bisexuality meant a physical attraction and an emotional relationship equally with both men and women. He was not sure about that himself.

Phyllis, who had already experienced relationships with both men and women (sometimes concurrently), responded that in real life people pragmatically chose one way or the other; but, she continued, that did not mean they became homosexual or monosexual. Shelly, the "guru," claimed that be it with a man or a woman, he could never differentiate the physical from the emotional. Rosanne, who was much liked in the group for her eloquence, warmth, and good looks, supported Shelly's statement as she revealed the tension she often experienced with close female friends. Since these were frequently heterosexual women, she had to be very careful not to overstep the border between emotional attachment and physical attraction. Once she had not been careful and had ruined the relationship. Her words seemed to leave a strong impression on both men and women, who shared her feelings. On that occasion, Rosanne expressed her own need to attend meetings because she could be in the company of people she could feel close to. At the end of the meeting, Rosanne and Shelly affectionately embraced each other.

Roger was instrumental in raising another frequent issue: How does a man who has mostly experienced relationships and sex with women start relationships with men? A simple answer often suggested was "Exactly as you do it with women!" But Roger disagreed. It might take him months until he got to bed with a woman, while it was well known that gay men were mostly interested in sex and got to it immediately, and this was why he avoided gay establishments. Nancy offered an explanation for the different behavior of men and women. Women were socialized to say "No!" otherwise they were considered "sluts," but men had been trained to be sexually aggressive, "to be a stud."

The group's position as stated by the regulars, who presented an "undefined definition"—a sort of a kaleidoscopic perception of bisexuality—was highlighted when compared (by the participants) with that apparently suggested by the psychologist who facilitated the support group that seemed to be competing with their own meetings. According to reports told by the veterans, but no less by newcomers, his definition of bisexuality was far narrower. Roger, who once attended the support group, related an unpleasant encounter with the facilitator. When the latter asked him what his definition of bisexuality was, Roger responded that everyone was more or less potentially bisexual and cited the Kinsey Reports as evidence. The facilitator rejected that idea and claimed that only 15 percent of the population were potentially bisexual. Moreover, when Roger told him he considered himself bisexual although he had not had sex with men, the facilitator recommended he seek therapy. A woman who came a week after she, too, had attended the psychologist's support group told us she came out shattered because he claimed bisexuals were unable to maintain a monogamous relationship. He also argued that when they were with a woman, they yearned for a man, and vice versa. The veteran regulars resented the professional therapeutic orientation that had been introduced in the other group. Not having attended the support group, I can only rely on the reports and reactions I observed at the bisexual social group. I avoided attending the support group to escape embarrassment or faking an identity, since the facilitator was known for his inquisitive manner.

The fate of bisexuals was a leitmotif at most meetings. "We are the marginals' marginals," Nancy claimed once; "The lesbians resent us, and the men [heterosexuals], once they discover we're bisexual, don't take us seriously anymore." Hazel suggested that bisexuals raise heterosexuals' anxiety in much the same way as the discomfort and alarm they experience watching somebody in a wheelchair: "When people see the crippled, they fear they might also be injured in a road accident and be crippled themselves," Hazel said. "So, for the heterosexual who discovers that his neighbor or colleague, the good looking father of three children, is attracted to men, and taken by surprise, it evokes the anxiety that he might also have a similar inclination!"

A newcomer, who elaborated on the resentment expressed by homosexuals for bisexuals, as well as the loathing of heterosexuals, concluded that he wished there was a pill to transform him either to full-fledged homosexuality or heterosexuality. "It is better to choose between right and left rather than get stuck in the middle," he said. He would have taken the consequences, be it gay or straight. He insisted that he would be unhappy to relinquish his right to a "dual attraction," but were he forced to choose, he would prefer being gay. To that he added another complaint—there is a clear manual of behavior for gays, lesbians, and straights, but where is the manual to guide bisexuals?

Many other participants concurred with the last speaker and told of the unpleasant reactions they experienced once their bisexuality was revealed. Barry showed an article he clipped from a newspaper that disparaged bisexuals who apparently enjoyed both worlds and could not be monogamous. Hazel, who as facilitator felt she had to make a final statement—probably on my account, likened their situation to the fate of another group she had learned about on a visit to Israel. She referred to Israeli emigrants, disparagingly nicknamed Yordim "because they are considered traitors; they were with us, but betrayed us and moved away." The same was felt about bisexuals, the defectors from the heterosexual tribe.

The assumption that bisexuals could not be monogamous was often brought up, raising bitter resentment or humor. "If I like both blue-eyed and black-eyed people, does it mean I can't be monogamous?" "If I like somebody, does it mean I am immediately unfaithful to my lover?" "Does commitment mean you stop breathing?" These were some of the reactions to the belittling stereotypes apparently held by heterosexuals, but also by homosexuals (lesbians in particular).

On other occasions the atmosphere of the group was more cheerful. Shelly, in particular, always had a far more optimistic view. He related his affair with a married French man who was a great lover. When Shelly told him he must be bisexual, the guy responded, "No, I am sexual." At that point somebody else added: "We bisexuals are more complete!" Ruth was less enthusiastic about that statement. She argued they should be careful not to develop an arrogant position reminiscent of the heterosexual conviction that they are more complete than all others.

Occasionally somebody would suggest socializing after the meeting at the nearby restaurant. One Sunday, James suggested seeing a film. Hank, Robin, and James went along (and so did I). Roger, Kevin, and Hazel were invited to join us, but they opted out due to other engagements. In the meantime, we learned that Robin (a newcomer from South Africa) usually avoided gay bars because he assumed that gays in such places acted in an effeminate manner. We decided to show him a gay bar so he could see for himself what they were like. As we walked there, Hank told us about his habit of visiting the porn theaters in the Village, where despite his own disgust, he allowed strangers to engage him in anonymous oral sex. Hank, who seemed attractive, educated, and eloquent, thus openly expressed a deep frustration with his present situation, which made him look for company in sleazy places and ended up in anonymous sex. He told us that at the bisexual group he developed an attraction to a young, good-looking female participant, but unfortunately, coming from a heterosexual lifestyle, she was more interested in finding a woman. In any case, Hank assumed it would be easier to start a relationship with a bisexual woman than to succeed with women from the straight milieu.

This outing, which lacked any erotic involvement, revealed a deep intimacy experienced among complete strangers. It seemed to display the other face of anonymous relationships so close to the notorious gay scene beside the Hudson River. At that point, the bisexual matrix that brought us together proved wholly irrelevant. I was particularly impressed by that impromptu harmony between strangers.

Great disappointment awaited an activity that was expected to recruit a large crowd of bisexuals. In a recent newsletter, the bisexual group advertised a Cocktail Time for Bis to Meet Bis at an elegant Village bar in the early evening hours of 7:45 to 9:45 p.m. Hazel and Phyllis expected more than fifty people to come, but only six showed up, including Shelly, Roger, myself, and a man who had attended the previous Sunday meeting for the first time. We did not discuss the failed event much. It was considered mainly a failure of advertising. For example, it was not announced as planned in the *Village Voice*.

Acting Out a Bisexual Fantasy—"The Sensual Bisexuals"

A few weeks later, at a regular Sunday meeting, the group seemed at last about to fulfill its most cherished promise—to bring together men and women to initiate and consummate the experience of emotional and physical communitas. It all started during the get-together that followed the formal meeting. As we were talking around the table at Papas, the nearby restaurant, Bruce expressed his desire to take part in a group whose members were able to display and share physical affection without necessarily exhibiting sexual lust. Shelly and Jane immediately reacted enthusiastically, and Shelly told some stories of his past experiences with nude and massage groups. Roger came up with some sexual fantasies about men and women together in one bed, and Jane laughingly confessed she also imagined sexual fantasies but didn't dare let them happen. Now Bruce and Roger were arguing: why not realize our fantasies? What are the forces that prevent people from implementing their fantasies? Bruce's first "wild" idea attracted serious consideration. Roger was pushing to go ahead and suggested screening erotic (though not pornographic) films. Bruce repeated his wish to be able to hug and feel physical intimacy with other people. He did not specify a sexual preference. He commented to me that we had lost the ability to feel comfortable with our nudity in the company of other people and particularly with people of different ages.

Leaving for home, five of us got into Shelly's car. Ruth promised to prepare a list of names and phone numbers of the more active members in order to proceed with future events. I noticed that Roger and Bruce were touching each other's knee though in a restrained friendly manner. Somebody pointed out that we were evolving into a separate group, but that was considered OK (particularly since Shelly was among us). Roger argued critically that there were already those at the regular weekly meetings, Hazel included, who had actually used that forum as an opportunity to work out their personal problems. In a happy mood, suggestions were raised for names for our group: The Deviant Bisexuals, The Sensual Bisexuals, The Creative Bisexuals. Bruce now suggested having the first event for the new group at his Long Island residence. It was decided to meet for dinner the next Saturday in order to rethink and prepare for the event on a Saturday one or two weeks after that.

But the next Saturday evening, I felt it was all really a fantasy. Only Shelly arrived at the meeting place. We waited a long hour before departing for dinner. Bruce and Roger did not show up, nor did Jane, who was out of town and relied on the other four to prepare the event. Shelly was very angry, but I assumed that Roger and Bruce had had their own affair.

However, at the next regular meeting, I learned that the Saturday rendezvous had failed due to a wrong address (I still believed that although it happened by accident, that mix-up might have enabled Roger and Bruce to meet more intimately). In any case, Bruce had already invited the core group of the Sensual Bisexuals and a few other candidates to come along the following Saturday to spend an evening at his place. I identified in his list Shelly, Roger, Jim, Erik, myself, Jane, and two other women who had attended the meeting that evening. As it turned out, Bruce did not invite anyone from the formal leadership of the group. Except for Shelly, it was mostly a circle of newcomers, particularly those who had never complained about their predicaments and were not already too closely related as friends and organizers. Bruce wanted to build a group of "normals," relatively adjusted and presentable folks. Even Shelly, the oldest man in the group, suited that picture of well-being, of enthusiastic, adventurous, and hopeful people. Shelly represented the quintessential role model for the group. He had no regrets about his past life; he had a continuing successful career, loved his family, was in good health, and acted upon his desires with no inhibition and with both men and women. He stood out among the founders of the bisexual group in his eloquent and coherent positions concerning the theory and practice of bisexuality. He stood apart as a maverick, a tireless rebel, and behaving young despite his advanced age, and thus he added a sense of security and respectability to the new venture.

The next Saturday I arrived at Bruce's apartment in a manicured Long Island neighborhood, away from Manhattan's gay concentrations. The apartment was nicely decorated and had many books related to Bruce's professional interests. His guests included Shelly, Jim, Larry (a man in his mid-twenties), myself, and Ellen, a woman in her early thirties, whom I met for the first time. Larry and Ellen attended the meetings at the Center only irregularly. Other participants who were on Bruce's list and who were among the founders of the Sensual Bisexuals, Roger and Jane in particular, could not attend or opted out for other unspecified reasons. Altogether, we were five men and one woman who got together to initiate Bruce's fantasy of affection and intimacy.

Shelly and Ellen had planned the program of the meeting. Ellen had prepared a list of questions for discussion, for example, what would you do if somebody you love (a man or a woman) lived elsewhere and to join him you must leave behind family and friends? Another more relevant question: what was the participants' first priority, men or women? Shelly responded that in recent years he was leaning more toward men. Jim, not answering directly, expressed his wish for a world where one could freely choose men or women according to one's immediate urge. Larry related a recent experience with a couple of friends who had come to visit him with their baby when he was on a business trip and staying at a guest house close to their town. They stayed overnight and shared the king-size bed. It was a wonderful adventure. But he also had another story: he had gone to a movie with a friend from work, a "he-man" in looks and demeanor. When during some erotic scenes the guy leaned a bit against him, he did not dare move for fear of being rejected.

Bruce reported that in his fantasies he moved between a man and a woman. Ellen claimed she had never really had a relationship with a woman but had mostly been involved with men, and she was looking forward to having sex with a woman. She claimed that men's erotic behavior lacked affection. She thought that women could better understand other women, but those with these inclinations were mostly the lesbians one could meet more easily than bisexual women. Bruce agreed with her and also lamented the insufficient affection he had experienced so often with men. He thought that the deficiency started with his father, who never displayed warmth toward his young son. He reminded us of his original idea for their first meeting: to indulge in mutual affection.

Now Bruce's collection of pornographic films was discovered and caused much excitement. Larry announced that he was tired and took his rest on the carpet. Shelly offered him a massage and was telling us about his own female and male masseurs. He even had with him poems written by his admired massage therapist—a black man—who sometimes also offered sexual services. The atmosphere was getting more erotic when Ellen expressed an interest in meeting the attractive poet. We ordered Chinese food and were watching a porno film when Shelly, who had commented before that nothing exciting was really happening, made the move that most others were expecting but were too shy to initiate themselves. He asked if anyone was interested in getting physically close. Ellen and I remained silent and stayed seated somewhat removed from the others, who got closer to each other as they watched the porn. Larry expressed his excitement and seemed to start masturbating under the blanket spread over his legs. Sitting next to Shelly, it was clear that Larry was now also being gently massaged by our older mentor. Bruce joined the motion as he took a seat close to Shelly, who also massaged his head as Bruce himself gently stroked Jim, who was seated close to him. Ellen was now seated close to Bruce, who had his arm affectionately about her shoulder, and I had Jim putting his arm gently over my knee. But only Shelly and Larry were more explicitly engaged in sexual activity, whereas the rest seemed to display Bruce's original desire for affection.

I could not determine to what extent Ellen's presence had restrained the erotic atmosphere. She herself seemed reserved, as if representing the anthropologist's mate. However, her presence seemed important, since it supported the participants' self-presentation as bisexuals. I wonder what would have happened had Ellen not been the only woman present. I believe that Jane, for example, would not have adopted a passive role. Actually, a few commented disappointedly on her absence. Ellen was also not particularly attractive— tall, very slim, somewhat "bookish" and severe-looking, she compared poorly with Jane's more feminine and provocative appearance and style. Before we left for home, Shelly and Bruce voiced their wish to institutionalize this type of meeting and invite other members to join them.

As we were on our way back to Manhattan, waiting for a late night train, Jim told me what he was thinking: why could kittens cuddle together, while human beings, the most developed animals on earth, were unable to show that act of affection. He also told me that earlier that evening he wanted to suggest that we all move to the other room, get together in bed, and cuddle affectionately. He told me that Jane visited him at home, but he also mentioned again his desire to "put his hands on Erik" and went on to describe Bruce as one who urgently needed to "be laid." The messages I got at that late hour on a deserted train platform were indeed very mixed: gay, bisexual, and a clear call for affectionate relationships.

However, at the next day's Sunday meeting, no one mentioned the previous night's event at Bruce's place. Twenty men and women attended, including ten of the main core and a few other familiar faces. During the go-around, Jane, who had missed the previous day's gathering, told us she had just come back from a national convention for police officers. Assuming she would spend most of the time in the company of macho men, she had not imagined that she might encounter an interesting woman of similar orientation, though that was exactly what happened. They had a wonderful time together. Jane now concluded that spending all day at work in a male macho society, she seemed to prefer women's company for relaxing after work. This is why she was often drawn to end a long day of work in a lesbian bar. Barry, who dominated the meeting, argued that in real life there is a deep division between men and women: men are more oriented toward sex, they are "sex hunters," whereas women are more romantic in their relationships and expectations. The question was therefore how to integrate these two desires and appetites, and that, he suggested, was probably the root of their "dual attraction."

On our way to Papas, Jim caught up with Jane. As I walked behind them, I could hear him telling her about yesterday's meeting at Bruce's place. He told her how much he enjoyed the "snuggling" and how much he envied the cats who could do it without training, whereas man, the glory of creation, lacked that most elementary skill. I later spoke to a newcomer, Julio, a computer expert, who claimed that he had been mostly involved with men but also wished to get involved with women. I asked his opinion about the meeting and, more specifically, what had he learned that day. He responded that he was "confused," but he also felt that some descriptions raised at the meeting were very familiar in his own experience, particularly Barry's claim that men were sexual predators, whereas women were more inclined to love and affection.

The four of us stayed on at the restaurant after the others had left and had a lively conversation on various subjects, from the politics of AIDS to literature, computers, etc. While occasional visitors were sometimes difficult to understand, on the whole most of the core group, as well as most of the infrequent attendees, were educated and worked at various professional, artistic, and other white-collar occupations. Regardless of the sexual agenda, one could feel comfortable and often spend a nice afternoon in the company of pleasant and intellectually stimulating strangers.

I soon left New York, but as far as I know, this was the last meeting of the Sensual Bisexuals. Bruce was before long engaged with other groups in the Center and the intimate circle he initiated quietly evaporated. I met him a few years later at a meeting organized at the Center by Dignity House dedicated to discussions on various political and intellectual issues related to gay identity. He was still looking for a more satisfactory social environment, though obviously also scouring the opportunities offered at the Center to meet potential partners for love and sex.

Confronting the Bisexual Riddle

One is naturally puzzled, if not somewhat confused, about the sexual identity of the participants described above. What are the indicators one can suggest to confirm the validity of their claim for bisexuality? Moreover, why is an identity label so important for people who decided they were bisexual, often on the basis of some fleeting attraction or an unsatisfactory liaison? Certainly, a considerable number of participants acknowledged they were gays or lesbians (actually more men than women) who were trying to find a new outlet for their sexuality. In this category I have described, for example, Hank, Jim, Bruce, and Hazel. Another group consisted of the married or otherwise heterosexually engaged men and women who wished to experience a long-suppressed or newly discovered urge to have a same-sex relationship, like the young couple who attended a few meetings or Robert who attended only one meeting. Close to them, if not identical, were the men and women who were presently free of a committed heterosexual relationship and who had defined themselves as heterosexuals but who now also wished to experiment with a same-sex relationship. Roger, Jane, and Rosanne are good examples of that category. A minority, though mostly members of the veteran core group, appeared to have comfortably engaged in bisexual sex. This describes Nancy, Barry, Phyllis, James, Ruth, Rose, and Shelly. However, more women seemed to have experienced sex with men than men had with women.

On the whole, my observations reveal much similarity to some major demographic characteristics of the bisexuals described by the authors of *Dual Attraction*. I can also affirm their conclusion that "unlike being heterosexual or homosexual, there is no predominant sexual profile that described most of those who adopt the label 'bisexuals'" (Weinberg et al. 1994: 154). The information the participants divulged about themselves ranged from almost exclusive homosexuality to heterosexuals who had never experienced a same-sex erotic relationship. However, more women in the San Francisco research had sex also with men. In the New York group, although many women had experienced heterosexual sex in earlier years, they were mostly involved with women at the time of my study.

Weinberg et al. focused on the role of social scientists in revealing the social factors or circumstances that encourage or restrain the potential of a bisexual orientation and showed the changes over time (from 1983 to 1988) among the people they studied in San Francisco. Under the impact of AIDS, they concluded, many of the men and women had been drawn either to the heterosexual or the homosexual fields of sexual preference. My observations cannot display changes over a long period. I could only observe the cravings and "actual" behavior as displayed over a short period of time.

Already in 1983, the bisexual men and women studied in San Francisco reported more sexual encounters with men. As the authors interpreted it, men were more easily available as sexual partners for both men and women. Gay sex in particular could be easily obtained at the many establishments still operating, even in the AIDS era of the late 1980s and early 1990s. Lesbians never had as many meeting places and organizations as gay men, which explains their better chances of meeting heterosexual or bisexual men. Also in New York, Hank, who so wished to leave the gay scene (of anonymous sex in particular), is a good example of that observation. He started to attend the bisexual group activities regularly but was soon involved with a man he met at his first Friday visit to another group at the Center. That appeared much easier than beginning a relationship with a woman, bisexual or heterosexual.

On the whole, one (the anthropologist at least) could not deny the overwhelming impression that most attendees had a better experience or a stronger attraction to same-sex relationships. Their experiences with same-sex partners were more vividly reported, and the social relationships that evolved in the group were mainly same-sex bonds. Bisexual experiences were less compellingly displayed and often related as past relationships, particularly by those who were divorced. The few events that were supposed to implement the group's ethos failed or ended up with a same-sex ambience. The party at Bruce's place is most revealing. The women and a few men among the organizers did not show up. Were they suddenly uncomfortable when they had to act out their fantasies instead of just talking about them? In any case, in the absence of most women the event was almost inevitably dominated by a gay male atmosphere.

Most scholars and other writers, as well as the participants themselves, have described bisexuals as stigmatized and rejected on all fronts—by the heterosexual, the gay, and the lesbian. Repeating an opening query, why then did the people described above, who were mostly educated, employed, of all ages, and "adjustable" by any visible criterion, choose to attend these meetings and claim a bisexual identity? If apparently gay or lesbian identities are more tolerated by heterosexuals and homosexuals alike, and since they could more easily find mates for friendship and sex in all gay/lesbian organizations, what made these people spend their time with the bisexual group? Why look for gays and lesbians, or for the opposite sex, in a group that might never offer a "good" choice compared with that available in same-sex institutions or in heterosexual bars?

Except for AA and other groups dedicated to addictive behavior or the town meetings, the bisexual group was the only one I attended at the Center that maintained equal membership of males and females. Women were present also in some other groups, but their numbers were small (see Chapter 4). Most regular meetings at the Center were exclusively male or female. The bisexual group was very different in the sense that it represented an amicable place for the meeting of both sexes at a site where most other meetings were immediately marked as gay or lesbian. But at the same time it was also a gay and a lesbian space, because many, if not the majority, of its regular participants and many casual visitors were well acquainted with the gay/lesbian world and had also attended other gay/lesbian groups on the same premises.

The bisexual group offered a safe entrance to the Center for those who had been searching for their "true" sexual identity and were eager to start exploring the Center. It offered a new place also for those acquainted with the Center but who wanted to get away from the familiar gay/lesbian crowd. Bruce, who had little chance to change his sexual habits, could nevertheless entertain the idea of finding a mate for friendship or sex regardless of the guy's announced sexual identity. Roger was no less eager for an affair, perhaps even more so with a male partner. However, it was far easier for him to start a relationship with a man he met at a bisexual group than attend an exclusively gay organization. He was not yet ready for that. He might have been far more hesitant to approach Bruce, an openly gay man, had it been an exclusively gay environment.

The above interpretation might present the bisexual group as cover or disguise for many people who were too embarrassed to acknowledge their gay or lesbian preferences. Even if that were true for some, declaring themselves bisexual was not a purely pretense. These men and women were anxious to leave the door open to the possibility of becoming involved, physically or emotionally, with an attractive other-sex candidate. But Bruce's party also indicated another terrain of feelings and desire: the search for affection. True, the argument and complaints about men's insensitive search for sex, devoid of affection, were not new. But why among the bisexuals, whatever their "valid" identity, was there an attempt to try to transform these habits and experiment with a more compassionate style of sexuality? Why the disguise of bisexuality to escape from casual or anonymous sex?

I return here to the query I posited earlier concerning the bisexual role. The publication of the first Kinsey Report (1948) undoubtedly carried dramatic consequences that supported the demands made by homosexuals for public recognition of their status as individuals and as a collectivity. But surprisingly, that revolutionary scientific manifesto made little impact on the development of a strong bisexual movement. Common wisdom or protagonists of a bisexual identity might naturally relate that phenomenon to the severe constraints initiated by the more powerful sexual constituencies, of both the heterosexuals and homosexuals. However, the ethnographic evidence, though limited in scope, displayed a great confusion of sexual presentations and of erotic expectations among those who claimed a bisexual identity. The participants who related their recent experiences or demonstrated a desire to experiment with a new sexual orientation had practically given up, at least temporarily, their previously announced sexual preference. Moreover, in most cases they seemed also to have moved closer to the homosexual matrix.

A Foucault disciple, I assume, would argue that these observations exhibit the pressures exerted by mainstream society, which maintains the sexual status quo of a dominant heterosexual majority versus a tolerated homosexual minority. But whatever the structural constraints, my observations, as well as those reported from San Francisco, indicate that the obscure category of bisexuals seems to facilitate the process of learning about and integration into the world of nonconformist sexuality, homosexuality in particular. At the same time, the bisexual venue, regardless of its institutional efficacy, seems also to blur the apparently unequivocally assumed characteristics, presentations, and behavior that construct the hegemonic hetero/homo division and public discourse. Ironically, it is mostly in societies that deny the role of the homosexual, such as in South America or in Muslim societies, that erotic bisexual gratification, among men in particular, seems far more prevalent and, to an extent, tolerated.[2]

I cannot avoid drawing the conclusion that the equal presence of both men and women inevitably played an important part also in the learning process of acquiring the skills to express homosexual or, though less frequently, heterosexual desires. Bruce's pleading for affection immediately garnered the support of women who had often complained about the lack of affection in men's sexuality. His call was appealing to women looking for a more congenial sexual and emotional experiment with both men and women. He equally gained an enthusiastic response from men who had sought out the bisexual group seemingly because they were already exhausted and emotionally frustrated with the gay scene of casual and anonymous sex. He was no less congratulated by men who were too hesitant to experiment or to start a gay career in the more ordinary scene of male gay life either outside or inside the Center.

The easy availability of casual sex in male gay society has been explained variously: as a response to the denial and persecution of male sexual bonding that has led to the separation of sex and intimacy; as enabling the full expansion and joy of free eroticism; as instrumental in the building of male bonding free of the boundaries of class, age, race and education; and as instrumental in the building of the gay community (e.g., Altman 1986; Seidman 1991: 157–91; Newton 1993). However, gay men have often also been described as representing an insoluble contradiction: frantically sexual in their actual behavior but romantic and emotional in their sexual dreams (e.g., Seidman 1991: 170–71). The bisexual circle—ephemeral in its operation (as also reported in *Dual Attraction*) and sometimes feeble in its members' assertion of their dual attraction—nevertheless seemed to offer the opportunity to combine the two faces of their sexual persona: actions and dreams. Regardless of the elusiveness of the "true" personal identities and sexual desires proclaimed by the participants, one could not dismiss the ambience of freedom and mutual confidence to express contradictory self-descriptions as well as the generosity of the listeners who served as flattering mirrors to men and women trapped in the predicament of unhappy sexual relationships and confused erotic attractions.

Recalling the SCA participants, who assembled to convey their degrading experiences and share their stigmatized standing even among other homosexuals, the participants who claimed a bisexual identity equally represented a problematic existential position in both homosexual and heterosexual societies. However, sharing with others their unresolved self-identity predicament seemed to offer them a sense of legitimacy in their display of "bisexual identity" as a viable and "true" presentation of social reality.

Endnote

Since the 1970s, for better or for worse, bisexuality has become a publicly recognized phenomenon. Its protagonists have also gradually but successfully gained a prominent seat in the politics and the logo of GLBT society. However, the study of bisexuality is a difficult task, as evidenced by the various disciplines involved in that subject. We need a far wider scope of ethnographic evidence to suggest a more authoritative assertion "from the anthropologist's point of view" about that type of human sexual behavior and its presentation in contemporary society, as well as the social and cultural conditions that stimulate or suppress its various manifestations. What else could better realize the visions of the prophets of "postmodern society" at the turn of the twenty-first century? However, while ethnographic research in that field of behavior is a tempting mission to undertake, what is possible to accomplish beyond the very limited opportunities that my own and earlier researchers have illustrated remains to be seen.

CHAPTER 6

The Interracial Gay Men's Association: Men of All Colors Together

Once I was Black
Proudly embraced
Then I loved a man who was white
I would be defined as different
No longer fully embraced
Black with an asterisk
This was my fate

—Tony Glover (1993)

The membership of Men of All Colors Together (MACT), an interracial association, also gathered once a week. However, its meetings on a weekend evening and at a later hour (8:00 p.m.) enhanced the potentialities of that group as a site for sociability and entertainment. The participants, by and large, almost equally represented "blacks" and "whites," though a few were Latino of different skin shades or others of mixed ethnic origin. The proportion of whites versus blacks varied at each meeting, but the attendance of blacks or whites had never been less than a third at all events. There were usually twenty to forty participants, the lowest attendance often being at the last monthly meeting, which was assigned to newsletter mailing. That one rarely recruited more than fifteen attendees.

Sexual/romantic attraction among members of different races, heterosexuals and homosexuals alike, is not surprising in a multiethnic society. This fascination has been related, in particular, by novelists and playwrights (as far back as Shakespeare's *Othello*). But this erotic/romantic desire carries a particular, sensitive implication in America. I mention only James Baldwin, who in *Another Country* (1962) describes most evocatively this powerful fascination and passion—both heterosexual and homosexual—as basic to the construction of American society, representing one of the most serious yet enticing violations of social taboos. His narrative about homosexual attraction culminated in two of the most profound breaches of identity categories possible: the sexual and the racial.

Gay identity is less conspicuous in same-race, same-sex bonding, while the more visible gay interracial mating carries greater stigma in a society that is both racial and homophobic. Although we have no statistics for the frequency of interracial gay couples, other reports and representations portray the attraction between and the bonding of white and black men. Among literary works, antislavery literature first eroticized black men and generated a sentimentalist vocabulary of benevolence, affection, and intimacy (Saillant 1999). In the visual arts, Mapplethorpe's pictures have greatly contributed to the eroticization of black men. Gay folklore has invented particular stereotypes, for example, "snow queens" (blacks attracted to whites), and "dinge queens" (whites attracted to blacks).

Research on black gays in the United States remains marginal in gay studies. It reveals, however, that their position is far more difficult than that of white gays. Most reporters claim they have to confront both a homophobic black society and a racist white gay community (e.g., Peterson 1992; Boykin 1996). Hawkeswood's ethnography (1996) focuses mainly on gay men in Harlem who prefer to socialize in their home neighborhood: he defines them as "black gays" rather than as "gay blacks"—their black identity comes first.

Black gays have no formal organization or exclusive bars, and they rely for sociability mostly on informal networks of friends. Gay blacks are apparently those who look for gay life away from Harlem. Black observers, however, have described those who choose the identity of gay black and look for the gay world beyond the black community as subject to discrimination across a wide array of gay institutions. Moreover, gay blacks have often complained that whites are attracted to black men because they expect them to have large penises, thus "objectifying black men only as sexual objects rather than as human beings with emotions and the capacity to think" (Boykin 1996: 216); "They just want their fantasies . . . to be dominated by this dark man with this big dick" (DeMarco 1999: 112–13).

In any case, the reality of race relations in the gay community is not encouraging. Even today, only a few gay institutions considered safe and

desirable are racially mixed. Most gay bars on Christopher Street (the mytho-
logical gay center in Greenwich Village), for example, are clearly demarcated
by ethnic composition. White men in black bars, like blacks in prominently
white ones, seem to advertise their search for sexual partners. Confronting
that reality, MACT, a national organization founded in 1980, promised a special solution. As argued by its founder: "White men who are into black men
are isolated in the community. The only time we recognized each other before
was when we'd lock horns over a trick in the bar. And for black men our organization offered a safe environment where they knew they weren't going to be
rejected because of their race" (Beame 1999 [1983]: 192).[1]

My observations—spread over many months during longer and shorter
visits to New York in 1995, 1996, 1999, 2001, 2002, and 2005—allowed me to
record the plans and hopes of its leadership to maintain the organization's existence and growth despite considerable obstacles that seemed to work against
their project (the proliferation of gay ethnic associations in particular). Arriv-
ing late for my first 1995 meeting, I was welcomed immediately by a friendly
black man (later identified as Thomas), who invited me to take a seat next to
the facilitator. At the next meeting, I mentioned my professional interest in
gay institutions in New York. Erik, an active member I had met also at the
Gentle Men's association (Chapter 7), became fully aware of my work, and, I
assume, filled in other participants. On a later visit in 1999, I attended a board
meeting and informed the members about the stage of my research. They were
welcoming and suggested I publish a piece in the MACT newsletter about my
work in the gay synagogue. They also invited me to address a membership
event dedicated to the anthropology of gay life. The title and an abstract of my
presentation appeared in the monthly newsletter (March 2000).

The participants were mostly in their thirties and forties, but some were
younger or older. The majority seemed to represent a lower middle class,
though not a few enjoyed a better professional status, for example, employ-
ees of various city and state social services. While most regulars were gain-
fully employed in white- or blue-collar occupations, some were unemployed
or were in professional training. Among the younger blacks, in particular,
I identified participants taking courses in programs leading toward college degrees. My perception of the group as representing a somewhat lower
socioeconomic status was, I suppose, influenced by the comparison with
other groups I observed at the Center. One should consider the average age
of the MACT participants, which was significantly lower than that of the
SAGE membership in particular. The mixed racial composition must have

also reflected the occupational situation among minorities in metropolitan America. That observation, I believe, was also on the mind of a veteran white member, a social worker, who once told me that, although the professional position of blacks had improved in recent years, if I looked around in New York's bank branches, for example, I would mainly see blacks as tellers, but not in higher positions, and those blacks would be mostly females.

The Weekly Meetings

The four or five monthly meetings were dedicated to activities advertised in the newsletter, mostly discussions that followed a short presentation by the facilitator of the meeting or followed a lecture by a guest specialist, a film, etc. The March 1995 schedule, for example, included (1) LES-BI-GAY and transgendered services today; (2) Consciousness raising discussion; (3) Concert by a member; (4) Poetry reading, listening to our sisters; (5) Newsletter mailing and social evening. The April 1995 program offered (1) Annual Passover Seder; (2) Games night, cards and board games; (3) Power dynamics in interracial relationships; (4) Newsletter mailing. The May 1995 schedule included (1) How to have a safe date; (2) "Gay rights, special rights"; (3) Anger—expressing it/hearing it; (4) Newsletter mailing. That monthly meeting structure has continued for many years, as attested in the latest advertised programs I checked out for 2013.

Other activities were also advertised in the newsletter, such as meetings of the various committees (the board, membership, etc.), films, picnics, receptions, or parties for friends who came for a visit or for new members. These activities were often hosted by members at home. Late in June, the group held its annual Sunset Cruise fund-raising event (a dinner and a dance onboard a Circle Line Cruise ship around Manhattan). On special occasions, the weekly meetings were scheduled as public events, such as the presentation on behalf of Mumia Abu Jamal,[2] the black activist sentenced to death in Philadelphia for the killing of a police officer in 1982. He was tried by a notoriously vindictive judge and a jury of ten whites and two blacks, on the testimony of questionable eyewitnesses, and on the basis of questionable circumstantial evidence. The execution was still pending regardless of the many protests and international pleas for clemency, and the MACT group organized a town-hall meeting in the center's main hall with several guest speakers, who called for a retrial.

The group's regular meetings were scheduled in a large room on the top floor, a location that also offered a feeling of some seclusion from the many other activities taking place at the Center. Two participants, one black and one white, took care of the refreshments—a variety of cookies, cakes, pies and soft drinks. Homemade food prepared by participants sometimes added a party atmosphere. This tradition was different from most other weekly meetings at the Center, which offered food and drinks only on special occasions. All events were planned by the board and usually facilitated by members chosen for the task. Specific subjects were sometimes introduced by guests who specialized in these fields or were representatives of particular organizations. The meetings ended at about 10:30 p.m., but those who wished could join the after-meeting get-together of a late dinner or snack at a nearby cafeteria.

To the disappointment of its regulars, the registered membership declined from about two hundred in the early 1980s to about one hundred in the late 1990s. That decrease was often explained as a consequence of the emergence of many other gay organizations catering to the needs of the same population that was first attracted to the MACT's pioneering gatherings: the ethnic associations, such as GMAD (Gay Men of African Descent), HUGL (Hispanic United Gays and Lesbians), GAPIM (Gay Asians and Pacific Islanders), LGMNY (Latino Gay Men of New York), etc. It was suggested that among the early joiners, many were interested in meeting their own people, and once the opportunity came, they preferred the more ethnically exclusive groups. A few of these newer groups also scheduled their meetings on the same weekend evening, which further exacerbated the drop in membership. But some members divided their loyalties between the mixed and the exclusive groups. I met a few black men who attended both the GMAD and the MACT meetings, choosing attendance by the attraction of the subject of the weekly meeting. James, in his early thirties and equally attracted to the company of blacks and whites, told me he preferred themes relating to personal relationships.

The Discourse of Interracial Relationships

An important source of information available to me that complemented the newsletters, the weekly meetings, and other activities I attended was *Celebrating Diversity: A 10th Anniversary Journal*, which recorded the history of MACT and offered a lively discourse on the major ideals, issues, and conflicts that affected its history. The journal introduced a position paper containing these lines:

> Our organization is a vehicle through which individuals attempt to put multiculturalism into practice in the world. It encourages people to form a safer space to nurture multiculturalism. This safer space encompasses cross-cultural socializing and education in addition to reinforcing our commitment to challenging racism, sexism, classism, homophobia, and the other inequities of our society wherever or in whomever they exist. (1993: 13)

The journal bluntly confronted "the mythical notion of the group as a social club only dominated by older white men seeking sex with younger Black men" (17). It emphasized the group's attempts to challenge racist notions that come with eroticization and objectification of black men in particular. It also indicated the fierce opposition by white men toward the establishment of separate caucuses for men of color and whites that threatened the integrity of their group. The establishment of separate racial associations clearly exemplified this threat. According to the journal's evidence, from 1980 to 1986 this was the only group available to gay people of color seeking a community.

The above citation, as much as others I have chosen from the journal's pages, reveals some of the most acute dilemmas that have besieged the group since its inception. In particular, what in practice was the balance between the politicocultural agenda and the social-sexual agenda (offering individuals the opportunity to meet men of another race)? This issue seemed more problematic for the black membership, which could now opt out and join separate groups. The problem was openly confronted in the journal by a leading black member, who admitted that groups like GMAD "have stepped in a way that MACT probably could not." Namely, they offer black men venues of activity and discourse more closely related to issues relevant to the situation—political, economic, spiritual, and personal—of black people.

Veteran members, whites in particular, claimed the group's activities had changed since its early days, when they were more actively involved in fighting racial discrimination, such as boycotting bars that did not serve blacks. Now, however, not only had the situation of blacks had greatly improved, but new groups had taken over much of that political agenda. The journal was candid about the process that took away many members, "even our leaders," who, after going through the consciousness-raising activities sponsored by

MACT, left for other groups and activities that gave greater scope to the sensibilities and skills they had first learned with that fellowship. This might be a sophisticated interpretation of the gradual and sometimes quick turnover of members, as well as the decline in membership since its heyday in the early 1980s. No doubt too, as indicated by the veteran members, a good number of old-timers had been victims of AIDS. Despite membership attrition, a few of the old leadership and veteran members remained with the group and thus helped to maintain a sense of continuity. Moreover, at particular events, a few of the surviving leaders who became involved in other organizations were invited to address the audience. They were very happy to fulfill the role of successful elders and reminisce about the good old days.

The Erotic Ambience

On my first visit I was at once struck by the somewhat erotic atmosphere engendered by the speaker, a white man in his late thirties who facilitated the theme of "gay relationships." He continuously related his experiences as a gay male nurse in a major hospital. He was conspicuously feminine and campy in his demeanor, to the delight of his audience. He claimed that the doctors were strictly closeted and that he himself was careful, in spite of his otherwise flamboyant behavior, not to act out in public. He admitted he was always single and not looking for a long-term relationship. Proclaiming his independence and his free sexuality, he amused his listeners as he confessed their meeting room was too small to accommodate all the men he had had sex with. In that happy mood, somebody suggested putting his lovers together in Shea Stadium and another recommended Grand Central Station as the place to host them happily together.

This campy presentation raised conflicting positions: some supported the facilitator's attitude to free sex, indicating also that those marked as "passive" (relating to the facilitator's preferred sex as much as to their own sexuality) are not really passive. Others claimed there must be some norms of good and bad in sexual relationships and insisted that every group must build together the norms that form the basis for its community. Participants in the discourse were equally blacks and whites. The atmosphere was relaxed, friendly, and recreational in the erotic tone that seemed to pervade the meeting.

The Passover Seder was far more serious than I expected. About thirty people attended the well-prepared event. Most attendees—about ten Jews, ten blacks, and ten others—wore white shirts and were less casually dressed. Jews were as prominent among the MACT membership as much as among other groups at the Center, but the ethnic identification was never publicly spelled out during my stay. The Jewish identity of participants was usually conveyed to me privately. The Seder seemed fitting for a New York crowd and for an association dedicated to race relations. The tables were prepared for a festive dinner with the symbols and menu of a traditional Passover meal. The Haggadah text (narrating the Jewish mythical story of the flight from bondage in Egypt), as edited by a gay Jewish writer, was displayed at each seat. Harvey, the Jewish member who led the Seder, added a reading from *Tikkun* (a liberal Jewish monthly) about issues of freedom in our time. Incidentally, my portion of the reading contained the prospects of reconciliation between Israelis and Palestinians.

The Haggadah was read meticulously and the food was consumed with equal enthusiasm. I noticed one mixed couple who seemed to have met at the Seder table and left together before the end of the evening program. Sometime later I met the black man of that couple (a department store employee in his mid-thirties) at a mailing meeting and learned he had "come out" recently and was looking for a white mate. He told me he had divorced his wife and discovered the MACT group in the Gay Yellow Pages. As he mostly liked white men, he thought it might be an interesting place and one that could offer an opportunity to meet suitable candidates. He had had an affair lasting a few weeks with the young man he had met at the Seder table.

We had a good laugh at the end of the Seder when Thomas, a dedicated veteran black member, went in search of the basket for the collection of contributions (at all meetings participants were requested to give a five-dollar donation). Erik, a robust looking artist of mixed race, teased Thomas, who often displayed a feminine demeanor, as he looked down at his own pants and asked him if he was looking for "that" basket. As I soon learned, Thomas was often involved in risqué encounters with close friends, who also engaged other attendees in that mode of joking relationships. At the Seder table, another frequent black attendee described Thomas as a "subway character," meaning everyone had a ride on him. Thomas, who retaliated in kind, did not take offense at the teasing, which contributed to the relaxed and intimate ambience of the meetings.

The first meeting in May was "How to Have a Safe Date." The theme naturally carried an erotic significance. The program was facilitated by representatives of the Gay and Lesbian Anti-Violence Project. They started with a game intended to familiarize the participants with one another, and then the audience was divided into smaller discussion groups.

As we were soon split into smaller groups, I was engaged with six members who were mostly veterans. The blacks in the group were far more active during the ensuing discussion. They emphasized the need for "chemistry" rather than specific physical attributes in order to get involved with another man. They also claimed they had no memories of particularly painful experiences; they had never been assaulted by gay or straight men. But David, a long-time white participant, told us about a past uncanny event containing a mixture of exciting and scary experiences. One summer evening, as he was waiting at a nearby corner for a blind date, he was approached by a gorgeous black guy, and he took him home. He soon felt something was seriously wrong because his date wanted only to be serviced and also started to harass him. He was relieved to see him leave when a telephone call came from the man he had actually been supposed to meet. So it was a story of mistaken identity. The right date, however, was far less attractive than the wrong one. All seemed surprised with David's story. His manner was usually very restrained; now he had revealed something more intimate about his life and passions.

Black men were also very active at the next meeting, when a film made by right-wing and homophobic political activists was screened in order to display the strategy used to get the support of ordinary black churchgoers. The film's producers set out to prove that the gay liberation movement exploited the civil rights movement. During the ensuing discussion, a very eloquent speaker claimed the issue of homosexuality was irrelevant in black communities, either because they had to confront far more serious problems or because black gays were protected by their close family networks. A church minister, for example, would not offend somebody gay because he could not afford to slight the man's relatives. As this argument was debated some other opinions were raised, but on the whole, the event proceeded in a relaxed and friendly atmosphere. The erotic ambience was conveyed to me by Erik, who claimed that a number of participants, including the facilitator, had tried to get his attention through insistent eye contact.

Erik probably sometimes exaggerated the erotic interests displayed by the MACT participants, but the sexual ambience was certainly far more prominent in these gatherings than, for example, at the SAGE or even at the SCA meetings. Erik, however, was highly critical about what he considered the unrestrained behavior of the pre-AIDS days. He had no doubt that wherever one went in gay society, there were opportunities to meet potential lovers, but he argued that gays, no less than heterosexuals, must develop boundaries and constraints for their sexual behavior. He often reminisced about the wild 1970s, when gays believed they could do anything they fancied. He remembered his own sexual escapades with numerous partners he met effortlessly "everywhere." Erik became engaged in MACT activities during my stay and eventually joined the board. He claimed he did so for no other reason than to support the sociopolitcal idea of cross-racial collaboration.

A June meeting was titled "Our Multicultural Relationships." Major stereotypes were raised as topics for the discussion, such as "sexual prejudices and mixed dating," "money in the relationships of mixed couples," "class and mixed dating," etc. For example, somebody mentioned that when a mixed couple ordered a meal, the waiter usually left the check with the white guy, assuming that he was the one who pays. The friendly discussion got heated when the hypothetical suggestions seemed too close to real life. A black veteran complained he was tired of learning again that the old racial attitudes were still there. Another black participant made a provocative statement as he turned to his audience with the question: "Tell me, you Caucasian guys, when you enter a bar and you see at one corner an intelligent looking black man and at the very far end you notice a black stud, whom would you prefer?" It was clear he assumed they would naturally fancy the black stud, the stereotype of white men's attraction to the physical prowess of the mythical black body.

That contention was immediately contested by a Jewish lawyer who specialized in cases of sexual abuse and who claimed without emotion that gay people, as much as heterosexuals, had many tastes. He thus rejected the stereotypical approach about the taste of whites that categorized them all in one grouping for sexual attraction. Another Jewish participant with whom I spoke supported that position. He affirmed the basic sexual attraction that characterized their group but nevertheless did not consider that attraction as the only basis for the survival of their association: "No doubt, people who come here are first physically attracted to another race, but then they get interested in other things. I never had an affair with anyone here. I just like the people and the atmosphere here. It is free."

But the controversy about the prevalence of racial stereotypes reappeared in great force in the ensuing discussion when the audience split into smaller groups. A visitor from Chicago, a member of the local MACT chapter there, commented that it was a common assumption in Chicago that among racially mixed couples, the black partners were the "studs" and the whites "take control." His position caused a heated argument revealing unexpected viewpoints. The first was voiced by the Jewish participant quoted earlier, who now claimed that people, gays and heterosexuals, were attracted to what was different from themselves—"they do not look for somebody they see in the mirror." That raised a strong reaction from another white man, who was offended by the implication already voiced by the visitor from Chicago that blacks had the body and whites possessed the brain. His interlocutor was equally disturbed by that "distorted" perception of his own words.

Although all involved resisted these stereotypical implications, they nevertheless were well aware of the power of these notions, not only in American society at large but also in their own membership. Moreover, these stereotypes were part and parcel of the racial convictions of both whites and blacks. That revelation caused mutual embarrassment and a sense of resentment in both the blacks and the whites, who shared a space here designed to bring them together of their own free will and through a strong mutual attraction. A few days later I attended the annual Sunset Cruise fund-raising event. Blacks and whites were enjoying themselves together during the dinner and the later dance. Most couples on the dance floor were racially mixed.

The issue came up again during a later meeting. A discussion about racial stereotypes raised the myth of the oversized black penis. Thomas denied it, claiming that black and whites were equally endowed. Tim, the white cochair, a very eloquent professional, said he had recently had a disturbing encounter with a friendly neighbor. When he mentioned his lover, the neighbor responded, "You mean the Nubian guy of yours?" Offended, Tim reacted immediately: "No, he's not a Nubian, he's a Fulani." He considered the neighbor's apparently humorous statement equally homophobic and racial and decided on a strategy of education as response. Tim also assumed he was being stereotyped as a gay man who preferred a submissive role in bed.

The Harlem Tour

The tour of Harlem took place a week later. This was an annual tradition organized and guided by Thomas, who had been raised in Harlem. Only a few men, mostly whites, showed up that Saturday morning. We started with brunch at Sylvia's, a restaurant famous for its soul food. We noticed the arrival of the Reverend Al Sharpton, a prominent, controversial black New York leader; he joined a nearby table. As we readied to leave, Erik approached

Reverend Sharpton and greeted him. I assumed they had met before. But I soon learned this was the first time Erik had had an opportunity to get that close to Sharpton, so he wished to shake the hand of a great black leader.

To my surprised reaction, Erik explained that whites resented all black leaders: they hated Martin Luther King, Malcolm X, and all others who stood up for blacks. Erik blamed white America for depriving blacks of their history, their language, and their culture. He saw no consolation in observing the successful black middle class so prominently present at Sylvia's. He argued that an affluent minority did not compensate for the rest of the black community. I have already mentioned that Erik was racially mixed. In his own family, some had more visibly Caucasian features and others were noticeably black. He did not identify himself as black. and he lacked a "black accent," which he thought was the most important identifying racial attribute among the blacks themselves. To me he looked like a Middle Eastern man; I perceived him as white. However, he seemed attractive to men of both races. Most of his close friends were whites, and he mostly preferred white men as lovers.

This was indeed an educational event for me. I already had a dislike of Al Sharpton, first because of his involvement with the notorious Tawana Brawley case, the Long Island black girl who had accused white police officers of sexual abuse but whose story later proved fabricated. I also identified him as a Louis Farrakhan supporter and therefore felt more personally engaged in my resentment of anti-Semites and their associates. At first I was uncomfortable to discover that Erik supported a completely different attitude from mine. I assumed I was mostly guided by pure motives based on "rationality and justice." Was Erik a fanatic supporter reacting to the forces of primordial ethnic loyalties (which now made him a member of an antagonist racial group and deprived him of "rational" thinking)? But my friendship with Erik (with whom I could share experiences of attending other Center meetings) and my respect for his position in various previous debates soon made me aware that I was probably biased myself. I wondered if my reaction of indignation was not almost automatic, as well as insensitive to the feelings and viewpoints of those who more "naturally" supported Sharpton. I pondered whether that personal experience and its lesson were indicative of the ethos and practice of the MACT association.

That somewhat contentious exchange did not affect the rest of our pleasant day in Harlem. Thomas showed us his old school and was open about his unhappy experiences as a young boy who had already seemed different from and more delicate than the rest of his classmates. This was also an opportunity for another young white participant to relate his own story about the life of a gay boy at an ordinary city-center school. Erik, as mentioned before, was aware of the erotic atmosphere that often permeated the MACT meetings. As we strolled through Harlem's streets, he told me that I would miss a forthcoming meeting (as I was scheduled to be away at that time) called "Let's Talk about Dick." He assumed the meeting would draw a large attendance. The next monthly program that reached me a few days later offered the following synopsis for that title: "What do we like? Thick, thin, long, short, cut, or uncut? What kind of importance do we attach to penis power? Do we pay more attention to those men who are more endowed . . . ?"

But the coming meeting, dedicated, as mentioned, to averting the execution of Mumia Abu Jamal, was scheduled as a town-hall meeting in the Center's main hall. That event, however, did not draw many MACT regulars. Actually, the majority of the forty to fifty attendees were newcomers, including many black women. I assume many regulars were uncomfortable with a meeting that lacked the intimacy of the weekly, more secluded fourth-floor gatherings. The organizers preferred to explain the hot weather as the main reason for the poor attendance of their own membership. In any case, they did not regret their initiative in what seemed to be a most relevant activity for their group. It was good for their public image and offered an opportunity to recruit new members.

Reunion on a Snowy Day

On my return to New York a few months later, the cold weather interrupted a very promising program on the contribution of African Americans to American culture, particularly in music, poetry, and food. A prominent academic was scheduled to convene the meeting. Food, poetry reading, and musical performances appropriate for the event were part of meticulous planning. However, it snowed heavily, so only about twenty men showed up. Even the organizer was unable to get there. Nevertheless, those present tried to carry on with the scheduled program regardless of the missing highlights (much of the special food, performers, and the supportive audience).

The atmosphere was particularly intimate, and those attending were encouraged to reminisce about the past. I met Ed, a young and robust-looking black man who I soon learned had been one of the leaders of the group for many years. He had left the group for several years to take part in the promotion of new gay organizations, but he had never lost his affection for and loyalty to the first MACT association, though many of his old friends there had died of AIDS. He claimed he looked young because he had no regrets about being gay and was always looking for ways to enjoy life. He remembered, in particular, the MACT meetings dedicated to "dicks" (the program I had missed the previous August) and relationships—topics that always sparked emotion. It was now time for Ed to recount a meeting that had taken place some years ago, also on a snowy evening, when the brave attendees ended up at a sex club, where they stayed until the next morning. His story was later confirmed to me by another veteran, who remembered Ed as an influential member but one who had been "too much involved in sexual experiments" and whose close friends had paid dearly for their unrestrained freedom and lust for pleasures.

That evening brought more of the black members to display their eloquence. A few recited poems focusing on the African American experience, a Metropolitan Opera chorus member demonstrated the musical talents attributed to blacks, and others reminisced about the history of MACT, its role, and its contributions. The only white speaker at the event, a board member, was the former lover of the black man who had taken charge of the program in the absence of the scheduled organizer. They both displayed a dedication to the group and a civility that overrode their personal feelings.

Thomas's Birthday Party

I also attended a meeting with the group on Thomas's birthday. Among the most dedicated members, Thomas was in his late forties and was undergoing training for a new job. The party at his modest apartment was attended equally by whites and blacks. Among the guests I identified Harvey, one of my first acquaintances, the leader of the Seder, who came to the party with a young black man whom he introduced as "my husband." They had met a few months earlier at the Center, just as Harvey was on his way home from a MACT meeting. They had already registered as domestic partners, which allowed the partner, who was still at technical school, to take advantage of the generous health insurance provided by Harvey's employers.

I met another veteran white member who remembered the group in its early days. He had not attended much in recent years, since he had been engaged in a stable relationship. (A few years later, in 2005, I attended a board meeting at his home and met his black partner.) As we discussed the history and changes that he had observed, he repeated what almost seemed to me an official slogan: "People join because they are physically attracted cross-racially, but later they discover there is something else that relates to rights and other things." A few more veterans, who also rarely showed up, attended the party and were accorded much affection by the regulars.

Thomas entertained us with stories from his own biography, mostly related to his gay experiences. His first encounter had been at seventeen with a white man who cruised him during midday in a busy Manhattan neighborhood. He assumed the guy would take him home but ended up being unceremoniously screwed on the roof of a nearby building. He humorously described the miserable experience as he was sweetened by his seducer with chocolate that he consumed during the act. The next step was his presence at the Stonewall riots. He claimed he was there together with a few hundred ·gays and the many "queens," whom he liked in particular. Then he related the story of his imprisonment following the accusation that he had solicited a plainclothes policeman. Thomas spurned the charge that got him a six-month jail term. By his account, he had been cruising in Central Park and had targeted another man. He told us that in prison he was spared the humiliation and violence awaiting gays because he flirted with a brute to whom he promised love and sex after they completed their term at the penitentiary. Thomas's stories raised both doubts and teasing, but his intimate revelations, related in a campy style, added much to the hospitable and friendly atmosphere of the gathering. The same evening another active member handed out fliers announcing his forthcoming birthday party, which he planned as a fund-raising event for their organization.

An Activist's Withdrawal

Erik, who had rediscovered MACT after a few years of absence, felt it needed fundamental changes. He thought the group was being led by whites, who set programs for the black membership. He believed they could expand the membership, recruit people of "better caliber," and enrich the weekly programs through a more serious agenda of politics and culture and the introduction of new venues for entertainment. He was soon elected black cochair, although he could equally have stood for office as white cochair (he had a somewhat dark complexion and curled Afro hair, but otherwise he had Caucasian features and his racial identification was mostly situational).

After a short period of enthusiasm, he was disappointed by what he considered the limited investment and initiative displayed by his colleagues on the board. They were too hesitant about his proposals and seemed satisfied enough with the style of activity that had existed for many years. Erik resigned from office and focused his energies on promoting other activities at the Center. I was back in Tel Aviv when I received his letter expressing, not for the first or last time, disappointment and hope:

> I thought I informed you of my resignation from the Board as Co-Chair and as a member of MACT; everything I was trying to do— lift the caliber of people, increase membership, charge at the door, require much better programs and commitments and responsibilities and order—were being sabotaged . . . ; SO I QUIT. With that resignation and the thwarting grief, returning to myself as a whole with the freedom I have gained. . . . I joined the XXX Veterans who had been courting me, as Vice President of Development and President of the Membership Committee.

Erik's association with the group probably reflects the history of other joiners. This was his second attempt to make the group a more significant part of his social life. He was attracted by the gay atmosphere of jovial relationships and the unrestrained sensual tone. He also expected an investment by others in promoting the politico-cultural agenda of a group engaged in racial issues. He found the balance between the ethos and the practice concerning these two major venues unsatisfactory. However, with the proliferation of both smaller and larger groups that catered to various social needs and personal proclivities, he could easily look for other activities accessible at the Center and other places that might better satisfy (or equally disappoint) his expectations. He accumulated organizational knowledge and social experiences through his ongoing engagement with various associations operating at the Center (the Gentle Men included; Chapter 7).

Why Join an Interracial Group?

The MACT's space and events at the Center were a promising setting for romantic encounters. Most attendees acknowledged that its members were attracted to men from another race (mainly blacks or whites). The programs were also intended to raise some kind of sensual ambience, although they never promoted initiatives that allowed a public demonstration of sexual activities. The newsletters and programs had never displayed anything overtly sexual beyond risqué jocular talk. That restraint was noticeable compared, for example, with the Gay Bears (Chapter 8) or the public S&M monthly programs at the Center, which often displayed sexual gadgets and theatrical illustrations of erotic S&M habits. Even the dance at the annual cruise was not provocative in any way—most of those on the dance floor were couples or close friends. The expressions of sexuality that I observed were mostly verbal, in light-hearted relationships or through erotic parlance at the semiserious discussions such as "Let's Talk about Dick." No one concealed or criticized the search that engaged some or many participants, that is, the search for opportunities to meet a mate from another race for "a relationship." I met several who did realize that expectation for shorter or longer duration. In most cases, however, these relationships started with the hope for a stable love partnership.

Popular assessments notwithstanding, most gay establishments in New York are in fact racially segregated, though not by any formal discriminatory means. This was also plain at the Center's activities. As mentioned above, the founding of exclusive ethnic organizations had seriously affected the membership of the first interracial association. I was often told by black members that the MACT participants were criticized at the GMAD meetings, where they were derogatively nicknamed "snow queens" for their attraction, and by implication their submission, to white men. An acute awareness of the ambivalent, if not stigmatizing, attitude toward them was expressed in *Celebrating Diversity* (1993): "Some people continue to dismiss our group as a sexual set-up for men interested in cross-racial/ethnic dating. Others say it is no longer political. . . . We refuse to make [MACT] a place that condemns or stigmatizes cross-racial sexuality. . . . But we once again assert that we are not solely a sexual group."

Looking for an intimate companion from another race immediately evokes a somewhat sordid allusion in most gay establishments. It suggests the social-sexual stereotypes prevalent among gays, as well as heterosexuals, which are accentuated by the history of blacks in America. Men and women of African descent have for centuries essentially represented the body as a major human asset. The strong and well-endowed bodies of blacks paraded at the market place and employed in manual tasks in the service of whites naturally stimulated the image of body versus mind as two separate racial estates.

White men in black bars, as much as blacks in those that are predominantly white, give up the facade of indifference to the search for sexual partners—a pretension so often exhibited by patrons of gay establishments. From that perspective, the gay interracial scene seems far less attractive to the black male. He is often perceived in degrading and stigmatizing terms: the trophy of some better-off white man. Could that tormenting consciousness explain the growing popularity of the all-ethnic associations (GMAD in particular)?

The mythology, prejudice, and stigma that engage black-white interracial relationships remind us of Colin Turnbull, a famous anthropologist, who shared his life with an African American man. In the chronicle of a life of a great possessive love and acute suffering, the reviewer points to the predicament, revealed also in this chapter, when white men are sexually attracted to black male partners.

> A white man who prefers a black man is constantly confronted with the inquiry, often in belligerent tones "What do you see in them?"...
> Size queens and fanciers of bubblebutts find that the black man's reputation is not unwarranted.... Exoticism seems to have played a considerable role in the determination of Turnbull's sexual preference, but it is far from the whole story. (Horne 2004: 144)

The MACT association, which first emerged and continued to operate at the Center, seemed to offer a congenial and safe space for the manifestation of a complex orientation: cross-ethnic empathy and political convictions concerning race relations in America; and social commitment to interracial relationships, which might, but not always did, involve sexual passion and the undisguised search for a black or white Mr. Right. It operated as a rap group for political discussions that also allowed the free expression of an emotional infatuation. It was no less a cruising site for the accidental visitor and a safe ground for acquaintanceships far less hazardous than those made in public spaces and at the commercial gay establishments (the few bars of mixed cliental, such as the Monster Bar in the Village, included).

True, the MACT repertoire could not provide long-term satisfaction for the more ambitious participants, particularly because of the decline of its active political agenda and the availability of many other polyethnic activities also at the Center. But for those who continued to attend its activities, as well as for the newcomers, the weekly program had always been a place to spend or start a weekend night's entertainment. That was not much different from

what I observed, for example, at the Friday services at CBST (the gay synagogue); participants could stay on late after service and socialize in the synagogue, go on with friends for a late dinner, or end up in a bar or a sex club.
In sum, the relaxed ambience at MACT activities evolved into a comfortable
space for blacks and whites to try out a mutual erotic attraction or enjoy the
experience of affectionate relationships on a regular or a casual basis.

However, a basic issue engaging the MACT participants, who are embedded in a problematic personal and social space of sexual attractions, relates
this account to earlier chapters. Observed ambivalently by both white and
black, and gay and straight audiences, coming together in the company
of other men who admit the same erotic attraction offers a sense of social
approval and personal comfort. They feel empowered sharing a choice of the
"wrong" mates in a society still infected with racial prejudices.

CHAPTER 7

The Gentle Men's Circle

It was by default that I first attended a meeting at the Gentle Men's association. One Friday evening I went to the Center to attend a MACT meeting (Chapter 6). As I entered and checked out the location of the group, I noticed on the list of activities for the day a meeting of Gentle Men scheduled for the same time. I had seen the name before and assumed it indicated some sort of effeminate men's activity. But now, before taking the stairs leading up to my regular MACT meeting, I made a detour and walked down the nearby corridor to where the Gentle Men's meeting was due to take place. I saw a line of men waiting outside the room. I assumed it was not yet vacant from an earlier event, but I soon learned that it was being prepared for the GM activity. The one black man also waiting in line, observing my uncertain look, asked me smilingly what it was that I was looking for. Embarrassed, I asked him, "What is Gentle Men?" With an amused expression he handed to me a flier and suggested I read it. The short text included the following: "Our vision is to bring together caring, affectionate, emotionally available gay men who want to truly relate to one another. In doing so, we hope to find friends, lovers, and community."

As I looked around, the men seemed to be of all ages and definitely not effeminate. I also identified a CBST member and another man I had met at a Radical Fairies meeting.[1] I immediately changed my plans for the evening, assuming that not many people would show up for the poetry reading planned for the MACT meeting. Luckily I made my mind up quickly. The room was opened for those waiting in line; latecomers were not allowed in.

I paid the seven dollar fee for nonmembers and discovered that members paid only five. The room, of medium size, was dimly lit and carpeted with mats. After removing our shoes, we all, about twenty-five to thirty men, took seats around the walls, almost touching each other. We started the meeting holding hands for a few minutes of meditation and then introduced ourselves by name and were expected to express our feelings at that particular time. Most of those present voiced, in a few words, a feeling of security and relaxation, but a few expressed feelings of uneasiness and anxiety.

With that part finished (about fifteen minutes), we started with the exercise of the day to which about forty-five minutes were dedicated. The facilitator, Don, was a man in his late thirties, a social scientist. I soon learned from my neighbor that Don had initiated the group about a year earlier. He told us we should pair with whoever was closest to us, and for two to three minutes to caress the upper part of the body, shoulders, and upper chest. The active party was supposed to remain seated while his partner reclined on his knees and submitted to that friendly treatment. Don rang a little bell, meaning it was time to change positions; at the next ring we were to change partners. We were expected not to choose or reject partners, but to pair with the man closest to us. I estimated that we changed ten to twelve partners during that session. As I later noted: "It was a mixed experience of an infantile pleasure of being gently fondled, but it was also equally unpleasant sometimes when partners were somewhat repulsive because of weight, age, or other disagreeable characteristics."

On my first visit I was not struck by any erotic overtone. As I recorded in my notes, I did not observe anyone overtly using the opportunity of the physical intimacy to take the liberty of stroking more sensitive erotic zones of his partner's body. Neither did I observe any rejection of less attractive partners. At the end of the exercise we resumed our places around the room and had another round of sharing. Now participants related their feelings following the last experience, as well as about other things they wished to share in the meeting. For example, a newcomer in his mid-thirties told us he had lost his lover six months before and, presently emerging from a painful period of mourning and depression, he again desired something they all were looking for—a new loving relationship.

The man seated next to me, in his late forties, told me he had started attending a few months before and had also been at the party celebrating the first year anniversary of the group. He knew of people who came from far away and pointed out one sitting nearby who came regularly from East Hampton, Long Island. The group met twice a month, but as I soon learned, the facilitator added additional meetings on Sundays to satisfy the growing popularity of his initiative. I later discovered that there were informal meetings of smaller groups of members who developed closer friendships. My first "informant" also insisted, however, that the Gentle Men's meetings were not perceived or used as a place for fleeting sexual encounters. The final round of sharing was relaxed and jovial with many bursts of laughter, almost all participants expressing their satisfaction.

When my turn came, it seems I added to the convivial atmosphere as I declared that I had got there by default, not knowing what Gentle Men was all about. Alluding to the seemingly erotic environment I had stumbled into, somebody said that he forgot on which side he parted his hair, suggesting he had been thoroughly stroked during the previous activity. I could not stay later that first time to attend the after-meeting get-together at a nearby restaurant. But before I left, another man, who was sitting next to me at the final round, with whom I had spoken briefly and who was among the more pleasant partners during the exercise, gave me his card. I called him a few days later, we met for dinner, and he became among my closest friends/ "informants." This was the man I call Erik, whom I have introduced several times already in previous chapters.

Many Center meetings took place on Fridays. I also attended MACT meetings and sometimes services at CBST. My next visit to a Gentle Men gathering was made convenient by the addition of a few Sunday meetings, which attracted many newcomers. However, I identified a few participants from other groups, as well as some I had met on my first visit to GM. Don, the facilitator, opened with an introduction intended for the many newcomers, mostly in their early thirties to late fifties, explaining that the group was founded as an alternative for men who were tired of, or uncomfortable with, the gay bars scene. Here they were offered an opportunity to meet and socialize in a way that enabled gay men to become better acquainted and where they could learn to express affection. Don avoided a direct reference to cruising and anonymous sex, but his mention of the bar scene was sufficient.

The activity started as in the earlier meeting with holding hands and expressing feelings that were mostly ones such as "I feel comfortable," "I feel relaxed," ". . . scared," ". . . expectant," and so on. The exercise for the meeting was touching and massaging faces and was again differentiated by active and passive roles followed by the changing of pairs. The participants were expected not to reject anyone, but one could take a seat or stand outside the close circle and thus avoid participation as long as one wished. Though most participants took part without obvious rejections, they could make quick choices and grab a preferred partner among those closest to their location.

Those left without a partner nearby looked around for others without one in a more remote spot in the room.

Although I did not experience physical contact with any sexual connotation, I felt a strong expression of affection with a few partners, conveyed through the delicate yet insistent caressing of my face with their fingers and palms. They seemed immersed in the activity and also made continuous eye contact. Although this might have appeared to be directed at "the one and only," they repeated the same dedicated and affectionate caressing with other participants. As on my first visit, I sometimes waited desperately for Don to ring the bell and relieve me of the ordeal.

We participated in this activity for about forty-five minutes, after which we were engaged in one circle, then in another, sharing our experiences. The first round was dedicated to commenting on the exercise, while the second offered an opportunity to talk about other life events and desires. Most participants praised the activity, and some said it was the first time in a long while that they had had a pleasant experience with men. A man in his mid-fifties told us about a recent visit with friends to the Splash Bar, a large club in Chelsea. The place was terribly noisy and crowded, mostly with a young clientele. One could hardly see or hear the men one wished to communicate with. He could not stand it for long and quickly escaped. A participant in his early forties, a playwright on his first visit to the GM group, related his experience with his different partners in the exercise as he made comparisons between the responses to his gazing into his partners' eyes. He returned to that subject later, as we went on to a nearby restaurant for dinner. He told me that in a bar, eye contact does not allow you to see the true selves of people because they hide them.

In the last round of sharing, a few participants related their recent separation from their partners or the loss of their lovers; some added that attending the meeting was part of the first stage in their search for new mates. Others discussed their work situations, achievements, and failures. Don, the facilitator, confessed the incongruity between his own work life and love life. Success at work and a happy love partnership had never coincided for him. He thus enhanced the cozy atmosphere of openness and the notion of shared predicaments that affect gay life.

I identified Andrew, whom I had last seen when he clashed with the SAGE participants and angrily left their meeting. He was now affectionately holding hands with a young Asian participant. I also saw him later at the restaurant; we walked out together toward his car, which was parked nearby on Seventh

Avenue. He went home alone. I had no way of knowing whether the affection he demonstrated with the young Asian man was casual, an extension of the spirit of the meeting, or if he had made some arrangements to meet or call him sometime later. However, most conversations at the restaurant were neutral, dealing with daily or past life experiences in other parts of the United States. Some fifteen to twenty men attended this after-meeting get-together, most of them newcomers to that group—apparent strangers but who an hour earlier had touched each other in a very intimate though gentle manner.

A few days later, at the SAGE meeting, I met Carl, a regular, whom I had also met at the last Gentle Men event; I asked for his opinion on the group. He replied that he liked its activities, although, he clarified, the success of the meetings greatly depended on the crowd that happened to be there at each gathering (always crowded, many among those attending were newcomers). He told me he had made a few good friends there whom he met sometimes also outside the Center for dinner or a movie. He told me a close friend had met his lover at a GM meeting, a widowed doctor. His friend was the first man the doctor had met since he had decided to satisfy his hidden attraction and try his luck in the gay world.

I asked Carl, more specifically, what made the Gentle Men meetings different from other sites of anonymous sex. Carl replied that in the usual anonymous sex situations, people immediately "get down to business" (sexual activity), but not so in the GM group. He told me he had received a card at the previous Sunday meeting from a man who told him he did not plan to attend future meetings. Certainly, that was a far more delicate and safer method to suggest a relationship, whether casual or more serious, than setting up a date with a stranger met at a bar (where people do not casually exchange personal cards).

I learned from Erik (who gave me his card on my first visit) about the social networks that emerged among the regular members. He told me he was organizing a birthday party for a friend he had met at GM. A few other members and close friends were invited to the party at an Upper West Side restaurant. He also told me that a group of participants, five men, had been invited a month earlier to spend a weekend at the spacious Long Island home of one of the active members. The GM's active participants, he commented, had a good time traveling together, dining, and visiting local bars. Only once, he admitted, had he had sex with a man he met at GM, but he soon regretted that affair. He remained on friendly terms with the man after confessing to him he did not feel that they might establish an enduring relationship.

I missed a meeting two weeks later because I arrived five minutes late and was unable to join the crowded assembly. That practice of keeping people out was extremely unusual among most Center activities. In other cases of overflow, the activity was usually transferred to a larger room. Except for closed meetings intended to preserve the participants' privacy, such as support groups for HIV-positive individuals, my only other such experience was when I arrived on time to attend a reading group but discovered they had a waiting list for new members.

A month later, Gentle Men hosted its first dance at the Center. Unlike the regular meetings, no attendance restrictions were applied at the dance. I missed that crowded activity, albeit for other reasons, including my hesitation to participate in an all-male dance. As I was later told by a few participants, the dance was organized in part at least in a fashion somewhat typical of all other GM activities. During the first half of the evening participants were obliged to change partners every few minutes, but in the second part they could choose their mates and stay together without time restrictions. The dance was considered a big success, and the decision to reserve a bigger room for the next dance had already been made. My informants were happy to tell me that the atmosphere was far more erotic than usual, and some couples danced in an intimate and physical manner, hugging and kissing. Erik told me he had collected a few business cards by the end of the evening.

A few days later, when the SAGE participants met for their weekly gathering, the story of the GM dance was related by Carl and Richard, who had both attended the event. They told us the crowd included all ages, from young men in their twenties to those in their sixties. Carl added that he saw couples who left the dance together and many who exchanged telephone numbers. Their story raised much interest, so I assumed that more SAGE members would attend future GM meetings. I also met participants at other groups who mentioned their attendance at the GM dance. The occasion seemed to attract a crowd of men who I believe were uncomfortable at nightclubs, but who also avoided the dances frequently organized at the Center's main hall, in part because those events attracted mostly younger men and lacked the level of intimacy suggested by the GM dance flier.

This successful event also indicated a forthcoming change in the organization of GM. Don was planning to retire from his leadership position and devote himself to his professional career. It looked as if the group would be able to survive after his departure. Don could congratulate himself that during his time, more than a year since he began that activity, a strong core group had developed among the regular membership. They were convinced they could continue, and even expand, the membership with the growing popularity of the GM circle.

On my return to New York six months later, I could see that they were right. The room was crowded to its maximum capacity. Thirty-six men came in before the door was closed. The average age seemed to me somewhat older than before. The majority were in their late forties, fifties, and early sixties, but there were also a few younger and older participants. I recognized quite a few faces from my earlier visits and from various other groups I had observed. They all seemed to represent middle-class people, with only one black man.

Erik and Bill (also a GM veteran) were facilitating the gathering. As I soon learned, since Don had departed, the role of facilitator rotated among board members or other active participants. Joint facilitating was favored by the leading members who lacked Don's professional background. It was also more fun having to meet and prepare the activity. They structured the program in almost the same style I had observed earlier: the lights were dimmed, we held hands to form a tight human chain, and after a minute of silence we all introduced ourselves and expressed our immediate feelings. Comments included "relaxed," "peaceful," "serene," "tense," and "nervous." The exercise involved the caressing of fingers and palms, changing pairs every three to five minutes. During that activity, I felt that three of my partners were very intense as they proceeded with the exercise, and I found them agreeable, if not flattering, in their gentle attention. A few others were "tolerable," and with yet others I prayed for the ring of the bell to free me from their hold. In one case, I escaped a partner I wanted to ignore by reaching for a seat, but there my hands were grabbed by a seated invalid, an ageing regular participant. I accepted that unexpected and somewhat forced engagement in a civil manner, as was expected by the rules of the game. It seems that my reactions were influenced by the physical, behavioral, and social characteristics exhibited by my partners. I learned that others were also sometimes unhappy with a few participants because of body odors, sweat, looks, age, forced physical intimacy, etc.

I estimate that we had between ten and fifteen partners during that Friday evening meeting. At the end of that part of the meeting, we returned to our seats and shared feelings and experiences. Alan, for example, told us about the memories that came back to him during the previous hour. It was ten years ago, in this same room, that he first attended a meeting of the Forum of Gay Fathers. He was then still married with two young children and in great emotional turmoil. But since that night, his life had taken a very different path; he divorced his wife and came out as a gay man. Others also repeated their pleasure at the opportunity to meet affectionate and caring men. At the end of the formal gathering, we were reminded about the forthcoming weekend retreat at a resort in upstate New York. Bill mentioned the fun and comfort that awaited the twenty men who had already registered for the event, noting that the quiet wooded site would be the backdrop for getting to know each other and making new friends.

The new leadership had started a tradition of having refreshments at the end of the meeting before departing for dinner at a nearby restaurant. This innovation offered an opportunity for casual socializing. I spoke to the only black man attending the meeting, asking him why no other African Americans came along. He thought they preferred the all-black organizations. As for his own choice of the GM, he emphasized his observation of its membership policy, which attracted men with a good education. Erik, who joined our conversation, also mentioned "the caliber" of the participants. He supported the policy of the entrance fee (five dollars for members and seven for visitors), which "keeps the bums away." Despite these considerable sums, he said, their meetings were packed; they had to send people away. Nor was he afraid of losing the "young and beautiful." Those who wanted to economize could get in free if they volunteered to help, for example, by preparing the room and taking care of the refreshments. Erik admitted that their meetings seemed to represent the more, if not the most, erotic activity at the Center, but he insisted it was not sexually or physically oriented. He believed it was mostly directed to develop and enrich the emotional intimacy dimension in the relations between gay men.

At the next SAGE meeting, one older participant related his experience at the previous GM gathering. He complained that only two guys had actually looked into his eyes with some warmth of feeling and touched him (fingers and palms) pleasantly. He specified that four others had avoided any eye contact and had hardly touched his hands. Sam took up the complaint and asserted it was proof that people didn't want to communicate, that they shut themselves off from the world. I was frankly amazed at Sam's judgmental reaction. I considered him a sensitive observer of other participants' behavior and feelings. I was surprised that he came out with that preacher's style explanation. Sam, who himself was attracted to much younger, good-looking men, might have empathized with the older man's cravings for the touch of men who, I suppose, may not have found him appealing.

However, I felt that he appreciated my rebuttal of his position, when during the final go-around I mentioned that I had also attended the last GM meeting and endured varied experiences there; I enjoyed, tolerated, and disliked some parts of the exercise. I rejected Sam's idea that these reactions had to do with one's opening up to or shutting off from the world. I was strongly supported by a few of those who had also attended the GM meeting (about five in the group), as well as by others who nodded in agreement. The GM activities were mentioned at another SAGE meeting after the dance that a few attended. They claimed that not all participants abided by the rules of changing partners, but mostly they expressed their satisfaction. No doubt, these enthusiastic reports influenced members of different groups to try out the GM events.

When I last attended a meeting led by the board, the attendees included a mixed crowd of young and old, one black and one Latino, and two newcomers in their early twenties, one of whom had recently arrived from India. I noticed these newcomers in particular, who waiting in line to enter the room approached me with questions about the program. Giggling embarrassedly, the Indian man asked if the activity took place in the dark and was there a lot of groping going on. Amused, I responded with vague messages. Sure enough, the shy visitor ended his first visit groping a young blonde in an open way I had never witnessed before at the GM gatherings. In the last go-around he also shared his story: he was a student from India who only recently had received a letter from his mother announcing the good news that she had found a charming girl to be his wife. He had replied, informing his mother he had a career to pursue first. She would have certainly died, he added, had she seen him here (still embracing his new attractive mate).

Nearly forty men had been admitted to the meeting room, and a board member facilitated the activity. The exercise involved touching and caressing one's partner's shoulders (and actually also neck and upper chest) with the two in a standing position, the active partner behind the passive one. That exercise left much body space for touching and caressing, as well as a comfortable position for full body engagement. That was the most sexually suggestive exercise I observed at the GM meetings.

Some participants were obviously enjoying themselves by way of engaging their partners with energetic massaging, including their chests and groping them from behind. One could equally observe the ecstatic response of the passive partners, who joyfully gave themselves to their enthusiastic partners. But no obviously "indecent" behavior could be observed.

I watched Al, a SAGE member who had struck me at most meetings as an unattractive aging man with an unidentifiable foreign accent and who confessed he had not had much success with men. At this GM meeting he seemed to have overcome whatever deficiencies had beset him in other sexual settings. He displayed a noticeable expertise through the very attentive massage he offered his partners. Although the men so devotedly attended to did not seem to respond in kind when the roles were reversed, they seemed to take pleasure from his enthusiastic massage. He must have enjoyed the opportunity to touch attractive men to whom he would not otherwise have had the possibility to get so close to. I saw Erik relishing both roles. He later told me he enjoyed the opportunity to be close to men but insisted these were moments of pure sexless pleasure. He noted that he had never had sex with participants. When he left for home, he went alone, though he seemed to have attracted much attention and potential partners for further intimate relationships.

I thought that Erik represented many of the participants who enjoyed the experience of erotic intimacy. Though much restrained in its physical expression, those meetings offered it openly and in a safe space. Had he looked for sex, I assume he could easily have found it elsewhere. He seemed to possess the looks and demeanor much appreciated among gay men. However, I reiterate my assertion about erotic engagement: it was strictly muted in its scope, duration, and meaning. There was no visible genital contact or undressing of any sort. Instead of the sexually ecstatic, short-lived, erotic encounters between unidentified strangers that led to orgasm in the sex venues that many participants had visited in the past (and present), the GM gathering was a short-lived experience of a different kind. It was an affectionate connection that made a strong impact in terms of the emotional intimacy it involved. Instead of "instant sex" with unidentifiable strangers, GM participants gained "instant intimacy"—indeed with strangers, but in clear view and easily identifiable as full social personae. Regardless of the overtone of the physical aspect of the group activities when compared with other groups meeting at the center, it was never confined to a strictly erotic dimension. Perhaps because of the warm feelings generated during the exercises, participants felt free and safe to share important issues affecting their lives in the company of numerous strangers.

Many had actually enjoyed the warm eye contact, the feeling of caring, the deep emotion displayed by their partners, and had tried to respond in kind. An innocent visitor might have assumed that some couples were in love, but that scene of loving relationships swiftly changed with the tinkling of the bell, when the partners so engrossed in an intimate bonding started it all over again with new strangers. These encounters were extremely egalitarian and far less prejudiced than in most sex establishments. No one was rejected in an offensive manner because of age, looks, or other characteristics so painfully degrading in the field of anonymous sex. Moreover, as with Al, "unattractive" men could reveal some hidden energies and get at least some of the pleasure they were often denied elsewhere. But, for some participants, these meetings also offered the potential for more enduring social and sexual relationships. The exchange of personal business cards, for example, was something one could not expect at cruising sites, where men were quick to disappear without revealing any trace of their social identity. It made all the difference compared with a lonely departure at a late night hour from a sex establishment.

On a visit to New York in spring 1997, I discovered that Don had successfully launched a new project at the Center that was advertised as the biweekly Saturday meetings of Date Bait. The flier elaborated: "Meet single gay men in a structured, fun, results-oriented mixer." I was not able to attend a meeting, but I was informed that the new activity had quickly gained popularity. After first introducing themselves and receiving a personal identifying number, those attending wrote down on cards the men they wished to get more closely acquainted with. After collecting the cards, Don withdrew to a nearby location where he could use a computer program and check the mix of mutual attractions. During his absence of about thirty minutes, the participants were assigned some socializing activities. On his return he announced the results. To participate in future meetings, participants were obliged to meet once one of those matched with their own choices. Obviously some participants went home without a date in hand.

That matchmaking activity soon drew much attention, and more than a hundred men showed up for the Date Bait events, and not all who came could squeeze into the packed meetings. The largest room available at the Center was "rented" to accommodate the big crowd who wished to participate in spite of the ten-dollar fee. More special events were soon announced, such as Date Bait gatherings for specific age groups: twenties, thirties, forty-plus; a lesbian event; and later, events for various professional and other categories of men and women. Don was careful to avoid a clash of dates with other popular activities at the Center. Date Bait special events were scheduled for the weekend but took place in the afternoons and were later hosted at other sites outside the Center. As one Gentle Men participant told me, the activity offered an indispensable service for the gay community. It seemed that no other method of search for gay partners in the public arena could compete with the Date Bait strategy in terms of safety and civility.

The Gentle Men meetings continued successfully for a few more years, as long as the first cohort of its membership led its activities. But gradually the board's "human capital" went into decline as prominent members passed away, left town, or became engaged in other activities. Erik told me bitterly that the new incumbent facilitators, whom he described as "ugly desperate men," were using the meetings as opportunities to snatch openly erotic experiences with innocent visitors. Don's professional rules and ethics of maintaining a society of men confined to a social scene of male affectionate relationships was elbowed out by a more vulgar approach that soon caused the group's demise. When I visited the Center in 2000 and spotted the Gentle Men meeting on the list of the day events, I discovered there were fewer than ten men, mostly newcomers, waiting for the activity to begin. The association had lost its attraction, got a poor reputation for its sleazy atmosphere, and was soon taken off the list of the Center's confirmed activities.

The GM project and its membership undoubtedly deviated from the associations described in previous chapters. The participants did not share a specific sexual proclivity or an identity representing a specific social enclave claiming legitimacy in the plethora of New York gay society. It drew its members from a wide spectrum of gay constituencies. The organization was free of any identifiable social, sexual, or spiritual agenda. The lack of an associational element of a shared specific categorical identity or of another joint interest helps explain its short existence. As stated by its founder, it was purely recreational, fulfilling the promise of playful, physical, affectionate intimacy, a civil substitute for the anonymous gay bar sociability.

Naturally, one would assume that I enjoyed the warm, friendly, erotic ambience that dominated the GM meetings. However, my surprise at discovering that activity calls attention to Moore's *Beyond Shame* (2004), which expresses his admiration for the lost gay scene of the 1970s. Moore came too late to take part in that celebration of sexuality unbound. However, the elapsed time and the survivors' stories he listened to enlivened Moore's artistic sensitivity. He could perceive the legacy of the burgeoning of gay venues (commercial and public) at the zenith of that era in terms of "cultural creativity." Earlier, in *The Rise and Fall of Gay Culture* (1997), a similar lament was expressed by Harris, who observed the growing acceptance of gays and lesbians in mainstream society and therefore envisaged the dwindling of the energies of gay sensibility. Without doubt, Don, who had invented the association of Gentle Men and later the popular and still practiced Date Bait, seems to represent the enduring creative power of gay people under the circumstances that have greatly curtailed the unrestrained expression of sexual liberty that signified the heyday of the Gay Liberation Movement. In retrospect, the GM association had actually realized Jim's dream reported in a previous chapter (in the company of the bisexuals): "Why could kittens cuddle together, while human beings, the most developed animals on earth, were unable to show that act of affection?"

CHAPTER 8

Cuddling with Gay Bears

Only at a later stage of my association with the Center did I attend a meeting of the Metro Bears New York. My participant observations among that organization were more limited than those among the other groups presented in previous chapters. However, the Bears, who have been the subject of inquiry by distinguished researchers (e.g., Harris 1997; Wright 1997; Manley, Levitt, and Mosher 2007; Hennen 2008), their agenda and activities seemed closely related to the major themes of my work.

I went into the Center one evening and noticed their meeting scheduled on the list of the daily activities. Not having heard about them before except when somebody at a SAGE meeting mentioned a group of "hairy men," I asked a man standing nearby what the Metro Bears stood for. He stuck a finger out at my short-sleeved and not fully buttoned shirt on a warm New York summer day and told me in an amused tone that it was a meeting for hairy men. So, I assumed I was in appropriate shape for that meeting (later discovering that my short beard made me even more suitable for full membership).

The room was too small to accommodate the nearly fifty macho-looking men. Actually, they were difficult to differentiate from an ordinary group of working men on their way home from some sort of blue-collar work. They were all casually dressed, mostly in their thirties, forties, and fifties, and only two were blacks. As I looked around, I noticed one dominant feature: all had a beard of some sort. Many were somewhat heavily built, many with bellies one rarely noticed in other gay groups. Only one or two were really significantly overweight. Jeff, my close CBST informant and friend, told me long ago that a flat stomach is a "must" in gay society.

The meeting, which was facilitated by four board members, was mostly dedicated to administrative issues dealing with forthcoming events: a film outing, a brunch, a Halloween party, and so on. To my surprise, once these issues were agreed to, the meeting ended.

I spoke to one of the board members, who told me the organization mostly concentrated on initiating social events outside the Center, such as socializing together in a particular bar, attending a film, spending a weekend together, and other activities that offered members opportunities to meet men they liked. They had started the organization in New York in mid-1995 and quickly expanded. They now had about a hundred registered members. He laughingly indicated that there was a lot of flirting going on at these informal meetings, and he assumed that a lot of sex took place among members. His description and my later experiences confirm the literature, professional and literary, available on the emergence of that society and about the habits of the Gay Bears in America.

About a year later I had an opportunity to attend a meeting and gain much better knowledge about the association, though not in New York. It was in a Midwestern town close to Iowa City, where I spent spring term 1997. That experience actually also reflected the claim as to the origins of Bear society in the smaller and rural towns remote from the major urban gay scenes.

I learned about that group in a flier I found on campus at the University of Iowa. A friendly phone response invited me to attend a meeting on a weekend afternoon. At this informal gathering, eight men came to spend the day together, among them two couples who had been together for a long time. They varied in age, from early twenties to early fifties, and also in appearance. They had beards or only mustaches, and they had a somewhat macho look. However, like the crowd of Bears I had observed in New York, they, too, did not exhibit the "gay look" of groomed men conscious about their weight and trendy attire. They did not wear anything particular or jewelry that could distinguish them from an ordinary group of men working in the same office or on the same shop floor.

The first meeting was mostly dedicated to administrative issues, such as checking on membership, planning future activities, particularly the upcoming annual Bear Pride in Chicago. Guy, the founder of the local group, who hosted the meeting at his apartment (shared with his partner of five years), told me about gay life in the rural and small-town environment of the Midwest. Lacking the variety of organizations and commercial gay establishments readily found in the metropolitan cities, gay life was maintained there in the "clubs," informal networks of gay men. These small groups, he explained, recruited to their annual party events members of other local circles, thus offering opportunities to meet with a wider cohort of gay men. As he told me, life can be very difficult in the Midwest "if one does not know," but once you come to know people, gay life is good enough for those who prefer to live in this part of the country (Howard 1999).

I was invited to read the newsletters and view the albums that recorded the members and the parties held since the group began eighteen months earlier. I was particularly struck by the notion of comradeship enhanced by the physical intimacy displayed at these parties and the extraordinary ease members seemed to manifest in accepting their own bodies. This was a celebration of play in informal clothing (shorts in particular), of nudity, and of affectionate eroticism among men uninhibited by the code of male bodily beauty. Good-looking men as well as those who seemed less desirable had a good time together. The photographs of sexual activity seemed to represent a kind of a cozy social game. It displayed eroticism in a relaxed campy fashion. This warm, sensual ambience seemed to emphasize affectionate sociability as a major goal, rather than a sexual hunt among strangers and an opportunity for instant sexual gratification. In any case, that weekend meeting indicated that sex as play in a more orgiastic manner was confined to the special events and celebrations scheduled in the annual cycle of the society of Iowa Bears.

Soon afterward, I was able to observe the Bear association activities more closely at the Bear Pride 1997 in Chicago (I introduced some details of that experience in Chapter 1). Organized by the Chicago chapter, it turned into a national and international convention drawing nearly 1,400 participants who gathered on Memorial Day weekend at a major Chicago hotel. This was also my first time attending a gay event of that magnitude. Bears of all ages and sizes formed a very unusual crowd. They all presented a somewhat macho appearance. One could not imagine anything more antithetical to that crowd swarming around the hotel lobby, elevators, and other public areas than the attendees at the National Convention of Cantors, which took place at the same hotel. Men in suits and yarmulkes and women in modest dresses, restrained in their public behavior, versus the robust-looking men in shorts, tight jeans, black leather garments, and chains, hugging and kissing old and new friends. The two conventions seemed to represent completely different human species thrown together by default.

Many Bear Pride participants undoubtedly displayed a sort of robust masculinity popular in both gay and heterosexual society. I was, however, impressed by the appearance of more than a few oversized participants, who seemed to "deviate" from the "authoritative" body code of both mainstream gay and nongay societies. Those men did not appear here as disadvantaged. On the contrary, they were no less surrounded by friends and admirers. A few of them also participated in the Mr. Bear Pride Contest. Their opportunities for the display of affection and for sexual encounters seemed no less promising than those of men who were more conventionally attractive.

During the many activities at the hotel and the bus rides to the various events in other parts of Chicago, I had the opportunity to establish friendly contacts with a few participants. Particularly illuminating were my conversations with Fred, who was in his late forties, from a southern city, and very reflective about the gay world. The humorous references we often made to our shared Jewish roots facilitated this impromptu communitas. We were attending the dinner cruise when I asked him to help me understand why I had the impression there was more sexual activity going on among the Bears than in other groups I observed. He looked around and responded, though apparently not directing his reply to my query: "These people, many of them are old and not beautiful in ordinary terms. They enjoy coming here because of the reassurance they will discover here that they can be loved and desirable." Several times he repeated that the element of desirability was important for both the beautiful and the less attractive who attended the convention. He pointed out one middle-aged man, whom he thought I would regard as old-looking and somewhat overweight, and said to me, "He is attractive in my eyes." He was clearly reacting to a remark I had made earlier—that if I hadn't known, I might have assumed it was a SAGE crowd. By implication, my comment seemed as sort of a derogative label for "retired" homosexuals. Fred's response resonates with Harris's (1997) depiction of the Bears phenomenon as a protest against the gay pathetic view of aging, as portrayed in the derogatory, "old queen" stereotypes.

I witnessed the easy get-together for sex play and the expressions of affection between strangers who met at the convention. They often retired to their hotel rooms and were not embarrassed if another roommate was present or came along. The accidental newcomer could join the lovemaking with no objection. Their private body parts seemed an extension of their personality not to be hidden from their friends. One afternoon, as I was preparing to leave my room, one of my roommates walked in. He was a pleasant-looking man in his early fifties with the appearance of a retired teacher or a bank executive. He attended the meeting with his partner of four years. As if talking to himself, he mumbled, "What am I going to do now, have a rest or fun?" I wondered, what he meant by "fun." Was it a delicate suggestion directed to the only other person present? When I came back a few hours later I found him in the arms of a big fellow Bear.

However, these were not men starved for sex who at last had the opportunity to satisfy a year-long deprivation. Many of them maintained a long-term relationship with men who had also come along and who were fully aware of and sometimes joined in their partners' sexual encounters.

I had recently received a message from a Center friend who, on a visit to Chicago, chanced into a Bear Party at the Steamworks gay sauna. He was overwhelmed by the encounter with 140 Bears, whose presence he was informed about on entering the place. He was moved by the comfortable demeanor of many overweight, often aged men who walked around the three-floor facility or lay on beds in lighted rooms, often with their "unappetizing" body assets in full view. It was a party he would otherwise not have attended, but he felt a sort of admiration for that brave expression of personal freedom and rejection of gay mainstream codes of physical attraction.

As indicated before, my association with the Bears was more limited in scope compared with my engagements described in other chapters. Their meetings were less regularly scheduled at the Center's premises and instead were more "active"—oriented to gatherings in specific bars and other public events. I could observe them sometimes at the Bear Night Bar Parties on Friday evenings at a Christopher Street venue. The scene was the same—men of various ages conforming to a casual dress code. They presented a mix of macho looks, free of the gay and the American mainstream "fetishism" of those absorbed with the desire to show off trim bodies and ruled by the codes of "gay" appearances. I often thought the Bears were happily and defiantly demonstrating against the nearby gay constituencies in particular.

It seems fitting to end the presentation of my experience with the Gay Bears with Harris's moving words: "The Bear phenomenon represents one of the most violent assaults that gay men have made to date against the over-groomed bodies of urban homosexuals. The bear is a man who allows himself to age in public, refusing to reverse the ravages of time by burying them beneath Max Factor foundation bases, face-lifts, Grecian Formula rinses, and hair replacement systems" (1997: 105–6).

My participation in the Bear Pride event in Chicago immersed me in an erotic atmosphere that transformed my role and the terms of my identity as an "innocent" observer (see Chapter 1). In an impromptu situation that evolved in my hotel room, shared with three other roommates, I succumbed to the friendly sexual play commotion. It was not akin in any way to an anonymous sex venue, of the rough genital interaction between strangers dominated by the unkindness of heartless relationships lamented by Saul (Chapter 4): "ending on his knees in a dark room begging for affection from men who were shut off from any emotion." The erotic ambience that dominated the Bears' activities turned into benign recreational sex play, connecting an affectionate circle of participants who experienced the sensual excitement, the emotional warmth, and a kinship of feelings, all sustained by basic human sexual energies. I was embarrassed by my loss of control, which might have betrayed the image of the "detached" observer, but I did not regret the experience that also made me part of the group. For the duration of the event, it became my rite of passage into the Bears' compassionate society.

In conclusion, despite my professional ethos anticipating a methodology of "thick description" in ethnographic writings, and although the Bears have been the subject of earlier comprehensive studies, I still felt I could not omit that part of my fieldwork, as I did with other groups with whom my involvement was short-lived (such as Gay Fathers or the Radical Fairies). I believe my observations among the Bears were sufficient and intimate enough to enable me introduce them in the ethnography and integrate their activities as part of my thesis about the life and role of contemporary gay and lesbian voluntary associations. Moreover, the account of my participation during the Bears' annual meeting in Chicago is an example of situational analysis—a Manchester School ethnographic research method: a composite case/event of social interaction, intensely observed, that seems to shed light on wider social circumstances and cultural signification concerning the studied society (e.g., Burawoy 1991). Like the members of most other associations on my list, the Bears participants assembled together to express and perform a distinctive gay identity, exhibiting intrinsic social and sexual elements, considered somewhat nonconformist in mainstream gay society.

CHAPTER 9

Listening to the Sermons
in Gay Congregations

Observers of gay life have revealed in recent years a new field of social activities and spiritual engagements among gays and lesbians occupied in a search for their lost roots in major world denominations or in recently established innovative religious congregations (e.g., Thumma and Gray 2005; Griffith 2005). My own attraction to the study of the gay synagogue, CBST, located in Greenwich Village, was triggered by the surprise discovery of a vibrant Jewish congregation founded by a group of men and women who wished to return to the cultural tradition they had abandoned when they came out as gays and lesbians (Shokeid 1995 [2003]).

My engagement with CBST confronted me with major human dilemmas of sex, gender, spirituality, ethnicity, and culture. In my adult years I have been deeply alienated from Jewish religious life, a position reflecting a deep divide in Israeli society (between the "religious" and the "seculars"). I assume I was comfortable at CBST services at least partly because that congregation stood against a major code of normative Judaism. Its mere existence was a permanent provocation against the Orthodox, whose worldview, way of life, and disciples I had venomously detested since completing religious elementary school in Tel Aviv. My perception of the gay synagogue membership was far removed from my view of an ordinary crowd in an Israeli synagogue. Actually, there are very few Israeli congregations that resemble a Reform or Conservative American service. Most Israeli synagogues are strictly Orthodox, albeit of diverse shadings.

I rarely considered my friends and acquaintances at CBST "religious." I cherished their wish to preserve a cultural heritage and the history of a tribe that occupies an important space in the texture of American society. Actually, most of my friends at CBST were constrained neither by food taboos (keeping kosher) nor by travel on the Sabbath—factors among the foremost distinguishing elements of religious life in Israel. As much as the services I attended reminded me of my own cultural background, bringing back memories of my youth, I considered CBST to be a socio-cultural-ethnic association and one of many venues of American gay society.

Not surprisingly, having completed the first version of my CBST ethnography, I became curious about the other gay religious organizations holding services in New York. It was also an older aspiration to better acquaint myself with Christianity, a religion that has affected much the fate of "my tribe" for the last 2,000 years. With the clout of an anthropologist who had already studied another gay religious institution, it seemed easy to enter the shrines of the gay Catholic, Protestant, and African-American congregations in New York. However, I did not conduct my observations with these congregations as I did with CBST. I did not attend services at only one location but instead attended different denominational services, often on the same Sunday. This made me sort of a "butterfly" observer. Though I developed a few intimate friendships at these sites, I did not cultivate the same close connections with the various organs of these institutions and their leadership.

So instead of the "traditional" ethnographic report of the workings of an institution and the relations among congregants, which I composed out of my CBST observations, here I concentrate on one major element in all services and its social role. I refer to the highly evocative spiritual and social messages conveyed in the sermons delivered to these various congregations. I consider the sermons I attended and the congregants' responses an embodiment of cultural performances shared by the clergy and their audience. That dialogical experience (though not equally expressed by the audience) constitutes an important public discourse among gay people, yet of a structure different from that in the other groups reported in this book.

Reclaiming a Neglected Subject

Based on the attendance at services, this chapter discusses the content and preaching style of the sermons and their social impact on four major gay and lesbian congregations in New York City: Dignity (Catholic), Unity (African American), CBST (Jewish), and, in particular, MCC/Metropolitan

Community Church (Protestant). The emphasis on and the mixture of religious, political, moral, and personal themes differ greatly among the four denominations and among individual preachers. My discussion expounds the sermons' potency, in Geertz's terms, of "sentimental education." Although they are passive listeners and often unable to follow the contents of the presentation, the congregants are nevertheless engaged in a "deep play" that reconfirms their identity and worldview as a morally sound community, worthy Christians and Jews, loyal American citizens, and proud gays, lesbians, and transsexuals.

Since the early days of ethnographic research, anthropologists have engaged in recording and analyzing socially sanctioned oral presentations—myths, folktales, public orations—delivered by religious and political leaders and the like. My own apprenticeship as an anthropologist was influenced by Middleton, who in *Lugbara Religion* (1960) interpreted the role of ritual addresses (which one might term "sermons") delivered at ghost invocation ceremonies by lineage elders in Ugandan tribal society. He argued that like myth and genealogy, these speeches were used by the Lugbara leaders to explain and validate present-day relationships and historical events. However, the bulk of this research has been conducted mainly in non-Western societies.

For many years the study of the major monotheistic religions—inquiry into the use of canonic texts, the attendance and behavior in churches, synagogues, and mosques—was by and large left to theologians and scholars of world religions and also, to some extent, to sociologists. Aspiring anthropologists have rarely chosen to research these areas (e.g., Antoun 1989). Mainstream anthropology has occupied a marginal position in what has become known as Jewish Studies (e.g., Heilman 1976; Prell 1989). My previous engagement in religious oral performances took place during my study of Israeli immigrants in New York who attended weekly Torah study sessions offered by Chabad (a Hassidic movement). The teachers' interpretation of the texts and other messages aimed to raise the participants' pride in their Jewish identity and to encourage a stronger affiliation with Jewish religious life (Shokeid 1988b: 139–60).

In recent years, the ethnographic projects that are close to my own interests have been conducted by scholars of Fundamentalism. I mention in particular Crapanzano (2000), who attended church services and Bible study groups. His subjects, however, exhibited a very different mode of employing and interpreting the words of the biblical texts from what I observed at gay religious services. By "literalism," Crapanzano claimed, Christian Fundamentalists have developed a mode of "puritanism" that engaged them in "an uncritical and rote allegiance to a reading of the Bible that deprived it of what many have found to be its deepest meaning" (324).

My study of CBST, though essentially aimed at revealing the social components and dynamics of a gay society in a metropolitan environment, inevitably directed my research to subjects of ritual and religious texts. Thus, a major chapter in my ethnography (118–42) is dedicated to the *drashah* (Hebrew: "sermon"; pl., *drashot*). I opened the chapter with the following statement:

> The most anticipated point of the service at CBST was the presentation of the sermon or drasha. The interpretation of the week's—or holiday's—Torah reading was the most personalized, least formulized part of the service, and allowed the speaker to express his or her feelings and attitudes toward God, Judaism, the synagogue, family and friends, homosexuality, and other shared experiences. Both the content and presentation of the drasha became a major topic of conversation among the congregants as well as a source of pride for the presenter.

During the initial period of my fieldwork (1989–1990) CBST conducted its services as a lay-led congregation. Any congregant in good standing could ask to deliver a drashah that was approved as suitable by the religious committee. However, the scene of sermon presentation at CBST changed greatly since 1995 with the installment of its first pulpit rabbi, and a few years later with the hiring of an assistant rabbi (Shokeid 2001). The synagogue had actually adopted a format close to that of the Christian denominations: sermons delivered by leading clerics.

As already indicated, I was tempted to observe the social and spiritual life in the gay Christian congregations in New York City. On prolonged research visits to New York over a period of three years (July 2003 to July 2006) I attended services every Sunday at one gay church or more. These included the Protestant-style morning service at MCC, an afternoon service at the black (Baptist-style), Unity New York, and an evening mass at Dignity New York (Catholic). Altogether, I spent more than forty Sunday mornings with the MCC congregation, fifteen Sunday afternoons at Unity, and twenty Sunday evenings at Dignity. In later years I continued to attend services at CBST and MCC on my visits to New York. I maintained friendly relationships with the veteran cohort of congregants and with Rabbi Sharon Kleinbaum at CBST. At MCC I remained especially close to a prominent deacon who had greeted me on my first visits, and I always enjoyed the warm welcome of Reverend Pat Bumgardner.

My observations of the services conducted at the three separate Christian institutions revealed different worship styles, but one element was shared by the services of all denominations I observed (Christian and Jewish): the public delivery of a moralistic statement aimed at creating an experience of spiritual awareness and delivered in most cases by the ordained clergy. The "sermon" at MCC (a movement founded in 1968), the "homily" at Dignity (founded in 1969), the drashah at CBST (founded in 1972), and the "celebration" at Unity (founded in 1985), all seemed comparable as to basis and intention. They all related, in one form or another, to the designated daily (Sabbath or Sunday) sections from the Old or New Testament.

The sermon is considered to be one of the oldest Christian teaching methods. The necessity of preaching the Good News was stressed by Jesus himself. The Protestant Reformation, in particular, emphasized the role of the sermon and made it a salient part of the service, while also attempting to have it respond to the challenges of a changing world and culture.[1] The sermon as part of the Jewish service and as the rabbi's task was adopted in the nineteenth century by the Reform Movement. Today it is an essential element of the service in most synagogues in the Jewish world.

The art of the sermon has attracted scholars and practitioners in the field of religion and homiletics, but these experts have conducted relatively little empirical social research on the preaching and hearing of sermons. The few studies that have been conducted have mainly employed quantitative and experimental methods, producing inconsistent results about the effectiveness of sermons according to age, sex, and education (e.g., Pargament and DeRosa 1985). The available research claims that listeners are frequently unable to comprehend the complex structure and associative connections made by the preacher. Avery and Gobble found that the preachers they studied seemed to be characterized by a "pervasive lack of clarity and consistency concerning the purpose of the preaching task" (1980: 46). Howden thought that when hearers stated that a sermon was "helpful," "meaningful," or even "good," they actually meant to say that it was no more than "pleasant" or "entertaining" (1989: 204).

My anthropological training and sociological imagination could not condone that verdict and supposition, which ascribe little value and meaning to a performance that seemed to me central to the social and spiritual activities of the service in all congregations. I set out to explore the presentation strategies employed by the preachers as well as their agendas—spiritual, moral, social, political, and so on. My objective was to inquire into the congregants' modes of response and their interpretation of the messages conveyed by the clergy.

Entering the Field

The venues of the services I observed were strikingly dissimilar in their decor and physical facilities. MCC and Unity had less impressive spaces in old, though somewhat refurbished, former industrial sites. Dignity conducted its services at the graceful sanctuary of St. John's Presbyterian Church in the Village. CBST had relocated its major Friday service to the impressive sanctuary at the Chelsea Church of the Holy Apostles.

The socioeconomic and ethnic background and the age range of these congregations also differed to some extent. MCC's crowd appeared the most varied, with a large constituency of African Americans and Latinos. Dignity's congregants were mostly white, middle-class, somewhat older men, with very few women. Unity was a fellowship based in the African American community, though I regularly met one other white man there. Its population seemed varied in age and economic status, and also had more women. The Jewish CBST congregation was mostly white of the middle and upper-middle classes, with men and women equally represented (a change from the earlier days of my research when men were the majority).

MCC, Unity, and CBST (from the mid-1990s onward) were organized according to a formal leadership structure, including officially appointed clerical staff. The services at Dignity were conventional in style, adhering to mainstream Catholic Church congregations, but they did not have a formally appointed local leadership of openly gay or nongay priests. The services were conducted by a number of ordained volunteer gay priests whose status in the church hierarchy was somewhat ambiguous.

I enjoyed the warm welcome and the jovial atmosphere that dominated the Unity church in Brooklyn. Nevertheless, I could not endure the ordeal of traveling by subway from Manhattan, as the long route was often changed over the weekend for maintenance work. My wish to attend a few different congregations on the same day (Sunday) also made it difficult for me to remain for the entire lengthy Unity service.

I gradually stopped attending regular services at Dignity. I enjoyed the stylish and smooth form of worship but somehow did not feel compelled to develop more intense ties with the congregation. The church members themselves also related to me that Dignity New York had not developed social activities beyond the schedule of religious services. Incidentally, I observed at Dignity another occasional visitor who, like myself, did not take part in the rituals as most other congregants did (taking the Eucharist, etc.). As it turned out, he was Jewish. He told me that he was uncomfortable at the gay synagogue due to its insistence on praying in Hebrew. He found the services at Dignity relaxing and conducive to spiritual contemplation.

When all the circumstances are considered—geographic location, attractiveness of the physical space, the spiritual atmosphere, and so on—all seem secondary to the accidental personal encounters that often take place at the early stages of fieldwork. Had I not met Don during my second visit to an MCC service and struck up a friendship with him almost from our first conversation, I believe I might have spent more time and energy on Dignity or Unity. An impressive African American professional in his early fifties, eloquent, friendly, and involved in the church organization, Don seemed an ideal informant in the age-old tradition of ethnographic fieldwork.[2] I regularly rounded off my attendance at Sunday morning services with brunch in Don's company. We kept to the same menu at a nearby diner, which became our traditional Sunday venue. In the afternoon we often strolled around the city, attending parades or visiting antique markets or mutual friends. The sermon we heard earlier that day was usually a starting point for our lengthy conversations. I communicated with other MCC participants as well (particularly during the social hour following the service), but these connections lacked the intensity of my relationship with Don.

At an early stage I realized that substantial research had already been conducted in MCC congregations (e.g., Wilcox 2003; Lukenbill 2005; Thumma and Gray 2005), and I did not wish to replicate it or compare various specific issues. However, the sermon seemed to be neglected in these studies. Listening to religious sermons is not easy for anyone reared in academia. Reconstructing these oral performances seemed an impossible task, unless one struggled to write them down simultaneously or record them using the various technical means available.[3] This difficulty has already been identified by other scholars who have attempted to describe sermons. A penetrating insight was presented by Trueblood (1958) and quoted by Reierson, who points out that "the difference between a sermon and a lecture is fundamentally a difference of aim ... whereas a lecture has a subject, a sermon has an object" (1988: 63).

I found it sufficient to assume the role of an accidental voyeur at both Unity and Dignity. My observations at Dignity, Unity, and CBST will provide comparisons for a discussion of my more extensive experience of sermon attendance at MCC, a sample of which (about fifteen short summations) is discussed next.

Preachers and Sermons at MCC

It became a Sunday routine I shared with nearly one hundred men and women assembled at MCC for the usually evocative service. The crowd, hailing from all walks of life, made an enthusiastic weekly appearance to meet with friends and enjoy moments of spiritual elevation that included the sermon's messages. They no doubt also benefited from the musical performance, which at times reached the heights of a powerful resounding concert. Except for one time at an early stage of my attendance, I did not take the Eucharist.[4] There were others who, for various reasons, also refrained from sharing that ritual. Nevertheless, I felt part of the congregation and enjoyed a warm reception.

On my first visit to MCC (July 2003), the service was conducted by a male assistant minister who was soon to leave for another post. In his sermon he referred to brief daily portions from the Old and New Testaments. He focused on the story of Jesus' arrival on the Sabbath ready to teach, which immediately arouses the congregants' resentment: "Who is that Jesus, son of the carpenter, who considers himself a teacher?" And Jesus responds: "The prophets lack respect in their own town and among their own relatives!"

The preacher made a connection between Jesus and the fate of homosexuals, both having been ostracized by their societies. I was struck by the relevance of scripture for gay Christians, who could closely identify with the life and suffering of the central figure of their religion. But the homily I heard later the same day at Dignity, although treating the same Bible story, did not emphasize the affinity between the destinies of Jesus and gays.

The following week's service was conducted by Reverend Pat Bumgardner (whom the congregants called "Reverend Pat"). It was a happy farewell sermon that celebrated the departure of the assistant pastor. Short and extremely thin, dressed in black (slacks and shirt), she reminded me of the crucified youth whom she often evoked in her sermons. During the sermons her voice carried to the farthest row of the long narrow hall, but there was something haunting in her strident style. In any event, at my first experience of her preaching she spoke about the daily Biblical portion on Jesus' admonition of his disciples not to take along any extra belongings on their missionary voyage. To the delight of her audience, she told a story from her youth about a bag lady who rarely changed her underwear but merely added one set on top of the other until she got involved in a road accident that revealed her strange habit and caused her considerable embarrassment. The departing minister and his partner were humorously advised not to take along even one other set of underwear. It was an engaging performance that left the audience in a good mood.

A week later (July 2003), the tone was different. Rev. Pat focused on the story of Jesus ready to take a break and rest with his disciples when a crowd of strangers surrounded him and forced him to stop resting and teach them. Rev. Pat used the story as a parable for our obligation to share whatever we have with the poor and needy and to help them. "This is what we always do at MCC: feed the hungry [through the charity services of meals and shelter regularly provided on church premises], and this is being symbolized today in the Eucharist." The Eucharist was thus presented as a ritual of sharing and as an expression of solidarity among the congregation. The sermon was softened by humor, which made it sound less strictly moralistic.

The homily I listened that evening at Dignity remained within the domain of textual analysis. It related to John the Baptist's and Jesus' differing views on the coming of the kingdom of God. Contrary to John, Jesus believed God's kingdom was already with us, and this was conveyed as a "good message" for us in today's world: "God is everywhere and with everything we do." The preacher made no specific reference to his listeners' membership of Dignity or its unique activities. The atmosphere remained solemn, with no breaks for humor or personal references.

In a lengthy sermon in August 2003, Rev. Pat started off with the story of Jesus identifying those among his disciples who believed in his mission and those who would betray him. She related this event to the present-day betrayal by the Vatican leadership of its true mission, stating that while exonerating their own emissaries who sexually abuse children, they fight homosexuals, who they claim endanger Christian morality. Moreover, Rev. Pat declared, the Church remains aloof regarding the real social problems in the world out there, while "we" [the stigmatized homosexuals at MCC] take care of the hungry and the homeless.

On my return to New York early in 2004, I attended a sermon in which Rev. Pat expressed her furious resentment against President Bush. This was brought on by the president's attack on the wave of gay marriages in San Francisco and his proposal to amend the American constitution in such a way that it would recognize only the marriage of a man and a woman as a legal act of marriage. This discrimination, she claimed, displayed only one of many expressions of inequality and abuse of human rights by the Bush administration. In particular, they were indifferent to the millions of Americans without medical insurance. However, Rev. Pat also directed her audience's attention to the gross abuse of human rights in other parts of the world, such as Uganda, Bosnia, Palestine, and so on.

A few weeks later (March 2004) the sermon was delivered by a visiting male minister. In a very relaxed tone he told the story of Esther, who had been admonished by her uncle that she must take care of her people before considering her own welfare. The minister tied this story to the lesson of Jesus, who seemed disturbed by the severe punishment of sinners in Galilee. He took these narratives as evoking the question of whether we have a religion of love or of fear. He stated that the religion of Jesus was one of love, but the religion of Mr. Bush and the Fundamentalists was one that could not comprehend the message of love as represented by the lives of homosexuals. He stated, "We are a movement of love," as exemplified by the many activities of MCC.

I attended the service at Dignity that same evening. The subject of gay marriage was not mentioned in the sermon, but one of my friends there, who was among the more knowledgeable in scripture, expressed his apprehension that the issue of gay marriage might jeopardize the chances of the Democrats in the coming presidential elections (he might have been right, because Kerry lost to Bush). However, at the end of the service, the congregants went in a procession, with lighted candles, to join a demonstration on the issue of gay marriage assembled at the square in front of Stonewall Bar, the landmark of gay liberation.

This was without a doubt a time when the leaders of all the gay religious movements were expressing their strong support of gay marriage. But the outrage against the Bush government's abusive rhetoric and active obstruction of gay marriage was nowhere expressed as vehemently as in the sermons preached at MCC. This issue was raised again by Rev. Pat in her sermon of March 21. It centered on the dramatic story of Sarah, the senior wife of Abraham's household, who demanded that Hagar and her son be banished.

God responded in contradiction to Sarah's unjust claim and promised Hagar that her son would beget a nation as great as that of Sarah's son. The lesson learned from this ancient episode was that no one had the authority to deny the rights of minorities. Therefore, President Bush and his team had no legitimate power to discriminate against gay people.

Rev. Pat diffused the tension created by her striking accusations by her sudden adoption of a calmer tone. She told her audience how she had been stopped a few days previously by a man who approached her with the appeal: "Father! I have sinned, but I am a good man—forgive me." Sure enough, Rev. Pat had fulfilled his request in the presence of passersby on the street: she rested her hands on his forehead, confirmed his claim that he was a good man, and prayed for his redemption. The congregants had a good laugh about her self-mockery regarding her boyish body that had been mistaken by the sinner for that of a man. But, she continued, urging the congregation to shout as loudly as they could, attend demonstrations and forward letters of protest to Senators Clinton and Schumer, who supported their cause.

The scriptural texts presented and discussed at MCC were a constant allegorical source of support for the position of homosexuals in American society. The main difference between Rev. Pat and other preachers was their more restrained style of delivery. A newly ordained pastor related the story of the adulterous woman who was brought before Jesus. Asked whether she should be stoned, as prescribed in the Pentateuch, Jesus responded that one who had never sinned should cast the first stone. The speaker compared the situation of the adulterous woman and that of "us—the queers." He claimed that gays were treated as sinners, as objects, were denied the right to marriage, and made easy prey for attackers as if they were subhuman.

On Easter Sunday 2004, the guest of honor was Rev. Troy Perry, the charismatic founder of MCC (see, e.g., Perry 1978). In a voice vibrant with the assurance of uncontested authority, Rev. Perry recounted the most dramatic revelation of Jesus' divine nature: Mary Magdalene's arrival at his tomb and her discovery that he had disappeared. Jesus had walked out of his tomb to take on his eternal role for mankind. Rev. Perry compared this imagery with the fate of gays and lesbians, who had now also "emerged from the tomb." It was a powerful evocation for his audience, as compared with the standard one of "coming out of the closet." This assurance of the imminent arrival of total liberation from the man who had founded the MCC movement and made it an international success seemed to offer more than a routine Messianic promise.

The following Easter week sermon was delivered by Rev. Karin,[5] the assistant minister, who differed greatly from Rev. Pat in both looks and demeanor. Feminine in appearance and soft-toned in delivery, she nevertheless related to scripture similarly to Rev. Pat. The story she presented on this occasion was that in which Jesus revealed himself after the crucifixion and blessed his disciples with the moving phrase, "Peace be with you." But the core of the sermon was the narrative regarding the disciples, who were hiding at home for fear of the religious authorities in Jerusalem. This was a reminder, Rev. Karin argued, of the fears in daily life shared by many of us; but the belief in Jesus liberated us from these fears in much the same way that it freed the disciples. In contrast to Rev. Pat, who usually used her sermons to illustrate political and social issues beyond the immediate needs of individual congregants, Rev. Karin related more specifically to personal issues.

A few weeks later, I spent a weekend in Washington. I decided to take the opportunity to attend a service at the local MCC congregation. The difference between the site and the congregation of these two offshoots of the same movement was immense. Compared with the modest old structure of the refurbished MCC New York site, the Washington congregation occupied a very impressive sanctuary built specifically for that purpose in a modern architectural style. The crowd also looked more affluent, seemingly composed of mainly middle- and upper-middle-class congregants. I did not espy anything of the more exotic attire seen on MCC-NY congregants (especially among the transgendered). The female senior minister who led the service presented a restrained combination of ritual and liturgy that reminded me more of Dignity-NY than of MCC-NY. During the sermon, no parallels were drawn between scripture and contemporary issues involving gay life or any other major political events of the day.

At the service in New York the following week I told a few acquaintances about my Washington experience. A young black woman commented that had MCC-NY taken a more amenable space for their church—in the neighborhood of Chelsea, for example—they would also have succeeded in recruiting more middle-class people (MCC-NY is situated at 446 West Thirty-Sixth Street, close to Tenth Avenue).

I asked a man sitting in front of me if he liked Rev. Pat's style of delivery. He replied that sometimes she was too thunderous in her enthusiasm, but that she was quite different face–to-face, when she projected a very gentle persona. One could hardly hear her voice on those occasions. For sure, Rev. Pat had the additional skill of making people feel she cared about them as individuals (myself included). Whatever the issue under attack, it was always made clear that those present in the sanctuary were among "the good people." I believe she knew the names of most of those who regularly attended services, and she greeted them warmly at the end of each one. A former MCC member, a black academic whom I knew from my MACT participation, had left the congregation after he separated from his partner (a congregant of Latino extraction active in the church organization). However, he could not replace his need for spirituality by joining Unity, although the style there was similar to the church experiences of his childhood and youth. He missed the combination of spirituality and politics represented by Rev. Pat's leadership.

On July 11, 2004, the sermon was delivered by a transgendered junior minister. The portion from scripture included the story of the lawyer who addressed Jesus with the question: "Who is my neighbor?" Jesus responded with the parable of the Good Samaritan. The lesson preached by the speaker was that we have to love our neighbors and that everyone around us is a neighbor! This is the message of MCC, the message of love, he said. We have to break down the barriers that divide groups, and develop instead "an anarchy of social relations" governed by love. It was a sermon close to Rev. Karin's manner of preaching.

I used the opportunity of "love your neighbor" to ask a congregant on his way back to his seat after the Communion what his reaction was to the day's sermon, compared with his response to Reverend Pat's sermons. The son of a Methodist minister, he answered, "It's like comparing oranges with apples." Reverend Pat had an especially powerful quality, he explained, but he liked both styles.

Two weeks later (July 25, 2004), the sermon was delivered by another veteran male minister. His voice was soft and warm. I got lost and possibly dozed off while trying to follow his chain of associations, which dealt with spirituality, the story of Sodom and Gomorrah, and other biblical events. However, I suddenly became alert again as he began dealing with the accusation sometimes made against their church that it was too political in its messages. Religion anywhere, he argued, is always associated with politics. The Evangelical movement, in particular, constantly interfered in American politics. As for MCC, it carried a message of spirituality that encouraged each individual to look into the mirror and judge his or her own actions in relation to other people. He emphasized, for example, that transsexuals were God's chosen people.

Don commented on this last issue at our brunch an hour later. He wondered aloud how he might have first reacted to accidentally meeting, in public, one particularly provocative transgendered MCC member. Our perception and treatment of other people, Don concluded, was often influenced by prejudices that were difficult to erase. His response made me reconsider some of the points the sermon raised, despite its length and its many digressions.

The last sermon I attended, given by Rev. Karin before we both departed at the end of summer 2004, exemplified how sharply she differed from Rev. Pat. Again, Rev. Karin emphasized the personal existential condition of the individual congregant. She posed the question, "Do you want to be well?" It is a matter of personal decision, she claimed. One can choose to be miserable, but one can equally choose to be healthy and happy. She revealed her own situation of personal afflictions that could have destroyed her life and how she had managed to overcome these misfortunes, including with the help of medication. It all went to show the need to fight back against adversity and how important faith in God was in finding the motivation for self-healing. This faith saved Noah from the Flood, secured the Promised Land for Abraham's offspring and blessed Sarah with a child long after the normal age of fertility. "Do not fear, but believe in God," was Rev. Karin's message.

During the social hour following the service I held a conversation with a close acquaintance who told me that the sermon reminded him of his split-up with his boyfriend, who had refused to consider medical intervention in order to overcome a personal condition that threatened to destroy their relationship. Actually, it was Rev. Karin whom they had consulted and who had tried to save their deteriorating partnership.

The accomplishment of the spiritual leadership at MCC seemed to hinge on both Rev. Pat and Rev. Karin serving the congregation with their combination of "hard and soft" styles and agendas. Together, they represented the global versus the local, the angry versus the more laid back. At a later period, when Rev. Karin left for another post, the man who replaced her filled a similar role of the "gentler" preacher.

On my return to New York in August 2005, I attended a sermon delivered by the minister who replaced Rev. Karin. His presentation concentrated, in particular, on his own extraordinary experience of divine revelation, an event of such magnitude that it filled him with a feeling of profound peace. The speaker's conclusion was that anyone could meet with God. At our brunch, I asked Don if he believed that one could have an encounter with the Divine Power, as suggested in the sermon. Don was positive one could and told me the details of an experience that he believed was a good example of such an event.

Grasping the Message

Naturally, I was puzzled by the effect of these performances on the four congregations. What did they really absorb? I wondered, and what remained with them of that oral battle at MCC with the "baddies" in American society as well as with the messages delivered in the other congregations?

Unity Sermons

At Unity, the sermon conducted in the African American church tradition of the "Celebration" (e.g., Moyd 1995) was a long event that combined songs, choreography, and an oral text that often repeated a short, focused message. The minister, who moved ecstatically around the hall with a megaphone in his hand, was supported by a powerful team of singers and musicians.

Despite the clamor created by the preacher's amplified voice and the strident musical support, I had no difficulty comprehending the messages of the Unity sermon. The preacher would often reiterate a phrase such as "It is a test," or "God is everywhere in what you do, you are sacred," while the audience would ecstatically respond with the same phrase. The minister often introduced his own life experiences into the sermon as proof of the power of a belief in God. His messages were mostly inspirational and firmly related to the participants' feelings and personal predicaments. Sometimes they displayed an even more dramatic affirmation of the preacher's words and promises by dancing around the hall in ecstasy (presumed to be the result of being possessed by the Holy Spirit). It was a joint venture, with the preacher, the choir, and the orchestra, as well as the whole congregation, creating an apparently spontaneous celebration. The cumulative effect was a sort of a collaborative art work, in which all present took on an active role in the script—the movement, the singing, and the musical accompaniment.[6] In sum, at Unity one did not find the division of labor that was prevalent at other services, where the congregants played a passive role when listening to the preacher's sermon.

Dignity Sermons

At Dignity, it was the identity of the participants rather than the style and content of service that characterized this congregation. As described in earlier studies, gay Catholics, although they felt alienated and disinherited by the Church, nevertheless remained loyal to its beliefs, practices, and values (e.g., Primiano 2005: 23).

Most of the homilies were derived from the daily scriptural portion. I often indicated in my field notes how the type of scriptural reference and the preacher's presentational tone at the evening service at Dignity contrasted with the same day's services at MCC and Unity. The delivery was usually shorter and only marginally related to the congregation's sexual orientation. As a result, the emotional ambience also remained restrained. Nevertheless, the seemingly more focused and restrained delivery was not necessarily easy to follow and remember. The world that was described and the moral conclusions that were deduced were rather remote from the context of the listeners' ordinary lives. Nevertheless, the ambience dominating that mostly male crowd immersed in a spiritual engagement revealed an overwhelming notion of queer communitas (experienced at a site in close proximity to a major concentration of gay venues, the neighborhood of Christopher Street in West Village). That supportive ambience invited the Jewish man who took the services and sermons at Dignity as an opportunity to meditate and relax.

MCC Sermons

At MCC I noticed that the audience responded with frequent laughter that indicated their identification with the preacher's jocular statements. But when I asked the people sitting next to me or other congregants for their reaction to the sermon, they often said that it was hard to concentrate during the presentation. These answers, however, did not imply that the listeners were frustrated or displeased with a delivery that still generated a mood of warmth and affection. I assumed sermons that lacked clear presentation and focus must nevertheless have aroused associations with memorable past experiences. I have presented examples of this above, such as Don's recollections of past encounters.

By the end of my stay in New York in fall 2005, I had become captivated by Rev. Pat's sermons, in which she consistently conjured a mix of doctrinal, inspirational, and moral elements.[7] The moral element, however, seemed to gain significance as Rev. Pat increasingly developed her presentations in the direction of contemporary political life. Neither Rev. Karin (who had also won my attention) nor the minister who replaced her followed Rev. Pat's pattern of presentation. Instead, they often highlighted inspirational and personal elements that were more directly relevant to their congregants' life experiences.

CBST Sermons

The doctrinal basis always seemed to be a starting point in all Christian congregations, as it usually offered a powerful identification with Jesus' personality, suffering, and teachings. At the gay synagogue, however, doctrinal elements could not offer an easy platform on which to base moralistic discourses. The Old Testament contains some of the most powerfully dramatic narratives in Western culture. However, it lacks the continuing presence of a major actor and his supportive disciples in a series of vivid scenes that become familiar to the audience as a sort of intimate family drama. Not surprisingly then, the sermons at CBST were generally based far less on scripture. Lacking the human characteristics of the divine Jesus figure, the presence of God was less prominent in the sermons at CBST. Thus, the drashot presented mostly by the rabbis often resembled lectures engaging inspirational, personal, and communal issues with a moralistic message. For example, a 1995 Rosh Hashanah (New Year) drashah made the following introduction:

> What does it mean to build a sacred community, a kehillah kedoshah? We need a community that is far more than a place where one can show up for a service here or a service there. We, gays and lesbians and our friends and families, understand the urgent need for real community, the urgent need to have a place that supports us in moments of crisis and sadness and a place in which joy—simchah—can be celebrated. (Kleinbaum 2005: 37)

A 1997 Rosh Hashanah drashah opened with the statement:

> I was struck this year by the number of times I have heard the following: "you know, I'm spiritual, but I'm not religious." Does that

sound familiar? "I'm really a very spiritual person, but I'm completely anti-religion." I'm not going to ask for a show of hands. . . . The truth is, I respect that statement deeply, because it is usually made in response to a religion that is—how shall we say it?—stilted. (Kleinbaum 2005: 53)

The Anthropologist's Dilemma

One may assume that the socioeconomic background of the congregation also influenced the style of sermons I attended at the four religious institutions. Thus, my sole experience at MCC-Washington revealed a different type of service and a far more restrained rhetorical manner within the same religious movement. In any case, Rev. Pat's sermons, colored by her relentless attacks on American agencies of power as well as on other leading world institutions, were not considered more or less satisfactory by the congregation than Rev. Karin's sermons, which were relatively relaxed and focused on personal issues. In all the congregations, the listeners were generally content with the preachers' performances. Most of the preachers at the congregations I visited were treated with respect and affection. Moreover, it seemed to me that most listeners did not expect an outcome, a "tangible product," in answer to Howden's (1989) query regarding what preaching "does or does not do." On the whole, I felt it was inappropriate to criticize sermons; I was careful in conversation not to seek a direct evaluation of them.

My observations of the sermons delivered by Rev. Pat and her colleagues did not reveal a departure from the Christian preaching tradition. As suggested by Van Seters, "Every sermon is uttered by socialized beings to a social entity in a specific social context and always at a social moment" (1988: 17). Moreover, he elaborated, "Preaching to the church is a form of public discourse in which God is recognized as being related to human beings not just individually but in the full context of their existence" (20). The discourse and social encounters that take place within the framework of sermons have been succinctly described by Brueggeman: "All parties to this act of interpretation need to understand that the text is not a contextless absolute, nor is it an historical description, but it is itself a responsive, assertive, imaginative act that stands as a proposal of reality to the community. As the preacher and the congregation handle the text, the text becomes a new act that makes available one mediation of reality" (1988: 138).

Brueggeman was aware of the potential traps involved in interpretation: "The preaching moment is a moment of great complexity, great danger, and great possibility" (1988: 142). Greatly different from the observations conducted by Crapanzano (2000) at Fundamentalist venues, Rev. Pat associated the potential freedom and risk inherent in the task of preaching with the field of American politics, in a mode far removed from textual literalism. She handled this project with an energy and force that other preachers applied to other areas of human experience.

The results of the obligation to preach and reproduce the Good News, the Word of God (or the "gift of God's grace," in Barth's terms, 1963: 21–22), are difficult to define and measure. As Nichols (1985: 228–29; quoted in Howden 1989: 204–5) admitted: "In terms of the living human 'documents' we work with, we really do not know what preaching does or does not do." Is preaching, as Howden suggested, a unique kind of communication that cannot be measured in the same terms as other forms of human communication?

Approaching the sermon event from an anthropological perspective, one naturally searches for interpretations and concepts of a category associated, for example, with Turner's communitas and liminality—his analytical insights for collective endurance—or with Geertz's deep play—his reading of the Balinese cockfight as a social text of status gambling. Observing the congregants at MCC, Dignity and CBST (in later years) assume the role of the apparently passive listeners, the query remains: what has been the product of that major segment of ritual in all services?

As I return to Geertz confronting his Balinese public square "congregations" enjoying a bloody fight between cocks, I feel we share a similar problem when he argues: "For an anthropologist, whose concern is with formulating sociological principles, not with promoting or appreciating cockfights, the question is, what does one learn about such principles from examining culture as assemblage of texts?" (1973: 448). And his conclusion: "Attending cockfights and participating in them is for the Balinese, a kind of sentimental education" (449). I follow a similar approach: I do not consider the congregants listening to sermons "passive" participants.

The Sermono-Musical Experience

As evidenced in my observations, the messages delivered by the preachers seemed to lack a standardized theme and a patterned style of presentation compared with the scene of cockfights in Balinese society. Geertz interpreted the cockfights' effects in terms of "sentimental education" related to the participants' perceptions of their social status and existential conditions. However, the emotions experienced during sermon attendance and its potential of sentimental education call for another category of responses. I suggest that the congregants' levels of attention and personal satisfaction, during and after the presentation of sermons, resembled a moment of emotional alertness comparable to the experience of an audience attending a classical music concert, enjoying the experience of listening to the creation of a composer they love.

I posit that the preachers' messages at MCC and other congregations— scriptural, spiritual, political, communal, personal, or poetic—made their first apparent impact on the listeners, which one might compare to a musical performance. I call it the "sermono-musical experience." Except for a minority of experts or people better musically educated, the majority of listeners at a classical music concert (myself included) cannot analyze the structure, themes, and specific roles of the various instruments throughout the performance. They emerge "pleased," "relaxed," "overwhelmed," or "moved," or, in the case of music with which they are not familiar, "confused" and "disturbed" (Slonimsky 1965). These reactions seem basically similar to those that I and other researchers observed when we spoke to congregants during or immediately after listening to sermons at all the venues.

With the above suggestion, I follow a trail blazed by scholars who have analyzed the sermon as an art form. For example, based on the sermon's use of image and story, metaphor, irony and paradox, evocative symbols, poetic and mythic language, dramatic rhetoric and based on the utilization of modes of knowing beyond the cognitive or rational mode, Reierson (1988) identified the sermon as a literary composition. The sermon, however, is only part of an elaborate service. Together with other components, it creates a dramatic performance with a script that is well rehearsed by both the clergy and the lay congregants. The stage is set with material and visual props—the stained-glass windows, the stone and wooden statues, the crosses, the canonicals, and so on—but the sermon plays a more conscious and intentional role in this performance. It is the one part that is not rehearsed in advance as a standardized repetitive text in the course of the prescribed ritual. Instead, it is a direct genuine communication between the congregation leader (pastor, priest, or rabbi) and the audience of congregants.[8]

Although their specific delivery style was very different, both Rev. Pat and Rev. Karin (and other preachers in all congregations, who were closer in style to one or the other) related to their listeners' major concerns as well as to the prevailing symbols of their denominational culture (Wardlaw 1988). Rev. Pat's powerful political discourse raised the congregants' awareness of their collective identity as a disadvantaged minority in the mosaic of America's social order. On the other hand, Rev. Karin's relaxed and personal agenda, evoked an emotional response to the situation of the congregants—gays, lesbians, bisexuals and transsexuals—as individuals who endured the difficulties of their specific position in American society.

Sharon Kleinbaum, the senior rabbi at CBST, titled her book of sermons *Listening for the Oboe* (2005). She used this musical metaphor to explain the complex journey toward religious knowledge and spirituality. In her sermon for Rosh Hashanah 1997, the rabbi made no use of scripture. It was an evocative discourse about the difficulties and passion involved in the process of learning Jewish religion and traditions (53–61). She compared this goal to the painful process she underwent when advancing from an embarrassing ignorance of classical music to some familiarity with Beethoven's Ninth Symphony. As indicated in the published text of the sermon ("Laughter" in parentheses), the audience laughed often during this presentation. As she tells in a humorous style, the rabbi's identification of the notes of the oboe was a sign that she had at last gained a deeper familiarity with Beethoven's great and complex work.

I assume that the congregants who listened to the rabbi's words on the eve of that major Jewish holiday were not convinced by her sermon that one could easily grasp Judaism and its traditions. As typical with most sermons in all congregations, I assume that by the end of her presentation they did not remember much of the less amusing content of that particular drasha. They seemed to emerge entertained, presumably exalted, responsive to their rabbi's ability to laugh at herself, and possibly also optimistic about the possibility of expanding their knowledge and understanding of Judaism. They had heard the voice of their religious leader, whom many of them loved and admired. It was a sermono-musical experience, a moment when their rabbi's voice and its subtextual messages inspired them as a cohesive community and as individuals seeking personal meaning in their lives. It was as though they were listening to an oboe in a synagogue symphony.

However, the audiences at the various congregations cannot be compared with the audiences attending musical performances anywhere—for one major reason. The concert hall crowd recruits strangers who have no common social bonds beyond the love of music. They do not constitute a "community" in any sociological sense. They enter the hall and leave it a few hours later with no further communication with the performing musicians or their neighbors at their assigned seats (unless they occasionally meet a few acquaintances during intermissions). The sermon event, in contrast, becomes the central dialogical segment in a communal gathering of people who share the vicissitudes of queer identities. In most congregations (Dignity being the exception), the preachers engage them in a narrative relevant to gay life experiences as individuals and as a social category. However, compared with other groups I presented in earlier chapters, the "dialogue" during the sermon keeps the audience at the status of listeners. But they are not a passive audience; they often respond spontaneously, expressing loudly their reactions by laughing, applauding, uttering sounds of support, and so on. Moreover, in all services, but during the sermon segments in particular, the congregants are engulfed in an atmosphere of affection toward their fellow men and women, uniting them in a sort of "deep play" as viable integrated communities.

Compared with most other groups introduced in previous chapters, the gay congregations engaged a wide mix of constituencies—men and women, young and old, various sexual and ethnic minorities, and more—a rainbow of queer singular identities. However, at this state of elevated consciousness, the participants, although passive and not always able to follow the details and structure of the intricate oral presentation, are nevertheless engaged in a "cultural performance,"[9] in a discourse engrossing them in a kind of sentimental education: it helps reconfirm their identity and worldview as a morally sound community—as worthy Christians and Jews, loyal American citizens, and in particular, proud gays, lesbians, bisexuals, and transsexuals.

Endnote

My participation in the various gay congregations confronted me with a situation I had not experienced in my previous ethnographic studies. On entering these sites, I lost the position of an outsider and the mental approach of studying "the other." My attendance at both Christian and Jewish services involved a life history of cultural edification that inevitably deprived me of the traditional position (or presumption) of the "innocent" anthropologist. I must have come with a preconceived idea about the type and quality of ritual practices and spiritual experiences I might encounter in these institutions.

But not surprisingly, the style and content of the sermons I attended during my first visits, as presented by the leading clerical staff at MCC, Dignity, Unity, and CBST, did not meet my conceptual expectations.

I have no doubt, however, that had I attended sermons in other, non-gay congregations, I would have been equally if not more confused or "disappointed." Academic life—entailing a more "positivistic" perspective—has deprived me of the ability to immerse myself in an evocative spiritual-moralistic experience. However, my growing rapport with Rev. Pat's and Rev. Karin's presentations revealed my own gradual induction into the art of sermons as contextual communications that arouse the emotional sensibilities of listeners about their existential conditions in a world they often feel is out of tune with society's social and moral codes.

Although a "complete" alien at MCC, Dignity, and Unity, also coming from another country and religion, I was overwhelmed by the warm reception I enjoyed at all gay Christian denominations. I observed a similar case with the Jewish man I met regularly on my visits to services at Dignity. At a later stage I left a copy of my CBST ethnography with the leading MCC pastor, Reverend Bumgardner. She never mentioned it or queried my interests. Remembering my name, on my occasional visits she was welcoming, in a personal manner, with the same warm attitude she expressed toward other, more regular congregants. It suited her ideals for MCC's mission as a religion of love, a message that I incorporate into my thesis about the unique presentation in gay culture—of affectionate relationships—a social commodity and a shared vision. This type of mutual emotional gratification among the participants proffers another response to the query "what do gay people want?" in their journeys to the Center meetings, as well as to the gay synagogue and church services.

With these lines I close my ethnographic voyage among LGBT organizations in New York. Although thoroughly secular in my worldview, I could still attend services at all denominations with a deep sense of empathy and, unexpectedly, even with a touch of contentment. In my perception, these were all public forums for people who got together to act out an identity and claim their equal share in their "tribal" social and cultural heritage. When Richard claimed of the Sexual Compulsives Anonymous meetings "These are our synagogues," he was expressing a similar feeling of solidarity with his fellow SCA congregants.

CHAPTER 10

Talking Sex, Imagining Love:
The Emotional Template

My aim in this chapter is to tackle a few themes that seem to impinge most profoundly on the life experiences and the existential visions of gay men, thus revealing an intrinsic facet of their subjectivity. We have often come across these issues in earlier chapters, but their manifestation was mostly expressed as part of a collective discourse. In the later part of this chapter, I will concentrate on the detailed life experiences and worldview of a few individuals, presenting them as full personas.

Impersonal Sex Revisited

In a volume edited by William Leap, old and new studies of anonymous gay sex detail a plethora of "public sex" venues, indoor and outdoor spaces including parks, beaches, rest areas, rest rooms ("tearooms"), bathhouses, back rooms in bars, video stores, and locker rooms. In his introduction, Leap presented the query that has occupied queer discourse for many years: "Is men-having-sex-with-men really the masterpiece of contemporary 'gay culture'"? (1999: 1). It was acknowledged and also sometimes celebrated by the early gay authors and later scholars as an affirmative display of gay life, gay culture, and gay men's social communitas and community building (e.g., Rechy 1977; White 1983; Altman 1986; Adam 1992; Newton 1993; Forrest 1994; Bech 1997; Delany 1999; Bronski 2000).

For example, Edmund White, a leading author and gay activist, asserted: "Sexual promiscuity, or at least the possibility of sexual adventure, has for a

long time now been the essential glue holding the urban gay ghetto together"
(1983: xiv). But other voices presented conflicting observations: a market
mentality, that is, depersonalization of attractive bodies and alienation (e.g.,
Levine 1979; Bersani 1998). However, in recent years, some gay advocates
have joined the heterosexual critics (see Rotello 1997 and Signorille 1997
in particular). They argue that the liberation of a sexual minority and the
assertion of gay identity in its expression of "free sex" between strangers—
"men who meet men"—have become synonymous with unbounded promiscuity, and consequently, irresponsible risk-taking in the era of AIDS.

Leap's query is only partly answered in his collection, which offers separate descriptions of gay desire and its consummation in the various sexual
oases. By contrast, I carried out my observations mostly at the Lesbian and
Gay Community Services Center in Greenwich Village, a public institution
not designed for sexual activities. The center gave me the opportunity to get
acquainted with a wide variety of groups representing many gay social and
sexual interests. As already set forth in earlier chapters, my data included
group discussions on gay erotic life, observations at sites congenial for more
or less anonymous sexual activities (outside the Center), as well as personal
narratives about the experience of varied sexual encounters. That diverse
type of intimate, verbal and nonverbal information at my disposal afforded, I
believe, deeper insight into the driving forces and the modes of gratification
that befall the participants on their sexual journey. In this exploration, I try
to reexamine the meaning of anonymous sex "from the native's point of view."

My query seems reminiscent of Leap's dilemma, but it also examines
the hypotheses suggested long ago: is anonymous sex mostly a "getting off"
method, namely an inexpensive and relatively safe venue for the release of a
sexual urge (e.g., Humphreys 1970; Delph 1978; Levine 1998; Hollister 1999)?
Is it a component of gay identity and an expression of gay society's communitas? Or does it, no less—and against the conviction of both straights and
gays, represent for many participants the desire for a paired male intimacy? I
suggest that participants in anonymous sex often are in search of emotional
and social bonding, a mode of sexual motivation far closer to the code of
mainstream society.

One might assume that I wish to "redeem" gay men engaged in the apparently endless quest for sexual encounters and that I also view their behavior in
terms of an emotional discourse. However, one wonders, is there something
unique about the emotional life of gay men? Is there a different sense of inten-
tionality, of feelings and other types of patterned emotional responses when

homosexuals meet their sexual partners? I will address the issue of the emotional template, its display, and the participants' self-awareness of that code.

Anthropologists Study Emotions

When I came to analyze my observations in terms of the previous anthropological studies of emotions, I could not ignore a few major dilemmas. In particular, which of the definitions of emotions is appropriate to my subject? How would my ethnography and interpretation relate to other studies of emotions carried out by anthropologists?

In recent decades, notable ethnographic studies of emotions have emerged in the aftermath of Geertz's seminal portrait of the socially patterned, restrained reactions of Balinese men to personal trauma and the orchestrated manner of their presentation of self. Geertz professed: "but emotions too, are cultural artifacts" (1973: 81). Subsequent studies presented evidence for the cultural construction of emotions, an idea developed by sociologists (e.g., Harre 1986; Hochschild 2003). Though they often criticized Geertz's work, these anthropologists have actually refined his insights while conducting their research by a more intensive, interactionist approach (e.g., Meyers 1979, 1988; Levy 1984; Rosaldo 1984; Lutz 1986; Lynch 1990; Wikan 1990; Wulff 2007). The vocabulary of emotions reported in these studies related to the demonstration or the suppression of behavioral responses to powerful sensations, such as, shame, anger, fear, compassion, grief, happiness, and kinship obligations. Much of the ethnographic research of emotions has concentrated on India, Southeast Asia, and other "classic" sites of anthropological research (exemplified in an issue of *Ethnos* 69, 4 [2004]).

My field of observation among gay men was remote both from the ethnographic sites and the type of emotions addressed in previous anthropological discourses. However, it seems relevant to be reminded of Malinowski. When dealing with themes of sexuality such as the "jealousy of passion" (1929: 322), he related directly to emotions. Of his theoretical premise he wrote: "The salient points which distinguish human attachments from animal instincts are the dominance of the object over the situation, the organization of emotional attitudes, the continuity of the building up of such attitudes and their crystallization into permanent adjustable systems (1927: 240). Also, culture depends directly upon the degree to which the human emotions can be trained, adjusted, and organized into complex and plastic systems" (236).

The neglected field of sexuality has been reclaimed by anthropologists in recent years, in particular by the protagonists of gay and lesbian studies. They have also gradually moved away from the old concentration in Third World "other" societies. However, emotions were not an initial focus in their endeavor. As already discussed in the introductory chapters here, the first studies of gay men's behavior in anonymous sex venues were dominated by Goffman's symbolic interaction methodology and interpretation, which left little space for an analysis of emotions in vivo. Other anthropologists who became engaged in the study of homosexuality, in both Western and non-Western societies, focused on the processes and the rituals of "coming out" and identity formation, community development, and other types of social interaction in the gay milieu. The issue of emotions remained, for the most part, the domain of the psychologists who were studying and treating the population "suffering" from the symptoms of homosexuality.

The subject of emotions seems particularly complex when considering a type of behavior that is so closely, if not inevitably, associated with the physical domain. A thorough discussion would lead us back to Plato, who first introduced the distinction between erotic love and sexual desire, a difference associated with the distinction between the animal and the rational motivation and demeanor (e.g., Scruton 2001). In simple terms, how separate is the sexual instinct, drive and orgasm from the realm of emotions, feelings, and affection? Not considering acts of rape, sexual abuse, and paid sex, how remote is the "pure" act of sexual intercourse from the Western concept of "lovemaking" (Weitman 1998)? In sum, can we apply the term "emotion" to the display of sexual attitudes, values, and actual demeanor with the same meaning as employed by anthropologists in other spheres of the manifestation of emotions? And as our last major research quest, can we identify a code of patterned verbal responses and of behavioral expressions in the landscape of gay men's mating interactions?

From among the sociologists, I suggest Hochschild's definition: "The concept 'emotions' refers mainly to strips of experience in which there is no conflict between one and another aspect of self: the individual 'floods out,' is 'overcome . . .' emotion differs from other adaptive mechanisms (such as shivering when cold or perspiring when hot) in that thinking, perceiving, and imagining—themselves subject to social influence—enter in" (2003: 88–89).

Among the various definitions of emotions suggested by anthropologists, I still favor Levy's broad perspective: "Emotions seem to be feelings which convey and represent information about one's mode of relationship as a total individual to the social and nonsocial environment: and they seem to involve sensations with essential autonomic nervous system components" (1973: 271).

I decided to address the field of emotions in the terms close to my subjects' perception of the different meanings they attributed to various sexual encounters in their own experiences as well as in the experiences narrated to them by their friends. I did not interview in any direct fashion or intentionally use the term "emotion" as I listened to reports on recent experiences or stories about past events. I sometimes asked questions for clarification, but as part of a natural discourse between close friends. In this chapter I intend to present the detailed stories of two of my close, single friends, who were open in my company about their search for sex and love (they were both introduced also in Chapter 2). For comparative illustrations, I will also present shorter descriptions of life experiences reported to me by a few other gay men.

I could of course employ a different strategy to introduce my data. In the earlier chapters, I presented gay men's attitudes to issues of sexual behavior, affection, and intimacy as expressed during meetings of members of voluntary associations. I could assemble my observations and a number of the stories I collected from my informants in various locations. However, I thought I could better substantiate my views about gay men's modes of emotionality in their quest for sex and intimacy through the presentation of two full research personas. By no means do I consider these two men representative of the world of American gay men. But I do follow a long tradition in anthropology employed by ethnographers who introduced the life history of one or a few individuals to illuminate some major themes in the culture of their studied society (e.g., O. Lewis 1967; Langness and Frank 1981; Shostack 1981; Myerhoff 1978; Crapanzano 1980; Eickelman 1985; Rapport 2003).

I met Jeffrey during my observations at the gay synagogue, while I met Nigel in one of the groups I observed at the Center in Greenwich Village. They came from very different social backgrounds and had different life experiences. My acquaintance with Jeff goes back nearly twenty years. I met Nigel more recently, and I will explore, here, the seven years since we incidentally attended the same group at the Center. I believe that my continuing communication with these two men reveals a reliable picture of their sexual and emotional lives. I am convinced that they treated me as a close friend and shared many details considered intimate and confidential. I was also open with them about myself as I had never been before in my ordinary daily life with friends. I consider Jeff and Nigel among my closest friends. I had many opportunities to test the reliability of their stories as I came to know individuals who participated in their lives. I believe that I am not betraying our friendship as I discuss their intimate life and feelings before an audience of strangers. They knew all along that I am a twenty-four-hour researcher and that our relationship was also part of my professional agenda. They both read my earlier ethnography on the gay synagogue and relied on my code of confidentiality, which would never allow a disclosure of their identity. Jeff, in particular, was familiar with my publications. I quoted him in my ethnography, and he was pleased with his role in the text. Naturally I changed some of my subjects' personal details that might easily have revealed their identity, and I refrained from reporting of some intimate issues that might embarrass or prove painful to them. Nigel, too, read an earlier version of this chapter and expressed his appreciation at my reliable recording as well as the narrative style of my presentation.

Jeffrey

I first met Jeff in 1989 at a Yom Kippur "breaking the fast" dinner, after services at the gay synagogue. Our hosts at the meal were a long-standing couple—a Jewish member of CBST and his non-Jewish partner. As I later learned, when Jeff was first introduced to the Jewish host years before, he was immediately infatuated with this good-looking and charming academic. When they engaged in conversation, Jeff became excited and hopeful, since the object of his desire seemed unusually warm and affectionate. But then the new acquaintance introduced him to his partner, and Jeff was crushed: "I felt the rug pulled out from under my feet." Nevertheless, he went on to develop a close friendship with both men and never pursued his attraction. It was part of his code—though not always followed—never to get involved with "married" men.

When I first met him, Jeff was in his late thirties. As our acquaintance deepened, he began to share his life history with me. He was raised in a lower-middle-class Jewish family. An only child, he had no close relatives when he was growing up, save a loving mother and a forbidding stepfather. His memories of family and youth were not happy. A college graduate, he was comfortable, but not really content, with his job in the New York State judicial bureaucracy. At the time of our first introduction, he was concluding a two-year relationship with a Jewish man about his age. His only other relationship had been of the same duration with a younger, less well educated, and less economically secure Hispanic partner. The latter conformed better to his ideal physical type: slim, boyish, and preferably, though not exclusively, of Puerto Rican or similar Latino extraction. As Jeff described it, he was always first attracted to the physical and erotic appeal of a potential mate. Everything else was secondary. That ordering, however, was often a source of later disappointment, when the sexual attraction of his partner was not matched with the personality and shared interests that could sustain a continuing relationship. This disparity, as well as his partner's later infidelities, ultimately doomed this first relationship.

As our friendship developed over the years, Jeff became ever more open about the intimate details of his life and his search for physical pleasure and emotional connection. In the summer of 2000, Jeff invited me to a sex party organized by the Golden Shower Association, an event described earlier (Chapter 1). Having described it before, I only emphasize here that I realized it was a place of sexual activity, but not of the "anonymous sex syndrome" I had anticipated. Many in the crowd knew each other as members of the organization: they had met each other at other sites. On the whole, there was a sense of familiarity, a feeling of mutuality. Jeff made it clear to me afterward that he did not consider the evening's events the quintessential aim of his sexual life. As much as he went there for sexual gratification and entertainment, he was hoping to meet someone at the event with whom he might pursue a continuing relationship.

In summer 2003 Jeff had just returned from a week-long retreat with the Gay Nature/Gay Nudist International Association (GNI), one of several organizations he had joined since we first met. As Jeff recounted, it was a great event of continuous entertainment and sexual activity. Gay men of all ages and shapes, 800 to 1,000 in number, got together to enjoy the pleasures of nature in a remote forested site. They were housed in comfortable cabins shared by groups of friends. They participated in grand parties as well as smaller cabin events. At one drag party, Jeff masqueraded as a lady-in-waiting to a cabin mate who came as the British Queen Mother. Jeff had sex with attractive partners in various more or less secluded locations and recounted how once, when he was sexually engaged with a handsome young man, he suddenly heard applause and realized they were being watched by an admiring crowd. Jeff admitted that this was all mostly about fun and pleasure. It was like taking part in a performance, though he was open to the possibility of pursuing a relationship with an attractive man he might meet at the retreat. Indeed, he had made a few trips to Boston during the previous year to get together with a fellow he had met at that camping event. As so often before, however, the attraction faded—in this case when distance as well as work and social obligations made it too difficult to sustain a continuing relationship.

Later in 2003, Jeff started a part-time after-hours job in a sex club he sometimes visited. Twice a week for a few hours, he worked an evening shift as a cashier at the entrance of the club. Although prohibited from getting involved with customers during work, he sometimes had an opportunity to communicate with patrons who seemed interested in his company. When we met in February 2004, he told me that a few weeks earlier he had noticed a very handsome man who made a point of telling him that he liked his looks and attitude. At the end of Jeff's shift, around 4 a.m., the man went home with him, and they enjoyed a great sexual rendezvous. Adding to his pleasure, Jeff discovered they were both Jewish. His partner was the son of Israeli immigrants. However, on their second encounter, he discovered that the handsome and pleasant man was a drug addict who sometimes went hungry. Jeff now avoided this once-promising partner. It was about this time that Jeff shared with me two failures in his life that made him feel "incomplete." The first was his lack of a career distinguished by professional achievement; the second was his failure to develop a stable love relationship. He missed the experience of going to bed and starting the next day stretched out next to a lover.

One evening in April, Jeff and I were having dinner when he noticed a group of men at a nearby table who were regulars at his club; he had had sex with some of them. "They come from a good stable," he commented, appraising them neutrally as sexual merchandise. This prompted me to repeat a question I had asked Jeff on various occasions: "Isn't there a show of feelings when gay men engage in casual sex?" He answered: "Heterosexuals naturally combine sex with feelings, but gays don't mix sexual pleasure with feelings. It is a cultural construct for gays!" But he added, "Sometimes following a sexual encounter a conversation might develop that reveals shared interests and consequently an emotional relationship might follow." On another occasion, however, he concluded that "sex can never be completely devoid of emotions."

Jeff's somewhat contradictory response was again reflected by events in his life. He had met an attractive Canadian businessman at the club, and after having sex, he invited him home. On later visits by the Canadian to New York, they continued to see each other. This promising relationship came to a sudden, disappointing end, however, when Jeff discovered his friend was using drugs. They were preparing to go off together for a weekend at a gay resort when the Canadian friend passed out in a New York bar. Jeff canceled his trip. He explained that he had lost faith in the guy's true feelings for him and suspected he might have been under the influence of drugs all along. He felt it was a betrayal of confidence in the relationship. Although the connection was based mostly on physical attraction, Jeff considered it special in its mode of affection and in the sense of humor and the worldview they shared.

Shortly after my dinner conversation with Jeff, I had a chance to resume its subject with an acquaintance from the LGBT Center, a professional in his late fifties. He was in a stable relationship of many years with a partner of similar age. They allowed each other to go out sometimes and have sex in their chosen venues. "We have an open relationship," he explained. I asked him whether there was an emotional component in his sexual encounters at the gay bath he occasionally visited. Without hesitation, he responded: "No! It's a fantasy of mutual attraction. Oh, sometimes a conversation may develop if you discover shared interests, but it all ends when you prepare to go home." His response reminded of Altman's observation years ago: "and many a man on his stomach at the baths for a night would then go home to (or with) his lover" (1986: 143).

Another frequent visitor to this same bathhouse, a single man, added some corroborative evidence of this attitude, though he himself seemed somewhat frustrated by it. On a few occasions he had felt a great sense of pleasure and a rush of affection for his sexual partners. When he asked if they wanted to meet again, they responded positively. But when he called them, they often apologized that they were busy and promised to call back, which they never did. When I told Jeff about that behavior, he explained it as a symptom of "a candy shop culture." In the heat of the moment the partner offers a positive reaction. But when he cools off, having consumed one sweet, he is looking for a new candy. In the rich market of New York's gay life, another novelty is always to be had.

Some years ago I was surprised to learn about a couple I knew from the synagogue being spotted separately at anonymous sex venues. Their "infidelity," as mainstream society would term it, however, did not appear to influence their relationship, which was marked by mutual support and affection. I later learned that another much-admired couple, who had been together for many years, had maintained an "open" relationship. Their ultimate separation was not a direct consequence of their fleeting affairs. A number of gay men I was acquainted with confirmed that they too maintained open relationships with their partners. They were aware that they were engaged in a type of behavior generally inadmissible in both heterosexual and lesbian society. I gradually reached the conclusion that the "open relationships" pattern was a credible feature in the local gay lifestyle repertoire.

I mentioned to Jeff that when I had walked by the Citicorp Building earlier in the day, it was surrounded by police. Jeff said he hoped it wasn't a target for a terrorist attack. Smiling, he explained it was close to a place he cherished—a popular bathhouse, one of the few left in New York. For Jeff, the place held many pleasant memories. When I asked him why he continued to go to the bath since he had free admission to the sex club on his off days, he explained: "In the club I already know most customers; there's more variety, more new faces in the bath."

A month later, Jeff told me about a new affair he had recently begun with a younger Latino he met at a private party. They had spent thirty-six hours together over the weekend on sex, food, long hours of conversation, and trips around town. Jeff was attracted to the man's physical beauty and was pleased with his role advising the younger man on personal issues. He was aware, however, of the difficulties that might block the development of this relationship. His new lover had unresolved family problems, only a basic education, and some traditional, conservative attitudes. His work schedule was also chaotic. Jeff explained to his new friend that they had very different lifestyles but needed each other for sex and intimacy. But after about a month of failed efforts to stabilize their connection, Jeff decided to let it go. He believed he had no need to keep the relationship going only because he enjoyed the sexual part. He could find his sexual needs gratified elsewhere with less effort.

Once in July, Jeff called me at midnight. He had just been with a man who had been coming to the club with his partner. For some time he had been trying to interest Jeff, who avoided him because he considered him "married." A few weeks earlier, he had handed Jeff his card, though Jeff still did not take him up on his offer. When he managed to reach Jeff by phone, though, Jeff at last "gave in" and invited him over. He discovered that the man was in a three-year relationship and his partner refused to engage in anal sex. Jeff said the man wanted to be penetrated. They had a good time, but Jeff had no plans to initiate further dates. They met at least one more time, but Jeff considered the relationship purely sexual.

Jeff was delighted later that July when he was at last approached by a man he had been interested in since first meeting him at a GNI retreat a few years before. Steven was an extremely attractive, educated professional in his early forties and physically Jeff's type. Until then, it had been a frustrating one-sided relationship, with Jeff repeatedly failing in his attempts to transform casual sexual encounters into a more serious connection. On three occasions in recent years, they had happened upon each other at various venues and had sex. But Jeff's suggestions that they get together for a date, and his flattering invitations and phone calls, had all been rebuffed. So it was a great surprise when Jeff, coming home very tired after a day of work preceded by a night of sexual activity, got a phone call from Steven suggesting they meet for dinner. Jeff forgot he was tired and immediately agreed to meet later at a popular Chinese restaurant in Chelsea. For years Jeff had been disturbed by Steven's attitude. Did he consider Jeff merely a nice piece of meat, only a body to use and discard? But dinner went well. They spent two hours in conversation and parted kissing in the rain and agreeing to call and make a date.

When Steven called, Jeff seemed elated. They arranged to meet the next week. Steven would come directly to Jeff's place from work and shower there before dinner. Without doubt, I wrote in my notes, Jeff is in love. Jeff added that he had learned from Steven that he was still in a relationship but his sex life was not satisfying. Jeff expressed excitement about the coming rendezvous. He hoped Steven would soon leave his rocky relationship. Then, he thought, the prospects for a new partnership with Steven were on his side.

But after a few weeks of sex and warm get-togethers, Jeff realized there was not much hope of a more serious relationship developing. Among the issues was the discovery that Steven was into S&M, an interest Jeff did not share. He described himself as attracted to pleasure, not to pain. He interpreted Steven's sexual inclination and inability to commit to a serious relationship as related to his history of abuse as a child. Nevertheless, they continued to meet occasionally and enjoy physical intimacy.

A year later, in summer 2005, Jeff seemed to have begun a new stage in life. He spoke of the preceding year as "my annus horribilis," quoting Queen Elizabeth's characterization of her own trying time. Not only had he been unlucky in love, he had fallen seriously ill, been hospitalized, and slipped into a severe depression (I was not aware at that time about the more serious details of his medical situation, described in Chapter 2). But out of this misfortune, he hoped, would emerge the buds of a better future. He had begun therapy, which helped him cope with old demons. "He saved my life," Jeff told me, referring to his gay therapist. Jeff concluded it was probably childhood trauma and low self-esteem that handicapped his professional and intimate life. He could now better perceive how self-defeating his choice of incompatible mates had been. And sure enough, soon after beginning therapy, he met a man at the club, a few years his junior, who seemed to be the partner he had missed for so many years. They were spending four nights a week together, but they still retained the freedom to pursue sex with other mates. Jeff had no hesitation about that open relationship. To my surprised reaction he responded, "Why not add some meat on the side?"

Jeffrey invited his "boyfriend," as he termed him, to join us for dessert at a Village restaurant close to the latter's apartment. The strong sentiment and physical attraction between them was readily sensed. The boyfriend, however, was not the "cute Latino" of Jeff's erstwhile erotic vision, but rather a blond WASP with a small bulging belly. As I walked with Jeff to his bus stop, he commented that I might feel the earth rumbling the next evening: he was getting together with his lover. When we spoke a week later, Jeff told me about their most recent time together. Jeff was working at the club in the evening and let his boyfriend in. After the friend "played around" a while, they left together for Jeff's apartment. "I washed and disinfected him, and we had wonderful sex for a long time." Jeff opened his eyes the next morning, his lover a few inches from him, with happy memories of the past night.

But that love story ended soon as economic and other issues of incompatibility became too difficult to accommodate. However, in 2008 Jeff met the mate he hoped and felt likely to stay with for the rest of his life. This event coincided with Jeff's retirement from his job and his move to an apartment on Long Island. It was there, at a party of local gay residents, that he met a man of his age who suited both his sexual and his social cravings. I met them a few times and came to believe they had a serious bond (see Chapter 2). Moreover, they eventually moved to an apartment they bought together in Florida. Whenever I call him nowadays (fall 2012), Jeff seems happy. Unless he one day fulfills his dream to visit Israel, I assume, sadly, that we might not meet again; still, we will continue to communicate by phone and e-mail.

In trying to predict Jeff's prospects for a stable couple relationship, I was reminded of an Israeli man I met a few years ago at the Center. A good-looking computer engineer in his late thirties, he had recently "come out" in New York, leaving behind a wife and children. He was now on an aggressive and endless search for sex across a wide variety of anonymous venues. I was worried he was risking his health in the process. When I met him two years later, with a younger man at his side, he was completely transformed. He had stopped visiting his earlier haunts and seemed engaged in a homey domesticity. "I've been married for the last two years," he told me, proudly introducing his partner.

Nigel

I first met Nigel in summer 2003 at a talk at the Center. He was among the few blacks present; we struck up a conversation debating the guest speaker's ideas. We discovered a mutual interest in each other's life experiences: a visiting academic from an area of international conflict (Israel) and a black American engineer in his early fifties with an interest in international affairs. I was impressed by his skill at interviewing me—a role reversal for an anthropologist and his potential subject. I realized I was open about myself in his company, as if with a therapist. I believe that our candid first encounter set the tone for our continued relationship, which has been one of shared confidences and intimate feelings. We met regularly during my visits to New York, often for dinner on Sunday. I also met a few of his friends at various events. Nigel's worldview included a belief in God in a very universal fashion and in reincarnation. He suggested that my having been black in my previous life explained my easy chemistry with black people.

Nigel was raised in a lower-middle-class family by a mother and a supportive stepfather. He went to college and pursued a career as a structural engineer. He was comfortable and generally content with life and work. At our second meeting, however, Nigel alluded to a painful personal event that had occurred about a year earlier: his separation from his boyfriend. He did not elaborate on the story, so I refrained from pressing him for details. The subject remained dormant for some time. A couple of weeks later, Nigel told me he had had a few long-standing relationships with men, which had all failed, including the most recent—the one to which he had alluded. That relationship was characterized by a strong bond that had lasted nearly two years. Though he did not regret the inevitable breakups, he would have preferred to remain in a stable relationship. As we were strolling down Sixth Avenue one Sunday afternoon taking in the annual Brazilian street fair, Nigel pointed out a few men he considered his "type." They were slim, dark, and masculine in appearance. He added that he liked men who looked and acted masculine but were submissive in bed. Nigel believed that his taste in men was taken from the image of his stepfather. He had an early memory as a toddler of watching this man's naked body. He never complained about his mother's mate, who treated him decently. When I arrived back home, I found an e-mail from Nigel with a few internet photos of men he found erotically appealing. They were of well-developed and well-endowed black male torsos.

When we met again in February 2004, Nigel was in the process of testing out a relationship with an attractive black man from Chicago, whose photo looked not unlike those Nigel had e-mailed me. But Nigel was frustrated that his interest was not being reciprocated. He had gone to Chicago to be with him, but his friend was caught up in pressing family problems. Nigel hoped that at night he would compensate for his aloofness during the day. But when they went to bed, the man fell asleep at once. This went on for a few nights, until he at last responded. Nigel, though, did not enjoy the idea of imposing himself on an unwilling partner. He was now anxiously awaiting his friend's visit to New York. Would the same dynamic repeat itself?

Nigel's report of the visit was not positive: "It was as expected, but not hopeful." He concluded that the fellow was not interested in having sex with him. When they were in bed together, he allowed Nigel to hold and caress him, but he did not respond. In deep disappointment and pain, all Nigel could do was roll over in frustration. It was a serious blow to his affections. Nevertheless, Nigel invited a few close friends (myself included) to a Harlem restaurant for a farewell dinner with his Chicagoan.

When I next met Nigel on our way out of a group meeting, we were stopped by a woman who asked "How's Peter doing?" "It's over," he responded tersely. Nigel explained that the woman had not seen him in a long time and naturally assumed he was still with Peter. I asked if Peter looked like the fellow from Chicago. No, he responded, he was an intellectual, older, and skinnier. Nigel continued to recount the sad separation, although it was he himself who brought about the breakup. They used to spend a lot of time together. Peter often stayed over in his apartment. When problems started to crop up in the relationship, they agreed to see a counselor, though Nigel felt Peter was not really responsive. His close friends were convinced that the relationship was doomed.

About a month later I got together with Peter, another acquaintance from the Community Center and the first black academic with whom I maintained a close contact. I had not seen him in a long time. When I first met Peter in 1999 I was impressed by his political convictions and we also shared professional concerns. Interested in my company, he seemed to be testing how sincere and empathetic I was with the problems of blacks and other minorities. We developed a close relationship, though probably less intimate than Peter expected. Nevertheless, we continued to communicate occasionally by e-mail.

At our get-together, I told Peter about my current research interest and the groups I was studying. He asked if I had come across a fellow whose description matched Nigel's. To my great surprise, Peter turned out to be the boyfriend Nigel had separated from the year before. In appearance and outlook they were quite different. Nigel looked like the corporate engineer he was, and he seemed content with his position in mainstream American society. In contrast, Peter's mode was that of a 1960s radical, and he often decried the treatment of blacks and other minorities in America. On learning of my friendship with Nigel, Peter immediately told me that he still lamented the breakup, which Nigel had brought about. He remained deeply in love with him. He asked me not to tell Nigel about our renewed acquaintance, a promise I soon regretted making. I kept this promise for some time but eventually revealed to Nigel that I had met Peter years before. To my relief, Nigel responded equably (see Chapter 2).

When I got together again with Peter, he soon returned to the subject of his life with Nigel. But first he argued that blacks have a problem with intimacy. They are unable to display feelings because they worry that anything of their inner self they reveal might be used against them. He went on to suggest that black men are taught to cruise women, something that is also expressed analogously in their gay relationships. Black women are used to looking "into the inside of their partners, but black men look to the outside appearance, and therefore they keep on changing their mates, women or men." He concluded that Nigel, like many other blacks, was not prepared for a long-term relationship. Peter's animated openness and his reflective attitude, I soon learned, were the result of therapy he had undergone since the separation from Nigel. He wanted to overcome some personal problems that he thought might have contributed to their breakup. Peter invited me to join him at several support groups he was attending for both gays and straights who wanted to break their addiction to various self-destructive habits.

I soon realized that therapy had not assuaged Peter's feeling of loss. He asked me if Nigel was seeing someone. (I refrained from the role of informer on Nigel's love life.) He believed that for several months Nigel had already been in a relationship with a younger man, for whom he bought presents and secured a parking permit at his building. Peter had e-mailed Nigel warning him that the new friend was taking advantage of him.

Asked whether his behavior was not obsessive, Peter argued that knowing about Nigel's present life would help him reconcile with the finality of the relationship. He complained that the breakup had been unwarranted; Nigel never explained why he wanted to end the relationship, instead asking only that he remove his stuff from the apartment. Peter phoned Nigel every day for a month pleading with him to resume their relationship. Looking for clues to Nigel's action, Peter reflected on Nigel's habits, which seemed to him selfish. Nigel was less accommodating sexually and less needy than Peter, who wanted to engage more frequently in sex with a loving partner. He was also aware of rumors that Nigel had complained about his moody character. Peter's disconsolation at losing Nigel was compounded by a belief that there were not many available gay black men who were healthy, highly educated, and well employed to replace him. Nevertheless, Peter had not given up the search for sex and love. He looked for prospects in various local support groups and social organizations. He also traveled out of town, attending conferences on gender issues and joining gay retreats.

Nigel had his own view of the breakup. He had lost his tolerance for Peter's demanding attitude and careless household habits. He had become concerned about Peter's increasing obliviousness to the world around them. He felt that Peter was also refusing to face emerging difficulties at his job and he was particularly disappointed when Peter refused to consider the counselor's advice to take up therapy—which he did only after the separation. To Nigel, it all meant that Peter needed help to overcome some personal problems. This view was only reinforced by Peter's behavior after the breakup. Nigel ultimately had to block Peter's phone calls and e-mails. Nigel had no wish to resume a relationship that could not be free of the pain and jealousy Peter displayed. Although he cherished the memories of his happy days with Peter, he would not consider reconciliation.

After the disappointment of his Chicago friendship, Nigel's search for a partner turned mainly to the Internet. He only rarely went to gay bars, usually in the company of out-of-town friends. He had no interest in gay baths or other sites that offered the possibility of short-term gratification, but there was little real prospect for a long-term relationship. At our weekly get-togethers, Nigel informed me of his successes and failures on the Internet. He showed me his personal ad on the Manhunt website. It contained his picture, dressed from the neck down, and listed his age, taste in sex, and other interests. It noted that Nigel was not interested in casual sex but was looking for a serious relationship.

The response was not overwhelming. Over the ten months of this project, Nigel calculated he had contacted about ten candidates a month and was approached by five callers. Of these, only about three reached the phone-call stage, and only one or two resulted in a face-to-face meeting. Only once did that lead to a sexual contact. Even then, Nigel was not really excited: "I went with the flow." In June 2004, however, a more promising contact arose on the horizon. Nigel received a positive response from a man whose profile seemed a match for Nigel's intellectual interests and sexual preference. Anthony was black, in his late forties, and a teacher enrolled in graduate studies at NYU. They met for dinner and seemed to hit it off. When Nigel got home, he found an e-mail from Anthony mentioning their mutual interest in golf and adding what seemed a sexual innuendo: "I have a club and balls." Nigel responded: "We can play with balls."

The relationship with Anthony took some time to develop. Nigel was careful to proceed slowly. He was aware that the lack of a sexual "tingle," as he defined the erotic chemistry between lovers, may ultimately lead to disappointment. But he had no wish to begin the relationship with the sexual test. He was aware that even when physical and social attraction exists, sexual incompatibility may be a stumbling block. He felt that the tingle could even overcome this. Both he and Peter had identified themselves as "tops," but they still found a solution in switching roles. Their ultimate separation was not a result of the ostensible sexual incompatibility.

It took a few more dinners and films that ended in hugs and kisses, before Nigel invited Anthony over one night and they had sex. Nigel told me it was "okay"—expressing neither excitement nor disappointment. "We have to wait and see how it develops," he concluded. They had many shared interests in sports and movies, and he enjoyed their developing friendship and intimacy. In the meantime, Nigel was pursuing an ongoing Internet relationship with an older white musician. They exchanged a few phone calls and eventually met at the musician's home, where they had a good time discussing music and other interests. They fondled affectionately, but Nigel was careful to stop before things went too far. Nigel now seemed more ambivalent about his conviction that the ideal relationship is one based on a spiritual communication that later leads to an erotic tingle. Would the tingle prove positive with Anthony? Ironically, it had already emerged during the first rendezvous with the musician, although he conformed less to Nigel's ideal of an attractive man. In any case, Nigel was not interested in recreational sex with any of his Internet acquaintances.

The relationship with Anthony developed in the next few weeks. They enthusiastically shared sporting activities and met each other's friends. A close friend of Nigel asked about the slow pace of the relationship: "Are you officially dating Anthony, or only exploring the possibility of dating him?" Nigel replied, "I am officially exploring dating Anthony." Anthony was away on business for a while, so Nigel went to see the musician, who lived nearby. At last Nigel could not resist his affectionate entreaty, and they had sex. When Anthony returned and he and Nigel started to meet more regularly, some minor problems emerged, including an incompatible schedule of sexual desire. Anthony slept late on weekends, while Nigel wished to start early and have sex. Anthony was willing to have sex in the afternoon, when Nigel was ready to leave for home and for other engagements.

Nigel told me that while they were happy socializing together, he rated his sexual satisfaction as four on a scale of ten. That compared with eight or nine during his happy days with Peter. He reminisced about those times—when he and Peter showered together, how good he felt, and how relieved of all other problems. The sexual fulfillment they experienced from the very beginning of their relationship was the "glue" that mended the minor difficulties that emerged. But then, he continued, more serious problems began that eventually ruined their happiness. That sexual bond seemed missing in the present connection with Anthony. In contrast, Nigel commented, the one full sexual encounter he had with the musician rated an eight, but he did not consider that a sufficient basis for a serious relationship. Nor did he consider it recreational sex; instead he deemed it "charity sex," an obligatory reciprocation of the musician's enthusiasm and affection.

Later in the summer, Nigel concluded that the relationship with Anthony could not lead to a satisfactory partnership. They remained in a friendly relationship but gave up sex. When I met Anthony about then for the first time, I discovered he did not fit Nigel's "type." He was tall, somewhat overweight, and had a large build—he was not the slim "cute" men Nigel had often pointed out as we walked around New York. In any event, Nigel was again looking for new candidates on the Internet, although he considered it a difficult venue for men his age. Visitors to the sites, both young and old, seemed to prefer younger males.

Nigel's experience on the Internet differed from that of his friend George, whom he had introduced to the gay dating websites. Nigel described George as a good-looking black man in his forties—a successful, politically engaged professional. He told Nigel he averaged fifty replies a month and had met a number of them, at short notice, for sex. He attributed Nigel's poor showing to his insistence on a drawn-out process of getting to know the other party first. Most men answering an internet ad, George claimed, wanted to connect right away, "within 30 minutes." That personal testimony confirms Gudelunas's report that, "advertisers were interested in interacting locally, eager to move from online to offline communication" (2005: 29). Nigel was puzzled that for all George's successful encounters he had no desire to meet any of these attractive and willing partners again. His friend replied, echoing Jeff's "candy shop" metaphor, "There are so many new attractive men to meet."

Nigel came to believe that this attitude was characteristic of many of the younger generation—gay and straight—who felt less commitment to their relationships. Many of those online already had partners but were looking for one-night stands. Interested in themselves and their careers, they took advantage of the growing availability of casual sex and neglected the obligations of fidelity and married life.

During my meetings with Nigel in later years, he introduced me to another boyfriend he had met via the Internet. He was of Asian extraction and worked in the catering business. Again, he was very different from the model of a slim dark man. That relationship lasted about a year. More recently (2010), Nigel informed me in an e-mail that he had met a tall white Englishman at a party, a computer whiz. They seemed to be developing a long-term relationship.

About the same time that Nigel was experimenting with online dating, I learned about another close friend of mine from the gay synagogue who was also searching for partners on the Internet. A retired academic in his late sixties, Adam never had anyone with whom to share a long-term relationship. He had been closeted throughout his professional career and remained obligated to his former wife and children. During the pre-AIDS days, Adam often patronized anonymous-sex venues. He spoke of the emotional excitement, the feeling of adventure, the risks, competition, victories, and embarrassments he encountered. He gave it all up when the AIDS epidemic started to take its toll among his close friends. His focus turned to the many gay social organizations he was active in and among whose members he often found partners for relationships of varying duration, none long-term.

When we got together in the summer of 2004, I told Adam about Nigel's experience with gay websites. To my surprise, he told me he was regularly searching the "silver-daddies" websites, which connect young and older gay men. He also related a recent experience with a man his own age he found on the Web. For their first meeting, they chose a cafeteria close to Adam's apartment. Adam was a few minutes late and was embarrassed to see his partner waiting for him at the entrance. To break the ice, Adam held out his hand and said, kiddingly, "I'm horny." His new acquaintance responded in kind: "Should we go back to your place now?" So the introductory phase in a neutral space was skipped over and they went directly to Adam's apartment. Once there, they lay back on the sofa, hugged, kissed, gradually stripped one other, and ended up in bed. Adam said it was just wonderful. Never before had he enjoyed a feeling of intimacy and sexual pleasure to such a degree. When they had a chance to learn about each other, they found they shared a similar professional and cultural background. Adam also learned, however, that his new friend was in a long-term relationship and that his website wandering was unknown to his partner. Adam did not mind the clandestine nature of the relationship, so they continued to meet at his place. He regretted that he could not introduce his new soul mate to his friends. He kept repeating that the sexual and emotional gratification he was experiencing now far exceeded anything he had known. Naively, I had assumed that Adam had reached a stage of life and of health that put him beyond an adventurous search for sex and love on the Internet. His bold quest proved me wrong.

The Emotional Contradictions in Gay "Sexual Culture"

Jeffrey, Nigel, Peter, Adam, and George were all looking to connect with other men, but what was the aim of their search—sexual gratification, an intimate relationship, a mix of both? If both, what was the interplay between the two? How did their behavior accord with their ideology and their arguments about gay men's physical and emotional connection? Did they share a vocabulary and a set of symbols to express the existential position and expectations of gay men searching for mates? This last query has occupied researchers of gay language: does the reality of sex life produce the language that represents it? Or is it the language that produces the categories that help organize our sexual desires, identities and practices (Cameron and Kulick 2003; Leap 2008)?[1]

The five men presented in this chapter were, apart from race, of similar background. They were of the same socioeconomic status and roughly shared the same generational experiences; however, they brought a wide range of different attitudes and approaches to their search for partners or connections. Which aspect was more representative of general gay society is difficult to assess. Nevertheless, they seemed to share an ethos about the habits and its contradictions prevalent among gay men in their sexual and emotional life.

From our limited view of him, George, whose online success Nigel envied, appears to embody most the paradigm expressed by Jeffrey and others that gay men separate sexual pleasure from feelings. His aim was solely physical, and to Nigel's puzzlement he had no interest in pursuing any further involvement with the men he met for sex. George had age in his favor, and perhaps other factors as well, but their comparative experience suggests that George's approach better conformed to the expectations of those aiming to connect online than did Nigel's.

Nigel, by contrast, seemed his friend's polar opposite. He was not looking for an encounter that was only sexual; instead, he was looking exclusively for a long-term relationship. He was not indifferent to the sexual component, however. He had a deeply implanted ideal physical type, and he believed in the importance of erotic chemistry—"the tingle"—and sexual compatibility in a relationship. He hoped the sex would rate high on his ten-point scale, both for itself and the strength it gave the social bond. But he had a firm belief that the ideal relationship was one in which the erotic emerges no less from the spiritual connection between the parties. This conviction was concretized into a code that precluded his acting out his sexual urge when first meeting someone to whom he was physically drawn. Instead, he would delay acting on the erotic attraction until he had tested his potential partner's suitability in social, cultural, and other personal terms. It was that incubation period, he believed, that allowed the emergence of the emotional bond. A partner who passed the first test but failed the later sexual test, however, would be relegated to the status of a friend.

Peter, I had the impression, was first and foremost looking for social, cultural, and personal camaraderie. He was more accommodating in his sexual taste and expectations and, when partnered with Nigel, had adjusted to his sexual preferences. Adam seemed to resemble Peter in his search for partners with whom he seemed, above all, socially and culturally compatible. However, he did not expect a full-bond relationship. He had long ago given up anonymous sex venues. His behavior in recent years, I believe, reflected changes in his personal circumstances—family situation and age—as well as those in the gay scene.

Jeff's behavior seemed more complex and more contradictory, but there is reason to believe he was not unique in this. On the one hand, Jeff was clearly searching for a long-term partner. Like Nigel, he believed that sexual attraction and compatibility were essential for a durable emotional relationship. But their approach to achieving that end differed markedly. For Jeff, no prospective relationship of any duration could materialize without the immediate realization of an erotic attraction. He had to have sex with the partner before any other quality could be considered. It was only when compatibility in this arena was confirmed that Jeff would look to other issues that might sustain or doom the relationship. For Jeff, a lasting emotional connection required "good sex" substantiated by other criteria of personal compatibility. A good sexual mate would be discarded and the emotional connection halted if the mate later proved unsuitable in social, cultural or psychological terms (see more details about Jeff's life history in Chapter 2).

On the other hand, Jeff was also a regular at sex venues where, in his terms, he "got his rocks off" with men he had no interest in forming a relationship with. He claimed—sincerely, I believe—that when he went to the bath or the club it was purely for an evening of sex. It was devoid of any emotional investment or expectation. In this regard, his behavior conformed to the "gay cultural construct," as he defined it, which separates sexual fun from "serious feelings." This division was borne out, in most instances, by the results of his and others' encounters at these sites. The statistics support his analytical supposition. But that claim may also have served both him and others as a defense mechanism against the potential disappointment or humiliation of being unceremoniously deserted after a sexual encounter.

Exceptions—and there were more than a few—sometimes prove rules. Jeff's claims notwithstanding, all the relationships he pursued (except the last) were with partners he had met in sex sites, venues that would seem to discourage, if not preclude, the emergence of lasting emotional bonds and the development of long-term, committed partnerships. This is not surprising given Jeff's insistence that the sex test was the first and most basic criterion for pursuit of a relationship. But it is at odds with his categorical avowal that sexual pleasure and feelings were separate at these venues. He did occasionally qualify this claim, however, with the acknowledgment that post-sex conversation sometimes revealed shared background, interests, and temperament that might lead to a relationship.

It seems that much has changed in the role of the venues identified as "anonymous sex" institutions. For many years gay connections remained invisible in the public domain. Anonymous sex venues, sleazy or more elegant in their decor, functioned in Humphreys' conception (1970) as vending machines—quickly, safely (to an extent), and inexpensively (both in social and economic terms) providing a needed commodity. They "saved" clients from risks, but also deprived them of the opportunities of developing emotional attachments. Many of the old establishments survived and many new ones have emerged since the days of gay liberation. The expansion of the commercial market of sexual gratification and the variety of new venues had a double meaning. The new liberation made it easier for these institutions to flourish with little public intervention and without the aura of stigma over its participants, but the expectations of its patrons were also undergoing an important change. The "vending machine" economy of sexual release and fun no longer excluded the prospects of expanding these casual connections into a new type of more stable relationships (e.g., Bech 1997). The reputation and the symbolic position of these sites, however, have not altered much despite the changing benefits of participation.

Of the gay male couples I knew from the various institutions I studied, many had first met at anonymous sex sites. These venues offered an opportunity to meet a wide variety of gay men who could be pursued with little introduction and free of the ordinary rituals and rules of interaction expected not only in mainstream society but in the more conventional gay social environments as well. However, as easy as they were to initiate, these encounters did not usually provide more personal sharing beyond the physical. Indeed, there was a deep-rooted belief there that sex and feelings would remain separate domains. This perception allowed them to be treated as safe spaces for long-term partners to act out their sexuality without threatening the emotional bond between the mates.

From a heterosexual perspective one might react in puzzlement, or perhaps in admiration, in view of the challenge to the Judeo-Christian credo that sanctifies sex in marriage, as demonstrated in our observations. A number of couples I knew or was acquainted with maintained an "open relationship," and, indeed, did take advantage of the presumed emotional neutrality of these places. Men in long-term relationships, with or without their partner's knowledge or consent, occasionally visited anonymous sex sites. They claimed that the sexual connections made there were devoid of emotional involvement. They used various metaphors to express that idea, for example, "these are fantasies," "infatuations at the heat of the moment," harmless temptations of the "candy shop society." Jeff, as we have seen, took his then new boyfriend to the sex club while he worked. Even the scrupulous Nigel got together with his musician friend while Anthony, with whom he was developing a relationship, was out of town.

Whether this represented the majority of gay society is a question well beyond this exploration, but it seemed prevalent enough to constitute an ethos among the men I came to know. The men profiled here often spoke of a type of behavior in what they defined as the "gay culture" that was carefree in its attitudes and activities in the sexual domain. This was not the heterosexual ethos, which in spite of its many transgressions, places sex (ideally at least) within an emotional connection. Nigel, whose own behavior conformed more to the heterosexual ideal, still recognized the prevalence of another ethos, one he decried.

This did not mean they were not interested in sex with affectionate intimacy or a long-term relationship. In fact, they were engaged in a continual search for long-term partners. This effort was a permanent element in their daily life and was conducted at a variety of venues. These included social organizations we observed in earlier chapters, such as the religious congregations, voluntary associations, and support groups of all types; commercial sites, such as bars and those offering "anonymous sex"; and the new rich field for cruising and matchmaking, the Internet. The details of this quest were also a field of experience that was shared with friends and even former lovers. The men in my company were remarkably open about their feelings and regularly analyzed and interpreted their fortunes in their quest for mates.[2]

The eagerness with which they pursued this aim at times belied their allegiance to what they deemed the "gay cultural" sexual ethos. Jeffrey, for instance, was concerned that he was being seen as a piece of meat by his erstwhile partner, though he himself described others in those terms. Even seemingly carefree, unencumbered encounters—"getting your rocks off"—could be charged with subtextual meanings as well as hopes for emotional intimacy. This was also likely the case for the wider population of men with whom they interacted in their search. The continuous trial-and-error process they were engaged in reflected a yearning for a stable relationship.

In sum, can we designate a pattern that indicates a cultural construction of emotions apparent in the perspectives and behaviors of the gay men presented in our ethnography? If there is a specific vocabulary for the culture of emotions in our observations, it made its impact in a set of symbols that projected, first, that gay men are necessarily and continuously hunting for partners for sex and intimacy. Under these premises it is also deemed that sexual compatibility is paramount whether it is tested at the first meeting or later (nevertheless, serious relationships were not necessarily with men who suited a preconceived personal fantasy of the erotic male body). That vocabulary informed its audience about the frequency of open relationships; it sustained the ability to talk about sex with friends and promoted the continuance of friendships with former sex partners. Different from the code of heterosexual mating and bonding, the contract of gay coupled relationships does not seem universally threatened by the sanctioned mainstream society's condemnation of extramarital fornication. The pleasure of "pure" sex, although indispensable for an ongoing bonding, nevertheless did not, in the narratives I collected, seem the monopoly of partners to a stable bond.

However, contrary to the popular image, the pleasure and the search for "pure" sex—the mythical legacy of gay liberation heyday and its survival in the still existent anonymous sex venues—the men described in this and other chapters were anxious to find that desire wrapped in civil affectionate interactions. The suffering narrated during the SCA meetings (Chapter 4) exposed the uncontrolled compulsion to patronize the scene of anonymous sex—sleazy, brutal, and devoid of signs of affection.

That deliberation on "gay culture,"—the personal narratives and the terminology applied to the vision and practice of gay bonding—seem to complement the discourse observed in the context of group meetings reported in earlier chapters. That culture and its contradictions seemed to dominate the discussions and other activities performed in a similar or different manner in the various associations presenting special interests and particular gay identity displays.

Negotiating Gay Subjectivity

The ethnographic chapters in this book have offered a view of gay life through the lens of an alien anthropologist who came to conduct ethnographic research in the metropolis of New York. I envisioned a project not much different from studies I had done before: in communities or organizations clearly demarcated within a visible space, with publicly recognized communal institutions, and with presumably shared cultural norms. Instead, I confronted the hectic communication and often confusing discourses that went on in various groups (though all except the Bears and the religious congregations operated under the same concrete roof), which satisfied diverse social, emotional, and sexual needs of gay people of different backgrounds thrown together into a metropolitan environment. These groups were not "organic" communities by any normative definition but mostly assemblies of strangers connected through their same existential quest. In addition, the life histories of a few gay men, participants in these associations who revealed their personal experiences, predicaments and dreams, have been narrated.

As stated in the Introduction, I was overwhelmed by the repetitious scene I observed in the various groups composed of veteran members and chance newcomers; that is, the desire and the ability of nearly everyone to publicly reveal their most intimate feelings and share their very private experiences with strangers. The other side of the same coin was the extraordinary generosity of other attendees, who were willing to listen attentively and offer their sympathy and good advice if requested. These oral sessions were not akin to the popular confessional TV talk shows or the tales of sexual suffering and survival communicated and advertised in various venues (Plummer 1995). Nor were the groups at my observation sites convened by professional therapists; rather, they were voluntary associations (often branches of national organizations) run by self-selected dedicated participants. This was true also of the gay religious congregations, whose doors stayed open to accidental visitors of all faiths, free of any pressure on them to become regular congregants.

My astonishment is naturally embedded in the ethnographic experience in my home society. Recent observations in Tel Aviv reveal that efforts by the emerging gay institutions (in particular the municipality-supported Gay Center and the veteran SPPR/LGBT Israel) to engage Israeli men in voluntary associations on the American model have been mostly unsuccessful. Most significant is the failure to initiate support groups for HIV-positive and AIDS patients. Yet such is also the case in the wider sphere of voluntary associations in mainstream Israeli society (except political, feminist, and various human rights nonprofit organizations). The much smaller Israeli society and its close-knit social construction, even in the major urban centers, do not present the landscape for many strangers available for communal interaction, which seems typical of contemporary voluntary association membership in urban America.

Moreover, Israeli "sentimental education" does not support the style of a therapeutic language. I mention in this context Israelis' reluctance to admit that they need or actually resort to the help of psychological therapists. In public discourse, that service is considered proper for seriously disturbed individuals, although its application has greatly increased in recent years. An assessment of that sociocultural modality was recently proffered by Illouz (2012), who studied the diffusion and globalization of therapeutic cultural models. Conducting observations at some Emotional Intelligence workshops in Israel, she concluded skeptically: "It is doubtful whether this workshop can single-handedly transform the emotional makeup of its participants" (220).

A leading gay activist in Tel Aviv suggested to me an intriguing comparison between Israeli and American gay men: "The American gay man is lonely, the Israeli gay man, however, is never lonely! He has nearby close family and friends, homosexuals and heterosexuals, whom he can meet on a regular basis. They are part of his unbroken chain of major associations— from school, the army, college and work—and who are readily available when needed." Thus he explained his own and others' lack of interest in joining voluntary or support groups composed of strangers.[1] Accordingly, Israeli social composition cannot permit anyone, heterosexual or gay, to "disappear," cutting off all ties of family and other relationships.

There are no publicly identified gay religious organizations in Israel. However, one liberal Orthodox congregation I observed—Kehilat Yachad Tel

Aviv (Together Tel-Aviv Community)—welcomes gays and lesbians. LGBT participants form a major constituency of the congregation (about a third according to gay participants), yet no evident sign in its public presentation and ritual acknowledges the involvement of homosexuals. I assume the occasional "innocent" visitor may not identify the presence of gay congregants.

These observations are apparently not in the realm of "news," informing about the habits of the "natives" in America. As indicated in the Introduction, the tendency to come together and organize voluntary associations was noted long ago by outside and inside observers. That impulse of "a nation of joiners" seems to persist, developing new venues for communal collaboration (e.g., Curtis, Baer, and Grabb 2001).[2] Thus, the emergence of the organizations presented in my ethnography has provided another layer of gay social venues, beside the array of recreational institutions and the public sex sites; this development accords with the old practice of American mainstream society. Wuthnow (1994: 25) argued that the "small-group" movement reflects the fluidity of social life in America and the search for a community to compensate for the loss of the traditional support structures. Small groups offer an easy way to connect with other people, but at the same time, their members can easily disconnect and move away: "It provides a kind of social interaction that busy, rootless people can grasp without making significant adjustments in their lifestyles."

Still, the communal agenda that dominated the meetings, and the role of these associations in the lives of their participants, seemed to differentiate the groups presented in this book from most of those in Wuthnow's study, which centered on religious affiliation. In particular, the groups I observed were often reluctant to define their activities as substitutes for family or community (where one does not, in fact, freely reveal one's innermost cravings). The people I studied were not looking for a gay Shangri-la—a Cherry Grove (Newton 1993) or a Provincetown (Faiman-Silva 2004)—in Manhattan. At the same time, however, they seemed to generate an alternative mold of social affiliation, mobilizing the more appealing elements attributed to mainstream kinship and community. That proposition recalls Weston's (1991) discourse on the emergence of new forms of family structure and kinship relationships among lesbians and gays.

Bellah et al. differentiated "a community of memory" from a "lifestyle enclave." They explained: "Where history and hope are forgotten and community means only the gathering of the similar, community degenerates into a lifestyle enclave" (1985: 154). I decline to adopt their term "degenerate." The participants in our groups bore different ethnic, cultural, economic, religious, and other social signifiers. Except CBST congregants, they did not share a community of memory. Yet Jews, including CBST congregants, were also represented in all other groups, such as SAGE, SCA, MACT, the Bisexuals, the Bears, and more. They all shared, however, the existential experiences and destiny of gay people.

We can identify some shared characteristics among the participants I observed, their status as single men and women in particular. However, in the various religious congregations, the membership included many gay and lesbian couples. Naturally, I cannot relate my reports and conclusions to "all" gay people. As in most other types of nonexperimental social research, I can speak confidently for those under investigation; however, I do feel it legitimate to consider my thesis relevant beyond the borders of the studied population. Be that as it may, many of the various groups' participants shared with other gay people the variety of recreational institutions considered major markers of gay life in New York City.

That said, our observations do suggest a novel divergence from the common public perception of homosexuals, men and women, as representing a monolithic identity, often defined as the "gay community" (except the "deviant" categories, such as transgendered, bisexuals, transvestites, etc.). I posit that the participants in the groups introduced above expressed and proclaimed their particular gay identity, which seemed to differentiate them from other gay people. However, they might sometimes have professed their adoption of more than one group's social and sexual agenda. For example, one could identify as a gay Jew—an active CBST member—but also be a prominent SCA founding member. As reported in my records, those individuals revealed a different social persona in either of these two communal arenas. Similarly, a SAGE devotee may also identify with MACT or the Bears. These specific identifications and loyalties offer a polymorphic perception of the "gay/lesbian community."[3] Indicating a wide variation of communal alliances, sexual habits, and erotic preferences, these associational memberships play an important role in the social, psychological, and emotional domains of gay personal identity. Moreover, that pattern of personal sociosexual consciousness seems unique to gay society.

Out of these focused gatherings, the evocative exchanges between those who shared an existential problem or a similar erotic desire, there emerged what I incline to define as "affective fellowships." My designation recalls J. Dean's (1996) characterization of "affectionate solidarity" in feminist circles, a term also employed by Plummer (2003), in contradistinction to "conventional solidarity" that develops from shared interests, and by Cvetkovich (2003) in her exploration of structures of affect and affective networks promoting associations of emotional affirmation (relating the case of lesbians engaged in ACT UP). In my observations, the varied texture of assemblies of strangers offered immediate admittance to a quasi-stable group of welcoming and supportive gay people who met at fixed intervals (weekly, biweekly, or several on the same day). For many joiners, these also afforded the company of a closer core of associates who got together for other activities on weekends and holidays in particular. Sam, a regular member of SAGE (as well as of other groups), expressed in his spontaneous apothegm "the group has a life of its own" the viability of these highly democratic, affectionate fellowships.

Like all other groups at the Lesbian and Gay Community Services Center, the SAGE circle's framework for social interaction differed greatly from the more familiar scene of gay interaction observed in urban settings: bars, sex clubs, bathhouses, cruising areas, and more. Avoiding a repetition of the well-known descriptions of the social ambience at these sites, I quote Bech, who succinctly expressed the experience of gay men in the city: "The city, with its crowds and mutual strangers, is the place where the homosexual can come together with others; and—at the same time and for the same reasons—it is the place that confirms his loneliness (1997: 98).

I ended my introduction by invoking two contenders from different sociocultural realms and fields of observation: Umberto Eco in Disney World, asking what the visitor takes away from his/her experience in this invented world, and Halperin, asking "What do gay men want" in their immersion into the dangerous domain of unprotected sex. Is it fantasy, or is it something real? Eco pondered. He believed that what visitors get/buy at Disney is indeed "goods, genuine merchandise, not reproductions," but he doubted the authenticity of the will to buy—an urge that he posits is manipulated by Disney's entrepreneurs. In contrast, I assume that the often fantastic architectural designs of sex sites in the days of gay liberation (the bathhouses in particular) souped up the excitement of going there, but there is no doubt as to the authenticity of the will "to buy the merchandise" they offered. This is also true of the less fabulous institutions that preexisted, or survived, the forgotten days of "uninhibited" gay sex liberation.

In any event, in the groups I observed at the Center's "gay marketplace," converging in the dilapidated Center building (before its refurbishment) and at the MCC, Unity, Dignity, and CBST religious services, both the merchandise offered and the drive to acquire it were genuine. The participants, who traveled from all parts of the city to attend these meetings, were gratified by a unique experience: the sharing of intimacy with other attendees, mostly strangers the first time they walked in, and also on later visits, but who also revealed the same basic sexual/erotic predilection that dominated their lives. These semi-tribal gatherings offered the participants the notion of a shared core identity beyond the undifferentiated status of "homosexuals." "Unconditional affection" was their mode of communication.

Not surprisingly, the messages coming from the religious organizations also continually emphasized affection and love as basic elements in the lives of the congregants—as members of the assembly, as American citizens in their relationships with their fellow countrymen, and as individuals seeking personal happiness in the company of friends and with loving partners.

But the gatherings at the Center and the religious services also held out the potential for erotic excitement similar to that expected at other recreational venues, the anonymous sex sites included: meeting new candidates for intimacy (friendship and sex), though not under the shadow of concealed personas.

Most revealing were the descriptions of individual life histories, in particular my two close friends Jeff and Nigel, whom I met in different voluntary associations. Nigel identified with one group only, which became the major arena of his social and spiritual life. Although not the only venue for the search of mates for intimacy and sex, that personal identification was still his major source of pride and emotional self-assurance as a gay man. Jeff, however, was more versatile in his erotic proclivities and the social spaces for his identification as a gay man. Both assiduously sought a love relationship, but in a most dissimilar manner. For Jeff, erotic attraction and sexual compatibility came first, as a trial for a more serious bonding. For Nigel, however, the personal compatibility (social, cultural, emotional) was the first test. True, the sexual tuning, the "tingle" in Nigel's terminology, was for him too the final brick in the construction of an enduring partnership. But the cherished project for both men was a search for love and the founding of a committed stable couple relationship.

I observed Jeff's longing for that goal for nearly twenty years. It was a story with many painful turns that brought him to the brink of despair and almost death. One not closely familiar with Jeff might have assumed that "the guy is only looking for instant sex," "he is a sex addict," or "he is a typical product of gay life of the 1970s." He promoted that false portrait of himself as a sort of shield. I observed Nigel for seven years, but I had been informed about his personal life a few years earlier. Nigel did not experiment as much as Jeff at the various gay venues to satisfy his sexual drive and search for a lover. However, in his restrained and "cool" way, he was equally persistent in his search for a suitable mate for sex and love. Luckily, my last communication with Jeff and Nigel, late in 2012, found each of them in a state of happy bonding.

"The group has a life of its own." "These are our synagogues." These emphatic "authentic" labels were ascribed to organizations with very different social agendas and by men of diverse age and life situation. They suggest reflexive metaphors for a social product and a mirror of a collective consciousness. They seem to propose a partial answer to the question: what do gay people want? These gatherings offered participants the opportunity to relate emotionally and to swap tales of intimate experiences with others who shared their existential position: the unique fate and its consequences—the positive and the negative, the pleasures and pains—of their particular gay identity in American society. Blacks and whites, men and women, younger and older participants with various sensuous desires generated solidarity in a communitas-type of focused gatherings, exhibiting, performing, and communicating some basic dimensions of gay subjectivity. In conclusion, I suggest that the "currency" tendered at these meetings was specific gay identities—personal valuable assets, comprising, besides the social camaraderie, a feeling of self-assurance about the validity of one's intimate compulsions, frustrating impediments, and erotic preferences. These associations established a network of active sub-communities within the virtual map of New York's (and other cities') "gay community."

I conclude my task as "navigator" among the gay arenas representing different existential circumstances and sexual/erotic gay identities but offering similar substantial social and emotional responses. As for our major queries, I wrap up my conclusions about the reality observed in poetic terms: Not so much a fantasy, more a way of life.

NOTES

Introduction

1. I am aware of T. Dean's (2009) interpretation of barebacking based on personal experiences.

Chapter 1. The Anthropologist in the Field of Sexuality

1. See Hastings and Magowan's (2010) review of major developments in the anthropological study of sexual intimacy and desire.

2. Famous in particular is the book by Karla Poewe about falling in love in the field, published under the pseudonym Manda Cesara (1982).

3. I approached a gay colleague in Sweden and asked his view of Henriksson's research. I was soon informed that the gay community, as well as gay anthropologists in Sweden, had bitterly condemned the early exposure of Henriksson's project on various grounds: it caused a public outcry against the apparent sleaziness of gay men and therefore enhanced homophobia; the media exposure of the report endangered the reputation of the uninformed subjects who were intimidated by the police at the raids that followed the press coverage; and the eruption of scandal curtailed public funding for gay organizations. Gay scholars also objected to the method of encouraging assistants to get information through active participation in sex. They accused Henriksson of sheer opportunism.

4. During my fieldwork the congregants made arrangements for recruitment of a salaried rabbi (installed in 1995). Today, however, the synagogue's leadership combines a few salaried professionals and a strong cohort of volunteers.

5. A similar approach, although in an unrelated field, was suggested by Jackson (1989: 3) who argued: "Unlike traditional empiricism, which draws a definite boundary between observer and observed, between method and object, radical empiricism denies the validity of such cuts and makes the interplay between these domains the focus of its interest."

6. My participation in that event brings to mind Stoller's (1997: 23) conclusion: "The full presence of the ethnographer's body in the field also demands a fuller sensual awareness of the smells, tastes, sounds and textures of life among the others."

7. I was able to comprehend his late discovery of my research interests in terms of "motivated missing of the point," a phrase I remembered from my early education in

social psychology. He knew about my professional background and my previous work in New York. He must have also noticed my passive yet attentive attendance at all meetings.

8. The different circumstances of my work and the closer relationships with congregants at CBST also enabled me to share with them the ethnographic text prior to its publication (Shokeid 1997).

9. I related to that issue at an early stage of my career (Shokeid 1971b). I was studying a community of Jewish immigrants in Israel at a time when most anthropologists ventured to remote continents to discover the "other." I tried to demonstrate the pros and cons that distinguish research in one's own society. I claimed the two perspectives are complementary and necessary. I believe the field of gay life is not basically different from most other fields chosen by anthropologists.

Chapter 2. Concealments and Revelations in Ethnographic Research

1. A phrase I borrowed from McLean and Leibing 2007.

2. See Freeman 1983; Oscar Lewis 1960; Redfield 1955; Tierney 2000.

3. I dedicated my ethnography to four close congregants who died of AIDS before its publication (1995).

4. Wolf (1992: 129) had succinctly expressed that professional perplexity: "When human behavior is data, a tolerance for ambiguity, multiplicity, contradiction, and instability is essential."

5. See, for example, Marcus, "Where Have All the Tales of Fieldwork Gone?" (2006).

6. See my discussion on this issue, Shokeid 2007.

Chapter 3. The Regretless Seniors

1. Under the auspices of SAGE, a few more groups met regularly at the center. SAGE groups differed in their declared categories of age and sex (such as forty plus, fifty plus, for men, for women) or in their different schedule during the week. All members contributed two to three dollars at the end of each meeting. These contributions formed a standard norm at most meetings at the Center and were dedicated to the "rent" of the meeting room as well as the support of the specific organization that initiated the group.

2. My observations at the SAGE and other groups' meetings introduce another methodological issue raised by Wax (1996: 3–41) as he considered the ethnographic authority of fieldwork carried out in focus groups: "Focus groups are low on the scale of MOP (Massive Over-determination of Pattern)". But this issue demands a wider discussion about the status of fieldwork under the changing circumstances of ethnographic projects. See, for example, Clifford 1997 and Ortner 1998.

3. On a more recent visit to the SAGE group, I discovered that for the previous six months Michael had been involved with a man from the Netherlands he had met on a trip to Africa.

4. Varenne's conclusions, which seemed to rely on somewhat obscure observations among young heterosexuals in a remote small town, were strongly supported by Bellah et al. 1985 and are continuously reflected in my own work.

Chapter 4. Attending Meetings of Sexual Compulsives Anonymous

1. Twelve-step recovery program—a nonsectarian spiritual program, the central points of which are trust in God or a higher power as each individual understands that concept, and the value of help to other sufferers.

2. Establishing the SCA groups at the Center in particular was not a difficult project. One participant commented laughingly that you only needed a coffeepot to start a new group when you were unhappy with the people you met at particular meetings. In fact, many participants, if not the majority, discovered the SCA through their engagement with the Center itself. Typical was the story of one young man sitting next to me. He had been with the program six months, but he told me he had started attending Center activities seven months before, volunteering to answer phone calls once a week. He soon realized that he himself actually had a problem, a sexual addiction.

3. Although Carnes assumed a mostly heterosexual audience, homosexuals can readily identify with his introduction of the method of recovery (based on the AA Twelve Step program) and his description of some major characteristics of sexual addicts' life histories and behavior. In particular, "addicts," heterosexuals and homosexuals alike, confuse nurturing and sex: "Support, care, affirmation and love are sexualized" (1992: 82).

4. My experience as observer at the SCA meetings contradicted my own convictions about the desirable relationship between the ethnographer and his subjects (Shokeid 1997). Exploring the ethical dimensions of fieldwork, Geertz emphasized in particular the inherent moral tension between the investigator and his/her subjects: "Usually the sense of being members, however temporarily, insecurely and incompletely, of a single moral community can be maintained even in the face of the wider social realities which press in at almost every moment to deny it. It is this fiction—fiction, not falsehood—that lies at the heart of successful anthropological field research" (1968: 154).

5. These later observations confirmed a continuity of my earlier experiences with SCA activities.

6. "The good old days"—memories as much as myth-making about the pre-AIDS years, when gay men enjoyed unrestrained sexual freedom consummated at a wide variety of commercial institutions and public spaces.

Chapter 5. In the Company of the Bisexual Circle

1. Rituals of homosexuality have also been employed in socializing the young into roles of masculinity and heterosexuality (see Herdt 1981).

2. In South American and Muslim societies, men's sexual relations with other men are often tolerated, and to an extent prove masculinity, just as long as one is not in the position of the "passive" partner. See, for example, Lancaster 1988; Shepherd 1987.

Chapter 6. The Interracial Gay Men's Association

1. A white scholar, businessman, and writer founded MACT, starting the movement with an ad in the *Advocate*. Four groups originated in 1980—in San Francisco, Chicago,

Boston, and New York. A year later, thirty groups existed, and the first convention was held in San Francisco (Beame 1999 [1983]: 187–95).

2. Mumia Abu-Jamal, a black journalist with no prior criminal record, awaiting execution on death row in Pennsylvania since 1982 for the alleged shooting of a police officer. Many supporters around the world believed he was innocent and repeatedly demanded a new trial, which would expose prejudice and vengefulness on the part of Pennsylvania police and courts. He was removed from death row in January 2012.

Chapter 7. The Gentle Men's Circle

1. An association of mostly gay men who emphasize, in particular, freedom of body and spirit in the closeness to nature (e.g., Hennen 2008).

Chapter 9. Listening to the Sermons in Gay Congregations

1. Some critics suggest that Luther and his followers may have focused more on spreading the Gospel and reaching the common people through simple speech and seductive rhetorical strategies than on the theological and biblical content of the sermon. See, for example, Hillerbrand 2004: 1541.

2. I have analyzed elsewhere (Shokeid 1988a) the role of the chosen informants upon whom anthropologists depend for the success of their ethnographic endeavor. These door openers to the communities they study may also influence the major subjects of their inquiry and writings.

3. At MCC, most services were recorded by the church and later publicized on the Internet. I decided to rely mostly on the memory of my experience during delivery. I assumed that this offered a perception and sensibility that more closely approximated that of the congregants, who experienced the oral presentations under the same circumstances. We shared the atmosphere of the actual performance and the audience's immediate emotional response.

4. I once received the Eucharist, when Don performed as deacon. I wished to demonstrate that I had no negative feelings about that tradition.

5. Except for Rev. Bumgardner, Rabbi Kleinbaum, and Rev. Perry, other names are pseudonyms.

6. Thomas 1997: 42 has succinctly described this African American sermon atmosphere: "It is through sense appeal that the physical matter (body, thinking, and emotions) of the preacher engages the physical matter (body, thinking, and emotions) of the listener, and the physical matter of the text."

7. These categories have all appeared in scholarly discourses classifying church sermons. See, *Encyclopedic Dictionary of Religion*, 1979: 3262.

8. An anthropologist, Bauman (1986: 7), suggested a similar approach. While he did not study sermons, his analysis of oral performances seems relevant to the present field of observation. He claims that his analytical strategy is rooted in a systemic conception of oral narrative performance as the indissoluble unity of text, narrated event, and narrative event.

9. See Heilman's (1983) study of Talmud classes and my investigation (1988b: 104–25) of communal singing of Israeli folk songs among Israeli immigrants in New York. We both interpreted our observations in terms of cultural performance.

Chapter 10. Talking Sex, Imagining Love: The Emotional Template

1. "[T]he 'reality' of sex does not pre-exist the language in which it is expressed; rather, language *produces* the categories through which we organize our sexual desires, identities and practices" (Cameron and Kulick 2003: 19).

2. That characteristic of close relationships among friends was reported by earlier observers. Nardi (1992), for example, claimed that intimacy and emotional support are far more prevalent among gay men than among heterosexual men who are constrained by homophobic stereotypes.

Afterword: Negotiating Gay Subjectivity

1. For further information about Israeli gay life, see, for example, Kama 2000, 2005; Kaplan 2003; Shokeid 2003.

2. I am aware of Putnam's (2000) counternarrative to the portrayal of "joining" in contemporary American culture.

3. See also Murray 1998 [1979].

REFERENCES

Adam, Barry D. 1992. "Sex and Caring Among Men: Impact of AIDS on Gay People." In *Modern Homosexualities*, ed. Kenneth Plumer. London: Routledge. 175–83.

Altman, Dennis. 1986. *AIDS in the Mind of America*. New York: Doubleday.

Amory, Deborah. 1996. "Club Q: Dancing with (a) Difference." In *Inventing Lesbian Cultures in America*, ed. Ellen Lewin. Boston: Beacon. 145–60.

Antoun, Richard. 1989. *Muslim Preacher in the Modern World: A Jordanian Case Study in Comparative Perspective*. Princeton, N.J.: Princeton University Press.

Antze, Paul. 1987. "Symbolic Action in Alcoholics Anonymous." In *Constructive Drinking: Perspectives on Drink from Anthropology*, ed. Mary Douglas. Cambridge: Cambridge University Press. 149–81.

Ariès, Philippe. 1985. "The Indissoluble Marriage." In *Western Sexuality: Practice and Precept in Past and Present Times*, ed. Philippe Ariès and André Béjin. Oxford: Blackwell. 140–57.

Avery, William O., and Roger Gobbel. 1980. "The Word of God and the Words of the Preacher." *Review of Religious Research* 22: 41–53.

Baldwin, James. 1962. *Another Country*. London: Corgi Books.

Barth, Karl. 1963. *The Teaching of the Gospel*. Philadelphia: Westminster.

Baudrillard, Jean. 1988. *America*. Trans. Chris Turner. London: Verso.

Bateson, Mary Catherine, and Richard Goldsby. 1994. "Thinking AIDS: The Epidemic and the Society." In *The Sociology of Health and Illness: Critical Perspectives*, ed. Peter Conrad and Rochelle Kern, 125–34. New York: St. Martin's.

Baum, D. Michael, and James M. Fishman, 1994. "Aids, Sexual Compulsivity, and Gay Men: A Group Treatment Approach." In *Therapist on the Front Line: Psychotherapy with Gay Men in the Age of AIDS*. Washington, D.C.: American Psychiatric Press. 255–74.

Bauman, Richard. 1986. *Story, Performance, and Event: Contextual Studies of Oral Narrative*. Cambridge: Cambridge University Press.

Beame, Thom. 1999 [1983]. "Interview." In *Black Men/White Men: Afro-American Gay Life & Culture*, ed. Michael J. Smith. San Francisco: Gay Sunshine Press. 187–95.

Bech, Henning. 1997. *When Men Meet: Homosexuality and Modernity*. Chicago: University of Chicago Press.

Beemyn, Brett, and Mickey Eliason, eds. 1996. *Queer Studies: A Lesbian, Gay, Bisexual and Transgender Anthology*. New York: New York University Press.

Bellah, Robert, et al. 1985. *Habits of the Heart: Individualism and Commitment in American Life.* Berkeley: University of California Press.

Berger, M. Raymond. 1996 [1982]. *Gay and Gray: The Older Homosexual Man.* New York: Haworth.

Bersani, Leo. 1988. "Is the Rectum a Grave?" In *AIDS: Cultural Analysis/Cultural Activism,* ed. Douglas Crimp, 197–222. Cambridge, Mass: MIT Press.

Blackwood, Evelyn. 2002. "Reading Sexualities Across Cultures: Anthropology and Theories of Sexuality." In *Out in Theory: The Emergence of Lesbian and Gay Anthropology,* ed. Ellen Lewin and William L. Leap. Urbana: University of Illinois Press. 69–92.

Boellstorff, Tom. 2007. "Queer Studies in the House of Anthropology." *Annual Review of Anthropology* 36: 17–35.

Bolton, Ralph. 1992. "AIDS and Promiscuity: Muddles in the Models of HIV Prevention." *Medical Anthropology* 14: 145–223.

———. 1995. "Tricks, Friends and Lovers: Erotic Encounters in the Field." In *Taboo: Sex, Identity and Erotic Subjectivity in Anthropological Fieldwork,* ed. Don Kulick and Margaret Willson. New York: Routledge. 140–67.

———. 1996. "Coming Home: The Journey of a Gay Ethnographer in the Years of the Plague." In *Out in the Field: Reflections of Lesbian and Gay Anthropologists,* ed. Ellen Lewin and William L. Leap. Urbana: University of Illinois Press. 147–70.

Borneman, John and Abdellah Hammudi, eds. 2009. *Being There: The Fieldwork Encounter and the Making of Truth.* Berkeley: University of California Press.

Boykin, Keith. 1996. *One More River to Cross: Black & Gay in America.* New York: Doubleday.

Brettel, Caroline B., ed. 1993. *When They Read What We Write: The Politics of Ethnography.* Westport, Conn.: Bergin and Garvey.

Brodsky, J. I. 1993. "The Mineshaft: A Retrospective Ethnography." In *If You Seduce Straight Persons, Can You Make Them Gay? Issues in Biological Essentialism Versus Social Constructionism in Gay and Lesbian Identities,* ed. John DeCecco and John Patrick Elia. New York: Haworth. 233–51.

Bronski, Michael. 2000. *The Pleasure Principle: Sex, Backlash, and the Struggle for Gay Freedom.* New York: St. Martin's.

Brueggeman, Walter. 1988. "The Social Nature of the Biblical Text for Preaching." In *Preaching as a Social Act: Theology and Practice,* ed. Arthur Van Seters. Nashville: Abingdon Press. 127–65.

Burawoy, Michael. 1991. *Ethnography Unbound: Power and Resistance in the Modern Metropolis.* Berkeley: University of California Press.

Cameron, Deborah, and Don Kulick. 2003. *Language and Sexuality.* Cambridge: Cambridge University Press.

Carnes, Patrick, 1992. *Out of the Shadows: Understanding Sexual Addictions.* Center City, Minn.: Hazeldon.

Carrier, Joseph. 1995. *De los otros: Intimacy and Homosexuality Among Mexican Men.* New York: Columbia University Press.

Cesara, Manda [Karla Poewe]. 1982. *Reflections of a Woman Anthropologist*. New York: Academic Press.

Chauncey, George. 1994. *Gay New York: Gender, Urban Culture, and the Making of the Gay Male World 1890-1940*. New York: Basic Books.

Clifford, James. 1997. *Routes: Travel and Translation in the Late Twentieth Century*. Cambridge, Mass.: Harvard University Press.

Crapanzano, Vincent. 1980. *Tuhami: Portrait of a Moroccan*. Chicago: University of Chicago Press.

———. 2000. *Serving the Word: Literalism in America from the Pulpit to the Bench*. New York: New Press.

Curtis, E. James, Douglas E. Baer, and Edward G. Grabb. 2001. "Nations of Joiners: Explaining Voluntary Associations Membership in Democratic Societies." *American Sociological Review* 66: 783–805.

Cvetkovich, Ann. 2003. *An Archive of Feeling: Trauma, Sexuality and Lesbian Public Cultures*. Durham, N.C.: Duke University Press.

Dean, Judi. 1996. *Solidarity of Strangers: Feminism and Identity Politics*. Berkeley: University of California Press.

Dean, Tim. 2009. *Unlimited Intimacy: Reflections on the Subculture of Barebacking*. Chicago: University of Chicago Press.

Delaney, Samuel R. 1988. *The Motion of Light in Water: Sex and Science Fiction in the East Village, 1957-1965*. New York: New American Library.

———. 1999. *Time Square Red, Times Square Blue*. New York: New York University Press.

Delph, W. E. 1978. *The Silent Community: Public Homosexual Encounters*. Beverly Hills, Calif.: Sage.

DeMarco, Joe. 1999[1983]. "Gay Racism." In *Black Men/White Men: Afro-American Gay Life&Culture*, ed. J.Smith, San Francisco: Gay Sunshine Press. 109–18.

Dominguez, Virginia. 1989. *People as Subject, People as Object: Selfhood and Peoplehood in Contemporary Israel*. Madison: University of Wisconsin Press.

Douglas, Mary. 1966. *Purity and Danger*. London: Routledge and Kegan Paul.

Du Plessis, Michael. 1996. "Do Bats Eat Cats? Reading What Bisexuality Does." In *Representing Bisexualities: Subjects and Cultures of Fluid Desire*, ed. Donald E. Hall and Maria Pramaggiore, 19–54. New York: New York University Press.

Eco, Umberto. 1986. *Travel in Hyperreality*. San Diego: Harcourt Brace.

Eickelman, Dale F. 1985. *Knowledge and Power in Morocco: The Education of a Twentieth-Century Notable*. Princeton N.J.: Princeton University Press.

Encyclopedic Dictionary of Religion. 1979. "Sermon." Sisters of St. Joseph of Philadelphia. 3261–62.

Eytan, Rachel. 1985 [1962]. *The Fifth Heaven: A Novel*. Trans. Philip Simpson. Philadelphia: Jewish Publication Society (first published in Hebrew).

Faiman-Silva, Sandra. 2004. *The Courage to Connect: Sexuality, Citizenship, and Community in Provincetown*. Urbana: University of Illinois Press.

Feldman, Douglas A. 1990. *Culture and AIDS*. New York: Praeger.

Forrest, David. 1994. "'We're Here, We're Queer, and We're Not Going Shopping: Changing Gay Male Identities in Contemporary Britain." In *Dislocating Masculinities: Comparative Ethnographies*, ed. Andrea Corrnwall and Nancy Lindisfarne. London: Routledge. 97–110.

Fox, Ronald C., ed. 2004. *Current Research on Bisexuality*. New York: Harrington Park Press.

Freeman, Derek. 1983. *Margaret Mead and Samoa: The Making and Unmaking of an Anthropological Myth*. Cambridge, Mass.: Harvard University Press.

Friedl, Ernestine. 1994. "Sex the Invisible." *American Anthropologist* 96: 833–44.

Furman, Mirta. 1994. *The New Children: Violence and Obedience in Early Childhood*. Tel Aviv: HaKibbutz HaMehuhad (Hebrew).

Gamm, Gerald, and Robert D. Putnam. 1999. "The Growth of Voluntary Associations in America, 1840–1940." *Journal of Interdisciplinary History* 29: 511–57.

Garber, Marjorie. 1995. *Vice Versa: Bisexuality and the Eroticism of Everyday Life*. New York: Simon and Schuster.

Geertz, Clifford. 1968. "Thinking as a Moral Act: Ethical Dimensions of Anthropological Fieldwork in the New States." *Antioch Review* 28: 139–58.

———. 1973. *The Interpretation of Cultures*. New York: Basic Books.

Giddens, Anthony. 1990. *The Consequences of Modernity*. Stanford, Calif.: Stanford University Press.

———. 1992. *The Transformation of Intimacy: Sexuality, Love and Eroticism in Modern Societies*. Stanford, Calif.: Stanford University Press.

Ginsburg, F. D. 1989. *Contested Lives: Abortion Debate in an American Community*. Berkeley: University of California Press.

Glover, Tony. 1993. "In Black and White for All to See." In *Celebrating Diversity: A 10th Anniversary Journal of Poetry, Narrative, Essays, and Photography*. New York: Men of All Colors Together.

Gluckman, Max. 1959 [1940]. *Analysis of Social Situation in Modern Zululand*. Rhodes Livingstone Papers 28. (First published in *Bantu Studies* 14: 1–30, 147–74.)

Godelier, Maurice. 1999. *The Enigma of the Gift*. Chicago: University of Chicago Press.

Goffman, Erving. 1967. *Interaction Ritual*. London: Penguin.

Goode, Erich. 2002. "Sexual Involvement and Social Research in a Fat Civil Rights Organization." *Qualitative Sociology* 25: 501–32.

Griffith, R. Marie. 2005. "Conclusion: Gay Religion as a Cultural Production" In *Gay Religion*, ed. Thumma Scott and Edward R. Gray, 367–77. Walnut Creek, Calif.: Altamira.

Gudelunas, David. 2005. "Online Personal Ads: Community and Sex, Virtually." *Journal of Homosexuality* 49: 1–34.

Gwenwald, Morgan. 1984. "The Sage Model for Serving Older Lesbians and Gay Men." *Journal of Social Work & Human Sexuality* 2, 2–3: 53–61.

Hall, Donald E., and Maria Pramaggiore, eds. 1996. *Representing Bisexualities: Subjects and Cultures of Fluid Desire*. New York: New York University Press.

Haller, Dieter. 2001. "Reflections on the Merits and Perils of Insider Anthropology: When Anthropologists Are Made Natives." *Kea, Zeitschrift für Kulturwissenschaften* 14: 113–46.

Halperin, David. M. 2007. *What Do Gay Men Want? An Essay on Sex, Risk, and Subjectivity.* Ann Arbor: University of Michigan Press.

Hannerz, Ulf. 2010. *Anthropology's World: Life in a Twenty-First-Century Discipline.* London: Pluto Press.

Harre, Rom, 1986. *The Social Construction of Emotions.* Oxford: Blackwell.

Harris, Daniel. 1997. *The Rise and Fall of Gay Culture.* New York: Hyperion.

Hastings, Donnan, and Fiona Magowan. 2010. *The Anthropology of Sex.* Oxford: Berg.

Hawkeswood, William G. 1996. *One of the Children.* Berkeley: University of California Press.

Heilman, Samuel C. 1976. *Synagogue Life: A Study in Symbolic Interaction.* Chicago: University of Chicago Press.

———. 1983. *The People of the Book.* Chicago: University of Chicago Press.

Hennen, Peter. 2008. *Fairies, Bears and Leathermen: Men in Community Queering the Masculine.* Chicago: University of Chicago Press.

Henriksson, Benny. 1995. *Risk Factor Love: Homosexuality, Sexual Interaction and HIV Prevention.* Göteborg: Göteborg Universitet.

Herdt, Gilbert. 1981. *Guardians of the Flutes: Idioms of Masculinity.* New York: McGraw-Hill.

———, ed. 1992. *Gay Culture in America: Essays from the Field.* Boston: Beacon.

———. 2003. *Secrecy and Cultural Reality: Utopian Ideologies of the New Guinea Men's House.* Ann Arbor: University of Michigan Press.

Hillerbrand, Hans J. 2004. *Encyclopedia of Protestantism.* "Preaching," Vol. 3, 1535–41. New York: Routledge.

Hochschild, Arlie Russel. 2003. *The Commercialization of Intimate Life.* Berkeley: University of California Press.

Hollister, John. 1999. "A Highway Rest Area as a Socially Reproducible Site." In *Public Sex/Gay Sex*, ed. William Leap, New York: Columbia University Press. 55–70.

Horne, R. A. 2004. Review of *In the Arms of Africa: The Life of Colin M. Turnbull* by Roy Richard Grinker. *Journal of Homosexuality* 48: 143–47.

Howard, John. 1999. *Men like That: A Southern Queer History.* Chicago: University of Chicago Press.

Howden, William D. 1989. "'Good Sermon, Preacher': The Effects of Age, Sex, and Education on Hearer Response to Preaching." *Review of Religious Research* 31: 196–207.

Huizinga, Johan. 1972 [1927]. *America: A Dutch Historian's Vision, from Afar and Near.* Trans. H. H. Rowen. New York: Harper and Row.

Humphreys, L. 1970. *Tearoom Trade: Impersonal Sex in Public Places.* Chicago: Aldine; enlarged ed. London: Duckworth, 1975.

Illouz, Eva. 1997. *Consuming the Romantic Utopia*. Berkeley: University of California Press.

———. 2008. *Saving the Modern Soul: Therapy, Emotions, and the Culture of Self-Help*. Berkeley: University of California Press.

Jackson, Michael. 1989. *Paths Toward a Clearing: Radical Empiricism and Ethnographic Inquiry*. Bloomington: Indiana University Press.

Jay, Karla, ed. 1995. *Lesbian Erotics*. New York: New York University Press.

Kalir, Barak. 2006. "The Field of Work and the Work of the Field: Conceptualizing an Anthropological Research Engagement." *Social Anthropology* 14: 235–46.

Kama, Amit. 2000. "From *Terra Incognita* to *Terra Firma*: The Logbook of the Voyage of Gay Men's Community into the Israeli Public Sphere." *Journal of Homosexuality* 38: 133–62.

———. 2005. "An Unrelenting Mental Press: Israeli Gay Men's Ontological Duality and Its Discontent." *Journal of Men's Studies* 13: 169–84.

Kaminer, Wendy. 1992. *I'm Dysfunctional, You're Dysfunctional: The Recovery Moment and Other Self-Help Fashions*. Boston: Addison-Wesley.

Kaplan, D. 2003. *Brothers and Others in Arms: The Making of Love and War in Israeli Combat Units*. Binghamton, N.Y.: Harrington Park Press.

Katriel, Tamar. 1986. *Talking Straight: "Dugri" Speech in Israeli Sabra Culture*. Cambridge: Cambridge University Press.

Kennedy Lapovsky, Elizabeth. 1996. "'But We Would Never Talk About It': The Structures of Lesbian Discretion in South Dakota, 1928–1933." In *Inventing Lesbian Cultures in America*, ed. Ellen Lewin. Boston: Beacon. 15–39.

Kennedy Lapovsky, Elizabeth, and D. Davis. 1993. *Boots of Leather, Slippers of Gold: The History of a Lesbian Community*. New York: Routledge.

Kinsey, Alfred C., Wardel B. Pomeroy, and Clyde E. Martin. 1948. *Sexual Behavior in the Human Male*. Philadelphia: Saunders.

Kleinbaum, Sharon. 2005. *Listening to the Oboe*. New York: Congregation Beth Simchat Torah.

Kulick, Don. 1998. *Travesty: Sex, Gender and Culture Among Brazilian Transgendered Prostitutes*. Chicago: University of Chicago Press.

———. 2003. "Language and Desire." In *The Handbook of Language and Gender*, ed. Janet Holmes and Miriam Meyerhoff. London: Blackwell. 119–41.

Kulick, Don, and Margaret Willson, eds. 1995. *Taboo: Sex, Identity, and Erotic Subjectivity in Anthropological Fieldwork*. London: Routledge.

Lancaster, Roger N. 1988. "Subject Honor and Object Shame: The Construction of Male Homosexuality and Stigma in Nicaragua." *Ethnology* 27: 111–26.

Langness, L. L., and Gelya Frank. 1981. *Lives: An Anthropological Approach*. Nevato, Calif.: Chandler and Sharp.

Leap, L. William, 1996. *Word's Out: Gay Men's English*. Minneapolis: University of Minnesota Press.

———, ed. 1999. *Public Sex/Gay Sex*. New York: Columbia University Press.

———. 2008. "Queering Gay Men English" In *Language and Gender Research Methodologies*, ed. K. Harrington, L. Litosseliti, H. Saunton, and J. Sunderland. Basingstoke: Palgrave. 408–29.

———. 2010. "Globalization and Gay Language" In *Handbook of Language and Globalization*, ed. Nikolas Coupland. Malden, Mass.: Blackwell. 555–74.

Lee, J. A.1989. "Invisible Men: Canada's Aging Homosexuals." *Canadian Journal on Aging* 8, 1: 79–97.

Levine, Martin. 1979. *Gay Men: The Sociology of Male Homosexuality*. San Francisco: Harper and Row.

———. 1998. *Gay Macho: The Life and Death of the Homosexual Clone*. New York: New York University Press.

Levine, Martin, and Richard Troiden, 1998 [1988]. "The Myth of Sexual Compulsion." In *Gay Macho: The Life and Death of the Homosexual Clone*, ed. Martin Levine. New York: New York University Press.

Levy, Robert I. 1973. *Tahitians: Mind and Experience in the Society Islands*. Chicago: University of Chicago Press.

———. 1984. "Toward an Anthropology of Self and Feeling." In *Culture Theory: Essays on Mind, Self, and Emotion*, ed. Richard A. Shweder and Robert A. Levine. London: Cambridge University Press. 137–57.

Lewin, Ellen. 1993. *Lesbian Mothers: Accounts of Gender in American Society*. Ithaca, N.Y.: Cornell University Press.

———. 1996a. "Confessions of a Reformed Grant Hustler." In *Out in the Field*, ed. Ellen Lewin and William L. Leap. Urbana: University of Illinois Press. 111–27.

———, ed. 1996b. *Inventing Lesbian Cultures in America*. Boston: Beacon.

———. 2009. *Gay Fathers: Narratives of Family and Citizenship in America*. Chicago: University of Chicago Press.

Lewin, Ellen, and William L. Leap, eds. 1996. *Out in the Field: Reflections of Lesbian and Gay Anthropologists*. Urbana: University of Illinois Press.

———, eds. 2009. *Out in Public: Reinventing Lesbian/Gay Anthropology in a Globalizing World*. New York: Wiley.

Lewis, H. B. 1971. *Shame and Guilt in Neurosis*. New York: International Universities Press.

Lewis, Oscar. 1960. "Some of My Best Friends Are Peasants." *Human Organization* 19: 179–80.

———. 1967. *La Vida: A Puerto Rican Family in the Culture of Poverty—San Juan and New York*. London: Panther.

Lipset, S. Martin. 1994 [1962]. "Harriet Martineau's America." In Harriet Martineau, *Society in America*. New Brunswick, N.J.: Transaction. 5–55.

Love, Heather. 2007. *Feeling Backward: Loss and the Politics of Queer History*. Cambridge, Mass.: Harvard University Press.

Lovell, Ann M. 2007. "When Things Get Personal: Secrecy, Intimacy and the Production of Experience in Fieldwork." In *The Shadow Side of Fieldwork: Exploring the Blurred*

Borders Between Ethnography and Life, ed. Athena McLean and Annette Leibing. Malden, Mass.: Blackwell. 56–80.

Lukenbill, W. Bernard. 2005. "Pluralism and Diversity: Music as Discourse and Information in a Gay and Lesbian Congregation." In *Gay Religion*, ed. Scott Thumma and Edward R. Gray. New York: Altamira. 167–80.

Lunsing, Wim. 1999. "Life on Mars: Love and Sex in Fieldwork on Sexuality and Gender in Urban Japan." In *Sex, Sexuality, and the Anthropologist*, ed. Fran Markowitz and Michael Ashkenazi. Urbana: University of Illinois Press. 175–95.

Lutz, Cathrine. 1986. "Emotion, Thought, and Estrangement: Emotion as a Cultural Category." *Cultural Anthropology* 1: 287–309.

Lynch, Owen M., ed. 1990. *Divine Passions: The Social Construction of Emotion in India.* Berkeley: University of California Press.

Lynd, Helen Merrell. 1958. *On Shame and the Search for Identity.* New York: Science Editions.

Malinowski, Bronislaw. 1927. *Sex and Repression in Savage Society.* London: Routledge.

———. 1929. *The Sexual Life of Savages.* New York: Halcyon House.

———. 1967. *A Diary in the Strict Sense of the Term.* New York: Harcourt, Brace, and World.

Manley Eric, Heidi Levitt, and Chad Mosher. 2007. "Understanding the Bear Movement." *Journal of Homosexuality* 53: 89–112

Marcus, George, E. 2006. "Where Have All the Tales of Fieldwork Gone?" *Ethnos* 71: 113–22.

Markowitz, Fran. 1999. "Sexing the Anthropologist: Implications for Ethnography." In *Sex, Sexuality, and the Anthropologist*, ed. Fran Markowitz and Michael Ashkenazi. Urbana: University of Illinois Press. 161–74.

Markowitz, Fran, and Michael Ashkenazi, eds. 1999. *Sex, Sexuality, and the Anthropologist.* Urbana: University of Illinois Press.

Martineau. Harriet. 1994 [1837]. *Society in America.* Ed. Seymour M. Lipset. New Brunswick, N.J.: Transaction Books.

———. 1838. *How to Observe Manners and Morals.* London: Charles Knight.

McIntosh, Mary. 1968. "The Homosexual Role." *Social Problems* 16: 182–92.

McLean, Athena, and Annette Leibing, eds. 2007. *The Shadow Side of Fieldwork: Exploring the Blurred Borders Between Ethnography and Life.* Malden, Mass.: Blackwell.

Meyers, Fred R. 1979. "Emotions and the Self: A Theory of Personhood and Political Order Among Pintupi Aborigines." *Ethos* 7: 343–70.

———. 1988. "The Logic and Meaning of Anger Among Pintupi Aborigines." *Man* 23: 589–610.

Michel, Fran. 1996. "From Performativity to Interpretation: Toward a Social Semiotic Account of Bisexuality." In *Representing Bisexualities: Subjects and Cultures in Fluid Desire*, ed. Donald E. Hall and Maria Pramaggiore. New York: New York University Press. 55–69.

Middleton, John. 1960. *Lugbara Religion: Ritual and Authority Among an East African People*. London: Oxford University Press.

Moore, Patrick. 2004. *Beyond Shame: Reclaiming the Abandoned History of Radical Gay Sexuality*. Boston: Beacon.

Morgan, L. H. 1851. *League of the Iroquois*. Rochester, N.Y.: Sage and Brother.

Moyd, Olin P. 1995. *The Sacred Art: Preaching and Theology in the African American Tradition*. Valley Forge, Pa.: Judson Press.

Muñoz, José Esteban. 2009. *Cruising Utopia: The Then and There of Queer Futurity*. New York: New York University Press.

Murray, Stephen O. 1996. *American Gay*. Chicago: University of Chicago Press.

———. 1996. "Male Homosexuality in Guatemala: Possible Insights and Certain Confusions from Sleeping with the Natives." In *Out in the Field*, ed. Ellen Lewin and William L. Leap. Urbana: University of Illinois Press. 236–60.

———. 1998 [1979]. "The Institutional Elaboration of a Quasi-Ethnic Community." In *Social Perspectives in Lesbian and Gay Studies*, ed. Peter M. Nardi and Beth E. Schneider. New York: Routledge. 207–14.

Myerhoff, Barbara. 1978. *Number Our Days*. New York: Simon and Schuster.

Nardi, Peter M. 1992. "That's What Friends Are For: Friends as Family in Gay and Lesbian Community." In *Modern Homosexualities: Fragments of Lesbian and Gay Experience*, ed. Ken Plummer. London: Routledge. 108–20.

Nast, Heidi. 2008. "Secrets, Reflexivity, and Geographies of Refusal." *Feminism & Psychology* 18: 395–400.

Newton, Esther. 1972. *Mother Camp: Female Impersonators in America*. Chicago: University of Chicago Press.

———. 1993. *Cherry Grove, Fire Island: Sixty Years in America's First Gay and Lesbian Town*. Boston: Beacon.

———. 1996. "My Best Informant's Dress: The Erotic Equation in Fieldwork." In *Out in the Field*, ed. Ellen Lewin and William L. Leap. Urbana: University of Illinois Press. 212–35.

Nichols, J. Randall. 1985. "What Is the Matter with the Teaching of Preaching?" *Anglican Theological Review* 52: 221–38.

Ortner, Sherry B. 1998. "Generation X: Anthropology in a Media-Saturated World." *Cultural Anthropology* 13: 414–40.

Pargament, Kenneth I., and Donald V. DeRosa. 1985. "What Was That Sermon About? Predicting Memory for Religious Messages from Cognitive Psychology Theory." *Journal for the Scientific Study of Religion* 24: 180–93.

Pepper, Carol, 1997. "Wanting and Not Wanting to Change: Conflict and Ambivalence in the Efforts of Sexually Compulsive Men to Modify Dangerous Self-Destructive Sexual Behavior." Ph.D. dissertation, City University of New York.

Perry, Troy. 1978. *The Lord Is My Shepherd and He Knows I'm Gay*. New York: Bantam.

Peterson, John L. 1992. "Black Men and Their Same-Sex Desires and Behavior." In *Gay Culture in America*, ed. Gilbert Herdt, Boston: Beacon. 147–64.

Pitt-Rivers, Julian. 1971. *The People of the Sierra*. 2nd ed. Chicago: University of Chicago Press.

Plummer, Ken. 1995. *Telling Sexual Stories: Power, Change and Social Worlds*. London: Routledge.

———. 2003. *Intimate Citizenship: Private Decisions and Public Dialogues*. Seattle: University of Washington Press.

Powell, D. A., ed. 2008. *21st-Century Gay Culture*. Newcastle: Cambridge Scholars.

Pramaggiore, Maria. 1996. "Introduction I: Epistemologies of the Fence." In *Representing Bisexualities: Subjects and Cultures in Fluid Desire*, ed. Donald E. Hall and Maria Pramaggiore. New York: New York University Press. 1–7.

Prell, Riv-Ellen. 1989. *Prayer and Community: The Havurah in American Judaism*. Detroit: Wayne State University Press.

Primiano, Leonard Norman. 2005. "The Gay God of the City: The Emergence of the Gay and Lesbian Ethnic Parish." In *Gay Religion*, ed. Scott Thumma and Edward R. Gray. New York: Altamira. 7–30.

Putnam, Robert D. 2000. *Bowling Alone: The Collapse and Revival of American Community*. New York: Simon and Schuster.

Quadland, Michael C. 1985. "Compulsive Sexual Behavior: Definition of a Problem and an Approach to Treatment." *Journal of Sex & Marital Therapy* 11: 121–32.

Rabinow, P., G. E. Marcus, J. Fabion, and T. Rees. 2008. *Design for an Anthropology of the Contemporary*. Durham, N.C.: Duke University Press.

Rapport, Nigel. 2003. *I Am Dynamite: An Alternative Anthropology of Power*. London: Routledge.

Read, Kenneth E. 1980. *Other Voices: The Style of a Male Homosexual Tavern*. Novato, Calif.: Chandler and Sharp.

Rechy, John. 1977. *The Sexual Outlaw*. New York: Grove.

Redfield, Robert. 1955. *The Little Community*. Chicago: University of Chicago Press.

Reirson, Gary B. 1988. *The Art of Preaching: The Intersection of Theology, Worship, and Preaching with the Arts*. London: University Press of America.

Rieff, Philip. 1990 [1960]. "Reflections on Psychological Man in America." In *The Feeling Intellect: Selected Writings*, ed. Jonathan B. Imber. Chicago: University of Chicago Press. 10–15.

Rosaldo, Michelle Z. 1984. "Towards an Anthropology of Self and Feeling." In *Culture Theory: Essays on Mind, Self, and Emotion*, ed. Richard A. Shweder and Robert A. Levine. Cambridge: Cambridge University Press. 137–57.

Rotello, Gabriel. 1997. *Sexual Ecology: AIDS and the Destiny of Gay Men*. New York: Dutton, Penguin.

Rust, Paula. 1995. *Bisexuality and the Challenge to Lesbian Politics*. New York: New York University Press.

———. 1996. "Sexual Identity and Bisexual Identities: The Struggle for Self-Description in a Changing Sexual Landscape." In *Queer Studies: Lesbian, Gay, Bisexual &*

Transgender Anthology, ed. Brett Beemyn and Mickey Eliason. New York: New York University Press. 64–86.

———. 2000. *Bisexuality in the United States: A Social Science Reader*. New York: Columbia University Press.

Saillant, John. 1999. "The Black Body Erotic and the Republican Body Politic, 1790–1820." In *Sentimental Men: Masculinity and the Politics of Affect in American Culture*, ed. M. Chapman and G. Hendler. Berkeley: University of California Press. 89–111.

Sanjek, Roger. 1998. *The Future of Us All: Race and Neighborhood Politics in New York City*. Ithaca, N.Y.: Cornell University Press.

Scheper-Hughes, Nancy. 2000. "Ire in Ireland." *Ethnography* 1: 117–40.

Schlesinger, Arthur M. 1944. "Biography of a Nation of Joiners." *American Historical Review* 50: 1–25.

Scruton, Roger. 1986. *Sexual Desire: A Philosophical Investigation*. London: Phoenix Press.

Seidman, Steven, ed. 1991. *Romantic Longings: Love in America, 1830–1980*. New York: Routledge.

Sexual Compulsives Anonymous (SCA). 1990. *Sexual Compulsives Anonymous: A Program of Recovery*, 1990. New York: International Service Organization, SCA.

Shepherd, Gill. 1987. "Rank, Gender and Homosexuality: Mombassa as a Key to Understanding Sexual Options." In *The Cultural Construction of Sexuality*, ed. Pat Caplan. London: Tavistock. 240–70.

Shokeid, Moshe. 1971a/1985. *The Dual Heritage: Immigrants from the Atlas Mountains in an Israeli Village*. Manchester: Manchester University Press. Augmented ed., New York: Transaction.

———. 1971b. "Fieldwork as Predicament Rather Than Spectacle." *Archives Européennes de Sociologie* 11: 111–22.

———. 1980. "Ethnic Identity and the Position of Women Among Arabs in an Israeli Town." *Ethnic and Racial Studies* 3: 188–206.

———. 1988a. "Anthropologists and Their Informants: Marginality Reconsidered." *Archives Européennes de Sociologie* 29: 31–47.

———. 1988b. *Children of Circumstances: Israeli Emigrants in New York*. Ithaca, N.Y.: Cornell University Press.

———. 1992. "Exceptional Experiences in Everyday Life." *Cultural Anthropology* 7: 232–43.

———. 1995/2003. *A Gay Synagogue in New York*. New York: Columbia University Press. Augmented ed. Philadelphia: University of Pennsylvania Press.

———. 1997. "Negotiating Multiple Viewpoints: The Cook, the Native, the Publisher and the Ethnographic Text." *Current Anthropology* 38: 631–45.

———. 2001. "'The Women Are Coming': The Transformation of Gender Relationships in a Gay Synagogue." *Ethnos* 66: 5–26.

———. 2003. "Closeted Cosmopolitans: Israeli Gays Between Center and Periphery." *Global Networks* 3: 387–99.

———. 2007. "From the Tikopia to Polymorphous Engagements: Ethnographic Writing Under Changing Fieldwork Circumstances." *Social Anthropology* 15: 305–19.

———. 2010. "Observing American Gay Organizations and Voluntary Associations: An Outsider's Exposition." Paper presented at AAA meeting, New Orleans, November 17–21, 2010.

Shokeid, Moshe, and S. Deshen. 1982. *Distant Relations: Ethnicity and Politics Among Arabs and North African Jews in Israel.* New York: Praeger and J.F Bergin.

Shostak, Marjorie. 1981. *Nisa: The Life and Words of a Kung Woman.* Cambridge, Mass.: Harvard University Press.

Signorille, Michaeangelo. 1997. *Life Outside—The Signorille Report on Gay Men: Sex, Drugs, Muscles, and the Passage of Life.* New York: Harper.

Simmel, Georg. 1969 [1908]. "The Secret and the Secret Society." In *The Sociology of Georg Simmel*, ed. K. J. Wolff. New York: Free Press. 307–75.

Simon, W., and J. H. Gagnon. 1969. "Homosexuality: The Formulation of a Sociological Perspective." In *The Same Sex: An Appraisal of Homosexuality*, ed. R. W. Weltge. Philadelphia: Pilgrim Press. 14–24.

Sinnott, Megan. 2009. "Public Sex: The Geography of Female Homoeroticism and the (In)Visibility of Female Sexualities." In *Out in Public*, ed. Ellen Lewin and William L. Leap. New York: Wiley-Blackwell. 225–39.

Slonimsky, Nicolas. 1965. *Lexicon of Musical Invective.* Seattle: University of Washington Press.

Slusher, Morgan P., Carole J. Mayer, and Ruth E. Dunkle. 1996. "Gays and Lesbians Older and Wiser (GLOW): A Support Group for Older Gay People." *Gerontologist* 36, 1: 118–23.

Steadman Rice, John. 2004. "The Therapeutic School: Its Origin, Nature, and Consequences." In *Therapeutic Culture: Triumph and Defeat*, ed. J. B. Imber. Chicago: University of Chicago Press. 111–36.

Stein, A., and K. Plummer. 1996. "'I Can't Even Think Straight': Queer Theory and the Missing Sexual Revolution in Sociology." In *Queer Theory Sociology*, ed. Steven Seidman. Cambridge: Blackwell. 129–44.

Stoller, Paul. 1997. *Sensuous Scholarship.* Philadelphia: University of Pennsylvania Press.

Storr, Merl, ed. 1999. *Bisexuality: A Critical Reader.* London: Routledge.

Style, J. 1979. "Outsider/Insider: Researching Gay Baths." *Urban Life* 8: 135–52.

Taussig, Michael. 1999. *Defacing: Public Secrecy and the Labor of the Negative.* Stanford, Calif.: Stanford University Press.

Thomas, Frank A. 1997. *They Like to Never Quit Praising God: The Role of Celebration in Preaching.* Cleveland: Pilgrim Press.

Thumma, Scott, and Edward R. Gray, eds. 2005. *Gay Religion.* Walnut Creek, Calif.: Altamira.

Tierney, Patrick. 2000. *Darkness in El Dorado: How Scientists and Journalists Devastated the Amazon*. New York: Norton.

Tocqueville. Alexis de. 1956 [1835]. *Democracy in America*. Ed. Richard D. Heffmen. New York: Mentor.

Trueblood, David Elton. 1958. *The Yoke of Christ and Other Sermons*. New York: Harper and Row.

Tucker, Naomi, ed. 1995. *Bisexual Politics: Theories, Queries and Visions*. New York: Haworth.

Turnbull, Collin M. 1973. *The Mountain People*. New York: Simon and Schuster.

Turner, Victor, 1967a. "Betwixt and Between: The Liminal Period in Rites de Passage." In *The Forest of Symbols: Aspects of Ritual*. Ithaca, N.Y.: Cornell University Press. 93–111.

———. 1967b. "Muchona the Hornet, Interpreter of Religion." In *The Forest of Symbols: Aspects of Ndembu Ritual*. Ithaca, N.Y.: Cornell University Press. 131–50.

———. 1968. *The Drums of Affliction: A Study of Religious Processes Among the Ndembu of Zambia*. Oxford: Clarendon.

Tuzin, Donald. 1991. "Sex, Culture and the Anthropologist." *Social Science and Medicine* 33: 867–74.

Valentine, D. 2007. *Imagining Transgender: An Ethnography of a Category*. Durham, N.C.: Duke University Press.

Vance, Carol S. 1991. "Anthropology Rediscovers Sexuality: A Theoretical Comment." *Social Science and Medicine* 33: 875–84.

Van Seters, Arthur. 1988. *Preaching as a Social Act: Theology and Practice*. Nashville: Abingdon Press.

Van Velsen, Jaap. 1967. "The Extended Case Method and Situational Analysis." In *The Craft of Social Anthropology*, ed. A. L. Epstein, 129–49. London: Tavistock.

Varenne, Hervé. 1977. *Americans Together: Structured Diversity in a Midwestern Town*. New York: Teachers College Press.

Wade, Peter. 1993. "Sexuality and Masculinity in Fieldwork Among Columbian Blacks." In *Gendered Fields: Women, Men, and Ethnography*, ed. Dianne Bell, Pat Caplan, and Wazir Jahan Karim. London: Routledge. 199–214.

Wardlaw, Don M. 1988. "Preaching as the Interface of Two Social Worlds: The Congregation as Corporate Agent in the Act of Preaching." In *Preaching as a Social Act: Theology and Practice*, ed. Arthur Van Seters, 55–94. Nashville: Abingdon Press.

Warner, Michael. 1995. "Unsafe: Why Gay Men Are Having Risky Sex." *Village Voice*, January 31.

Wax, Michael H. 1996. *The Professional Stranger*. 2nd ed. San Diego: Academic Press.

Weinberg, Martin S., Colin J. Williams, and Douglas W. Pryor, eds. 1994. *Dual Attraction: Understanding Bisexuality*. New York: Oxford University Press.

Weise, Elizabeth Reba, ed. 1992. *Closer to Home: Bisexuality and Feminism*. Seattle: Seal Press

Weitman, Sasha. 1998. "On the Elementary Forms of the Socioerotic Life." *Theory Culture & Society* 15: 71–111.

Westbrook, D. A. 2008. *Navigators of the Contemporary: Why Ethnography Matters*. Chicago: University of Chicago Press.

Weston, Kath. 1991. *Families We Choose: Lesbians, Gays, Kinship*. New York: Columbia University Press.

———. 1993. "Lesbian/Gay Studies in the House of Anthropology." *Annual Review of Anthropology* 22: 339–67.

White, Edmond, 1983. *States of Desire*. New York: Dutton.

Wikan, Unni. 1990. *Managing Turbulent Hearts: A Balinese Formula for Living*. Chicago: University of Chicago Press.

Wilcox, Melissa M. 2003. *Coming Out in Christianity: Religion, Identity, and Community*. Bloomington: Indiana University Press.

Williams, J. K. 1999. *Sexual Pathways: Adopting to Dual Sexual Attraction*. Westport, Conn: Praeger.

Wolf, Margery. 1992. *A Thrice-Told Tale: Feminism, Postmodernism, and Ethnographic Responsibility*. Stanford, Calif.: Stanford University Press.

Wright, Les, ed. 1997. *The Bear Book: Readings in the History and Evolution of a Gay Male Subculture*. New York: Harrington Park Press.

Wulff, Helena, ed. 2007. *The Emotions: A Cultural Reader*. Oxford: Berg.

Wuthnow, Robert. 1994. *Sharing the Journey: Support Groups and America's New Quest for Community*. New York: Free Press.

INDEX

ACKNOWLEDGMENTS

I have been working on this project for nearly fifteen years. The fieldwork took place during my sabbatical leaves from Tel Aviv University and on other stays in the United States as a visitor and research fellow at various academic institutions. I started to write up some of my observations during my 1997 sojourn at the University of Iowa as a Rockefeller Fellow at the Center for International and Comparative Studies. I continued writing during my stay in 1999/2000 at the Institute for Advanced Study in Princeton. Another productive period was my time in 2002 at the Institute of Ethnology at the Free University in Berlin. On my frequent visits to New York City, I enjoyed the hospitality of New York University's departments of Anthropology, Hebrew and Judaic and Israel Studies. However, I was able to integrate my disparate papers at the encouragement of Professors Virginia Dominguez and Jane Desmond, who hosted me first in Iowa and again in 2010 under the auspices of the International Forum for U.S. Studies at the University of Illinois in Urbana-Champaign. I owe them both a deep debt of gratitude for their friendship and generous intellectual support. I thank Anita Kaiser, who was a source of aid during my stay at the IFUSS center in Urbana-Champaign, and Melinda Bernardo, also at IFUSS, who assisted with editing the manuscript. I am grateful to Dr. Amit Kama for his insights on Israeli gay life, to Professors William Leap and Ellen Lewin for their helpful comments on the manuscript, to Edward Pass for his incisive comments on a large part of my writings, and to Murray Rosovsky for his help editing the final text. However, I am mostly indebted to the many individuals who are the subjects of this book and whom I cannot name. They welcomed me into their company of friends and shared with me their thoughts and feelings about the most intimate issues affecting their lives. I hope the following chapters will not disappoint them as misrepresenting individual personas or hurt their identities and worldview as gay people. Anthropologists of the contemporary, who conduct their work among people who can read what they write, do not enjoy the privilege of earlier generations of practitioners who told their stories from the field to an audience entirely alien to the subjects of their ethnographic narratives. In retrospect, I have gone to great lengths in my career searching for ethnographic sites and issues that satisfied my quest for subjects that evinced consequential social and moral relevance to my own personal worldview. This last venture has been most gratifying.

I thank the editors and gratefully acknowledge the publications in which earlier versions of the following chapters have appeared:

Chapter 3. "'Our Group Has a Life of Its Own': An Affective Fellowship of Older Gay Men." *City & Society* 13 (2001): 5–30.

Chapter 4. "Sexual Addicts Together: Observing the Culture of SCA Gay Groups in New York." *Social Anthropology* 10 (2002): 189–210.

Chapter 5. "'You Don't Eat Indian and Chinese Food at the Same Meal': The Bisexual Quandary." *Anthropological Quarterly* 75 (2002): 63–90.

Chapter 6. "Erotics and Politics in the Agenda of an Interracial Gay Men's Association in New York." In *The Anthropology of Values: Essays in Honor of Georg Pfeffer*, ed. Peter Berger, Roland Hardenberg, Ellen Kattner, and Michael Prager, 215–34. Delhi: Longman, 2010.

Chapter 10. "The Emotional Life of Gay Men: Observations from New York." In *The Emotions: A Cultural Reader*, ed. Helena Wulff, 299–320. Oxford: Berg, 2007.